Our Encounters with Madness

Edited by
Alec Grant, Fran Biley
and Hannah Walker

PCCS BOOKS
Ross-on-Wye

First published 2011

Reprinted in 2014

PCCS BOOKS Ltd.
2 Cropper Row
Alton Road
Ross-on-Wye
Herefordshire
HR9 5LA
UK
Tel +44 (0)1989 763 900
www.pccs-books.co.uk

Our Encounters with Madness

A CIP catalogue record for this book is available from the British Library

ISBN 978 1 906254 38 4

Cover artwork by Nicola Oliver who is an artist with bipolar disorder. This image is one of a set of
three which describe her breakdown, recovery and living with bipolar disorder. You can find more
about her and her artwork at www.artbynicola.co.uk
Cover designed in the UK by Old Dog Graphics
Typeset in the UK by The Old Dog's Missus
Printed by ImprintDigital, Exeter, UK

Dedications

Alec Grant
Mary, Kia, Millie, Amy, Anna, Charlotte, Mark and Julia.
You are all much loved

Fran Biley
Anna, Matthew, Jack and James; and the countless users of
the mental health system who have provided such an inspiration

Hannah Walker
My sister Dinah; and my long-suffering psychiatrist,
Dr Judith Townsend

Contents

On being a carer

Abuse and survival

Forewords

Professor Phil Barker and Professor Arthur W. Frank

Phil Barker

What does science make of a Rembrandt self-portrait or a Mozart concerto? Individual scientists can be art or music lovers but the discipline of science struggles with concepts like 'love' and all the other vague, ill-defined ideas associated with human encounters. Science needs to dismantle in its search for understanding. Paintings or music are analysed to reveal compositional structures, or colour or tonal schemes, from the surface back down to its interaction with the canvas support or relationship with the original musical notation. Such analyses might indicate, however crudely, how the pieces were made but offer no insight into its meaning or value, far less what the work might 'say' to the viewer or listener.

The same criticism can be made of all so-called scientific attempts to explain people. Like all works of art – whether masterpieces or not – persons are definably greater than the sum of their constituent parts. They are works in progress, shaped to some extent by the forces of nature and everyday experience, but also shaping and transforming their sense of 'who' and 'what' they are, as *persons*. This 'self' work is done through the ordinary art of storytelling. We tell ourselves and others stories about our human encounters. These stories contain the raw materials of our personal sense-making. Most of us do not know what to 'make' of many of our everyday encounters. We do not know what they *mean*. Over time – and repeated storytelling – we make some sense of the experience, however incomplete. That, certainly, has been my life experience. The academics may call this a *narrative process,* but it involves nothing grander than telling stories.

All a person can be is a story. Like all paradoxes, its apparent simplicity may belie its inherent complexity. To analyse such stories is to miss the point. Speaking of an American town Gertrude Stein once famously said, 'when you get *there,* you find there is no *there,* there'. The same is true of a person's story. The person is not to be found *within* the story, but there is no person *without* the story. All stories are mere signposts on the royal road of sense-making. Tramping the trail of storytelling is the point of human existence, not arriving at some final, complete understanding of who and what we are.

The various authors in this book are engaged in making sense of their encounters with madness, by telling stories. Read those stories and you may well appreciate something of 'what' they have encountered. Reflect on their stories and you may well appreciate better your own 'self' and your myriad encounters with life and its inherent madness.

Phil Barker set out to become a painter then fell, largely by accident, into the 'asylum trades', at the end of the 1960s, where he was captivated by the mystery of madness. After the most basic introduction to nursing he went on to train as a psychotherapist, became a university academic and, after 40 years, closed the loop by returning to painting. Largely self-taught, as painter, academic, nurse and psychotherapist, he believes that Life is the only real teacher.

Arthur W. Frank

Stories are good at scaring people, which is why ghost stories are a perennially popular genre. Storytelling is thus a good means of capturing what is fundamental about the collection of experiences, body processes, and institutions that we call mental illness: it's scary. Institutional psychiatry does not use the word *scary* much, at least in print. This book can teach anyone that mental illness is all about the toxic mix of one person being afraid of what may be inside him or herself, others becoming afraid of that person, and in the final twist, the now-designated ill person becoming afraid of those assigned to help.

Reading these stories, I could understand why theories of demonic possession made sense for so many centuries. These stories describe the demons inside people that lead them to thoughts and acts they wish they weren't thinking or doing. The stories also describe more visible demons outside people. Some of these may be demons only in the eyes of the beholder, but these stories make a compelling case that more than a few would be considered demons by any decent human observer. The responses of these external demons further incites the inner demons, even stirring up some that had been quiet.

But if stories are good at scaring us humans, they are also good at showing us ways out of the traps and dead ends we get ourselves into. Here it becomes easy to use words that I'm suspicious of, words like *resilience* and phrases like *the triumph of the human spirit*. I think of them as *yes but* words. Publishers want to put words like this on the covers of books about illness: *yes* he or she got sick, *but* it turns out fine in the end, so don't be scared. Certainly nothing is wrong with resilience – I wish I had a bit more myself – and the human spirit often is triumphant against the worst odds. The problem is when those words are used to make suffering reappear as a stage in some benevolent master plan, and it's people's responsibility to comprehend the plan, thus making their suffering all right. These stories show that suffering is not all right, but there can be lives after. Instead of *yes but*, I want to use the hopeful words in a spirit of *and this too*.

All the authors of these stories have suffered: some from what was inflicted on them as children, some from demons that seem to have been simply part of who they are or were, and some from the failure – at worst the betrayal – of what are supposed to be helping professions. The authors have also found resources for survival, and change, and the discovery of purpose in their lives. The problem reading these stories is holding onto both parts – the suffering and the hope – without fooling yourself that the second part takes way or compensates for the first part.

If these are to be stories that heal, readers must play their part. Health professional readers must be as willing to give up their defensive reactions as the authors have been willing to show themselves at their most abject. There are so many ways of reacting defensively to these stories: blaming individual mental health practitioners as simply being the low end of an otherwise correctly oriented profession; dismissing reports of abusive institutional practices because policies and treatments have changed since the author's unfortunate experience; and at worst, blaming the victim as not having cooperated in a reasonable way, thus inviting the diagnosis and treatment she or he received. Of course what's told in stories took place in the past and things change. The tough question for mental health professionals is, what are you doing today that will be written about in stories like these one or two decades from now?

For those who read these stories as part of their own work of healing, the stories can show you everything the author had to overcome, in order to tell his or her story as he or she does – but only now is able to. You can then ask what you need in order to be able to tell your story. Because while it does seem true that humans are natural storytellers, it is also true that conditions of life conspire against the telling of certain stories.

Some days I define *mental illness* as all that makes it difficult for people to tell stories in which their lives make sense. Which is why I understand this book as an exemplar of narrative healing. Maybe mental health needs to take seriously how much human learning occurs by imitating examples: seeing someone else do it, then taking your own faltering steps, and gradually gaining confidence. Professional intervention might begin with offering people the great gift of examples not to imitate, but from which to draw resources. Which is what this book does.

As a social scientist, I often find it useful to adopt the perspective of the anthropologist from Mars. If that non-human being read this book, I imagine it reporting to its colleagues: 'Terrible things happen to people down there on that planet. And yet these humans have this uncanny ability to make that terror their own, or what they call their *art*. Flawed as humans are, in both the vulnerabilities of their bodies and in how they treat each other, their beauty still shines through.'

Arthur W. Frank is Professor of Sociology at the University of Calgary in Canada. His first book, *At the Will of the Body* (1991), was a memoir of his own experiences of critical illness. His most recent book is *Letting Stories Breathe: A Socio-Narratology* (2010), a study of the symbiotic relationship between people and stories that are never quite their own. He is also senior consultant with Associated Medical Services, a Toronto-based foundation concerned with changing medical education and practice to make healthcare more responsive to patient needs.

Introduction: Learning from narrative accounts of the experience of mental health challenges

Alec Grant

Stories are important

As the titles of both the book and this chapter suggest, people can learn from narratives or stories and find them helpful. We are all storytellers, accounting for ourselves to ourselves and to other people, and these tales help us make sense of the past, present and future. Sometimes the stories we tell are from the reference point of the role or roles we occupy in the social groups that give our lives meaning. Groups of people tell stories about other groups. Sometimes these stories are negative, such as when a collection of people disparages another group in order to feel morally superior. Disparaged groups then become what the sociologist Erving Goffman (1963) described as 'stigmatised'. Stigmatised groups or people are labelled as unwanted, their 'spoilt identities' constantly excluding them from full social acceptance and membership of dominant groups. This cruel social trend has of course long applied to people with mental health problems, and is compounded when such people also belong to wider social groups, already stigmatised on the basis of ethnicity, sexuality, age, religion or culture.

Stories for healing, stories for knowledge, stories for action!

We can thus learn about ourselves and each other from the stories we tell, and the stories told about us. However, these tales do not have to marginalise, diminish or discriminate against us. Mental health narratives can be written as part of the healing process by people to help them recover and develop their preferred identities (Frank, 1995; Pennebaker, 2004). Another important function of mental health narratives is that they provide *testimony*. 'Testimony' is an ancient word, deriving from Latin. It means *giving witness to* – in the case of the stories in this book – the experiences of recovery, healing and endurance of sufferers of mental health problems. In the provision of testimony, both writers and readers are witnesses. This places an onus on both groups to treat stories with care and respect, learn from them as oral history, and take any necessary subsequent action in the spirit of social justice (Frank, 1995).

Stories of complexity, ordinariness and concrete detail

Stories of healing and endurance are also stories of recovery. The last two decades have seen the rise of the mental health recovery movement internationally (Campbell, 2005; Deegan, 1988). There is continual debate within this movement about what 'recovery' actually means. However, an important strand within the debate challenges the claim of psychiatry, in collaboration with the international pharmacological industry and the clinical psychology profession, to have the last word in labelling and defining the experience and reality of those suffering from mental health difficulties.

Some will no doubt argue that psychiatric diagnostic labels, and the mental health professional lens used for scrutinising those with difficulties, are helpful. This book will not contest this view, but will merely argue that this is only one form of knowledge among many to help clarify and understand the complexities of troubled lives. Formal labels might usefully be likened to black and white pictures of people. Despite their argued benefits in capturing human distress in relation to appropriate interventions, they don't discriminate well between the individual differences of those categorised under one grouping. Lacking the fine detail that comes with colour portrayals, diagnostic categories miss the complexity, the ordinariness and the concrete detail that contributes to the lived experience of someone struggling with, or recovering from, mental health difficulties, or of someone caring for such a person. Such aspects of lived experience are of course not trivial, as they define our humanity. Mental health service users and survivors are parents, partners, sons, daughters and friends, as well as 'schizophrenics', 'agoraphobics', 'manic-depressives', 'abuse survivors'.

The aim of the book

Our aim in this book is to provide stories which put the colour into what otherwise might be monochrome portrayals of human distress and resilience. The book will document in narrative first-hand form the challenging experiences of mental health problems and related suffering, including their beginnings through to recovery. Such a book is needed because most formal texts describing 'mental health problems' are written on behalf of 'mental ill-health sufferers' by either specialists in psychiatric medicine or in various forms of psychotherapeutic modality. These fail to get over what it really *means*, or *feels like* to have or care for someone with mental health problems, or suffer in response to abuse, in the context of a life. Formal accounts deal with human distress by proxy, and tend to have a narrow focus on 'illnesses' or 'disorders' – labels often rejected by those in receipt of them. Moreover, given the argument on labelling above, such 'expert' accounts often lead to a self-fulfilling prophecy: individuals who are *only* conceptualised, described and experienced by readers in a one-dimensional way – as *just* their illness, or *just* their disorder – are often treated as if *that's all they are*, all of the time.

The tendency for formal accounts to reduce people to their diagnostic parts in a 'capture and tame' way serves to strip individuals of their humanity, unless such accounts are balanced by 'fleshed-out' narratives of the experience of human suffering. The three examples below will hopefully illustrate this point. The first quote displays people stripped of their social context and reduced to the specific thoughts and moods prioritised as important by research authors. This is representative of the kind of accounts found in the quantitative experimental research underpinning the practice of cognitive behavioural psychotherapy. The two accounts that follow this are examples of narrative writing by individuals who have taken charge of telling the stories of their own troubled lives.

> Next we tested whether thought suppression significantly predicted time-2 distress over intrusions and time-2 negative mood ... when time-1 negative mood ... neuroticism ..., and pre-suppression distress over intrusions were held constant. We also controlled for time-1 distress over intrusions (assessed *before* thought suppression) when predicting time-2 distress over intrusions). As expected, thought suppression effort was a *unique* predictor of time-2 distress over thought intrusions. Thus, independent of baseline negative mood and neuroticism, individuals who suppressed their intrusive thoughts

experienced more distress outside the laboratory when those thoughts entered their minds … Contrary to expectations, high suppression effort did not uniquely predict time-2 negative mood. Instead, time-1 negative mood explained nearly all the variance in time-2 negative mood. (Markowitz & Purdon, 2008, p. 186)[1]

In the medical and psychological literature on bulimia, the voices of physicians and therapists speak. First they tell me about my 'troubled childhood'. 'Wait a minute', I say. 'I grew up in a stable and loving home.' Then they tell me about my 'psychological and behavioral problems'. 'But I'm a functioning, well-adjusted adult', I insist. I want their story to help me understand my participation in the dark, secret world of bulimia. But it doesn't. According to the story they tell, I have no reason (indeed no *right*) to be bulimic. But I am, and I know I'm not alone. For almost a decade, I have moved through this covert culture of young women, and I can take you there. I am not an 'authority' on bulimia, but I can show you a view no physician or therapist can, because, in the midst of an otherwise 'normal' life, I experience how a bulimic *lives* and *feels*. This renders my account different from theirs in a number of ways. Physicians and therapists study bulimia with laboratory experiments, surveys, and patient interviews. I examine bulimia through … my own lived experience …. They move toward general conclusions … [and] … use terms such as *causes, effects* and associations to try to explain, predict and control bulimia. I use evocative narratives to try to understand bulimia and to help others see and sense it more fully. They write from a dispassionate third-person stance that preserves their position as 'experts'. I write from an emotional first-person stance that highlights my multiple interpretive positions. Physicians and therapists keep readers at a distance. I invite you to come close and experience this world for yourself. (Tillmann-Healy, 1996, pp. 79–80)[2]

When I was eight years old, my father left us on Grandmother's (my mother's mother) doorstep. Shortly thereafter, he was arrested for indecent exposure. When news of his arrest appeared in the local

The author wishes to acknowledge the use of the above passages by kind permission of the publishers:
1. Lee J. Markowitz and Christine Purdon, 'Predictors and Consequences of Suppressing Obsessional Thoughts', *Behavioural and Cognitive Psychotherapy*, 36, 179–192, (2008).
2. Lisa Tillman-Healy, in Carolyn Ellis and Arthur Bochner, *Composing Ethnography: Alternative Forms of Qualitative Writing* (pp. 79–80), (1996). Lanham, MD: AltaMira Press.

newspaper, all of Grandmother's friends called to offer their 'condolences'. Although Grandmother was not wealthy, she came from a well-to-do family and had pretensions of being a socialite. My father's arrest humiliated her. In her anger, Grandmother informed me, 'Don't expect much from me. I have to take care of you, but I don't have to like it. I told your mother to have an abortion, but she wouldn't. You shouldn't be here. You shouldn't be alive. You just shouldn't be, given the way Suzanne and your father are.

I shrunk inside when Grandmother said this. I had fantasized about living like a regular little girl, in a regular house, attending a regular school. I wanted normalcy so badly, trusted the situation too much, and from the great heights of hope I plunged into new depths of betrayal. I really was a scummy little girl. I really wasn't ever going to be allowed to be regular, happy and safe. It was stupid to think it could all work out, since it never had before. I just assumed everything was going to be all right. Now, I feared something was wrong with me and it had to do with who my mother and father were. My new existence was to be one of walking on eggshells, just like my old existence; except now, instead of avoiding beatings and sex with my father, I had to avoid the furnace blast of my grandmother's blatant hatred of me. (Rambo Ronai, 1996, pp. 111–12)[3]

The above examples hopefully illustrate the important idea that the lived experience of human suffering, documented in the second and third accounts above, includes the complex social *meaning* of such suffering. This is usually missing from formal, 'expert' accounts, of the kind exemplified by the first quote. Tillmann-Healy's narrative allows readers to understand that the meaning of bulimia for her was inseparable from frustration with the professionals who were treating her. Equally, for Rambo Ronai – an adult survivor of childhood sexual abuse – an abusive and lost childhood among adults who should have loved and supported her was an integral part of her problem. Such stories are vital for individuals wanting to reclaim their identities and build a preferred identity. However, as argued above, this may not correspond to the one conferred on them by mental health workers operating according to a narrow view of 'the patient as problem'.

The author wishes to acknowledge the use of the above passage by kind permission of the publisher:
3. Carol Rambo Ronai, in Carolyn Ellis and Arthur Bochner, *Composing Ethnography: Alternative Forms of Qualitative Writing* (pp. 111–112), (1996). Lanham, MD:AltaMira Press.

The book's structure and content

In the following chapters, a wide selection of such stories will be presented. With one exception (Chapter 7), a fictional account based on the author's experiences, all chapters are written on the basis of direct experience, or by carers. They illustrate the rich, contextual, lived experience of negotiating, struggling with, and overcoming mental health problems and human suffering, while trying to maintain self-definition, self-worth, and family and social life.

At appropriate times, minor details have been changed in the text to protect anonymity. In all other instances, the authors' words and writing style have been honoured and subjected to a light edit only, to facilitate improved readability where and when appropriate.

For convenience, the chapters in the book will be grouped under a number of thematic sections. This will hopefully add to the sense of the pathway, or life course, of ordinary and sometimes extraordinary human beings living and struggling with madness, and will avoid 'medical model' language as much as possible. We use the term 'madness' not in a derogatory way, but with a sense of pride and fun, similar to its usage in the Mad Pride movement. Our employment of the term is as a 'catch-all' to both describe and celebrate individual differences.

The first section of the book is called 'On Diagnosis'. In the first of two chapters in this section, Andrew Voyce writes about coming to terms with his diagnosis of schizophrenia over the years, despite its initial and sustained dehumanising and life-constraining associations, and negative socioeconomic implications. In the following chapter (3), Amanda Nicol provides a retrospective account of negotiating the meaning of disabling episodes of manic depression over time. She describes her gradually evolving need to take charge of her own health, and her own life, on her own terms, including her decision to completely withdraw from medication.

The next section is titled 'Stories of Experience'. It begins in Chapter 4 with Richard Peacocke's narrative of living with post-traumatic stress disorder (PTSD), and the various ways that this has impacted on his life. In Chapter 5, Richard continues with this theme in a short, moving prose and poetic account of his lived experience of the pain associated with the disorder. Following this, in Chapter 6, 'Thom' narrates his experience of panic attacks and depression, which emerged towards the end of his schooling, and how this affected him and his outlook on life. Chapter 7, 'Marianne' is taken from Amanda Nicol's (2009) book *House of Bread*, and documents the depression, suicidal feelings and hospital experiences of the book's central character, Dan. In Chapter 8, Nicola Oliver writes about the doubts she has experienced as a mother of young children following the onset of bipolar disorder, and the steps she has taken in response to those doubts, and in reclaiming her life.

Following this, Andrew Voyce narrates 'On Schizophrenia' in Chapter 9. His account displays some of the ambiguities around illness and recovery, including the problematic experiences of discharge into the community when hospitalisation sometimes offers a better social and material option. In Chapter 10, Henry Laxton describes an epiphanal period in his life. This centred on his stay in a hotel, during which his alcoholism compounded his bipolar problems, resulting in a suicide attempt and a helpful, perhaps lifesaving, hospital admission. In the next chapter, Roxanna Mullick, a bipolar disorder sufferer, describes some of her colourful experiences from four months spent living on the streets in London in her late teens.

In Chapter 12, Sarah Nayler provides a resourceful account of what recovery means to her in the face of longstanding mental health difficulties. This chapter is followed by Hannah Walker's painful account of institutional stigmatisation and rejection on becoming mentally ill, following a very successful military career. Chapter 14 chronicles Terry Bowyer's behavioural and psychological steps to recovery in the context of his experiences of schizophrenia. Maggie Walker then describes in vibrant, humorous and colourful detail the effects of bipolar disorder on her day-to-day life in Chapter 15. In the next chapter, John Evans tells a moving story of his relationship, and battle, with anorexia from childhood through to young adulthood. The section ends with Ali Quant's vivid and detailed story of safety, checking regimes, and her relationship with faeces and voice hearing in Chapter 17.

The next section contains a number of chapters grouped together under the theme of 'Experiencing the System'. Chapter 18 is Helen Leigh Phippard's account of survival in a mental health system which she experienced for many years as oppressive. She goes on to write about a more positive period in her life in the context of her involvement in the recovery and service user movements, including being a mental health teacher. In Chapter 19, Diana Byrne describes her early experiences of forced hospitalisation, including the horrendous and often unexplained effects of psychiatric medication. Diana contrasts this with the people and steps that have been personally important to her in her subsequent recovery journey, which, again, have included involvement in mental health teaching. In the next chapter, Andrew Voyce describes his negative relationship with antipsychotic medication through the years, in relation to his experiences as a 'revolving-door' patient. In Chapter 21, Judith

Haire describes her treatment with electroconvulsive therapy (ECT) as an inpatient, and her ambivalent relationship towards this.

Chapters 22 through 24, written by Judith Haire, Alec Grant and Nigel Short respectively, are stories of the experience of being patients in acute inpatient wards. They document the feelings of alienation and isolation experienced by each writer as their basic needs for supportive human connection while inpatients resulted in a disappointingly mixed or non-response. Chapter 25 describes Andrew Voyce's simultaneous entrapment within psychiatric treatment, the criminal justice system and vagrancy, and the social and political changes that helped him eventually escape this pattern. In the next chapter, Jamie James' story revisits the theme of the vital need for and threats to human connection with her community psychiatric nurse (CPN), this time in the face of her perception of unfeeling bureaucratic healthcare rationing. The section is brought to a close in Chapter 27 with Richard Peacocke's simultaneously harrowing, earthy and amusing story of the tension between his lived experience and the advice he has received from medical and psychotherapy practitioners about his sexual dysfunctional problems.

The next section explores 'On Being a Carer'. In Chapter 28, John Major invites readers to join him on the 'dementia pathway' as he narrates his story of caring for his wife Helen, an early dementia sufferer. The next chapter is written by Sir Terry Pratchett. His story, told in 'Diagnosing Clapham Junction Syndrome', has clear implications for self-care and being cared for in exploring dementia from the direct perspective of the sufferer. Chapter 30 is Catherine Jenkins' account of the breakdown and subsequent hospitalisation of her beloved sister, a story which raises important issues around stigma and the need to humanise mental health services. The final chapters in this section, 31 and 32, are by Maggie Lloyd and her son Jonathan respectively. Their stories convey complementary perspectives on the harrowing years of heartache, frustration and worry over Stefan, Maggie's elder son. Against a backdrop of an enduring love for his older brother, Jonathan describes the shifting status of their relationship, from holding Stefan in awe and esteem as a child, to the times when he feared him and experienced him as embarrassing in young adulthood. Maggie talks with passion about the need for sensitivity in working with people with mental health problems, and about psychiatric services that, she argues, have constantly dismissed her as an 'over-anxious mother'.

In the first chapter of the section 'Abuse and Survival' (Chapter 33), Marjorie Holmes' narrative is 'bookended' with two of her own poems. She describes how poetry has been grounding for her, and in this context her overall story is rich in metaphor. In 'walking the tightrope between sanity and craziness', she describes her recovery from her past experience of physical abuse at the hands of an alcoholic husband. In Chapter 34, Keith King writes about the lifetime, desperately bleak and harrowing, and consequences of horrendous emotional, physical and sexual abuse as a young boy at the hands of an alcoholic mother and a sexual-abusing perpetrator.

Chapter 35, which ends in a poem, is written by Leonard Roy Frank, an articulate and vocal campaigner in the survivor movement in the USA. With reference to the Bill of Rights, he describes how his cultural and lifestyle choices in North America in the early 1960s resulted in a wholesale violation of his human rights with regard to enforced psychiatric treatment for 'schizophrenia'. In Chapter 36, Carol Rambo uses performance autoethnography to engage readers with an embodied experience she has named 'Twitch'. She makes links between Twitch and her childhood sexual abuse at the hands of a child-molesting father and mentally disabled mother. However, she suggests that it may be more useful to consider 'adult survivor' experiences as the stuff of everyday life, rather than pathologising, thus ghettoising, them.

Many of the chapters in the book refer to contact with mental health nursing staff, and two of the book's editors (Grant and Biley) originally trained in mental health nursing and continue to teach and write in this area. It seems appropriate therefore for the next chapter (37) to focus on this discipline. Fran Biley describes his professional lifetime quest for a model of mental health nursing mediated by humanity and based on the simple notion of people being with each other in a helpful, caring and facilitating way. He concludes that 'The Tidal Model' best fits this overall aspiration.

In the last chapter of the book, the epilogue, Fran Biley and Hannah Walker describe some of the strands that have contributed to the increasing humanising of mental health services since the 1950s. In this context, they celebrate the fact that all of this book's authors are experts by experience. They argue that this is reflected in the book's stories which, as testimony to the lived experience of human suffering and resilience, stand on their own merits, without the necessity for an added layer of 'expert professional' interpretation or opinion.

The book ends with brief biographies provided by most of the contributing authors and the bibliography.

Who is this book for?

Narrative ethics is an ethics of commitment to shaping oneself as a human being. Specific stories are the media of this shaping, and the shaping itself is the story of a life .... Thinking *with* stories is the basis of narrative ethics .... Narrative ethics seeks to remain with the story, even when it can no longer remain inside the story. The goal is empathy, not as internalising the feelings of the other, but [as having] 'resonance' with the other. The other's self-story does not become my own, but I develop sufficient resonance with that story so that I can feel its nuances and anticipate changes in plot. (Frank, 1995, p. 158)

The pedagogy of suffering means that one who suffers has something to teach ... (Frank, 1995, p. 150)

Essentially, our aim is to provide a classroom textbook for students of mental health. Beyond this, the text is also intended for mental health service users, survivors and carers, and abuse survivors, who wish to reclaim a 'voice'. It is hoped that it is written in such a way that makes it accessible to non-specialist readers and mental health workers alike. We hope that carers and survivors will find the stories in this book helpful in making sense of and developing their own stories, and in providing a good 'route map' for this endeavour. Equally, we hope that mental health professionals and students will gain a better and more empathic understanding from the book of what it really means and feels like to develop, suffer, endure and recover from mental health problems and related difficulties in the context of a life. May this result in better stories for you too!

ON DIAGNOSIS

On hearing my diagnosis

2

Andrew Voyce

I can't remember exactly when I was told my diagnosis was schizophrenia – it certainly wasn't until after I had been a revolving-door patient for a number of years. Maybe the first time was when I was alone in one of my father's detached houses. I went into the room used as an office and opened a filing cabinet to find a file with my name. In it was a letter from a consultant psychiatrist, from Haringford Hospital, which stated that 'your son has schizophrenia'. This was not good news that such information had been disclosed to my parent, a one-time plumber who had got Burma veterans to build houses for rich people with finance from the bank and who hence spent his days driving his Jaguar to The Black Boy pub in Sevenoaks.

My part in this had been to do all manner of labouring tasks on the building sites on weekends while at Sidcup Grammar School. I later appreciated that this was exploitation, what had I to gain from this? The disclosure of my diagnosis did not result in the considerable resources of the building company being used to give me the best of care that money could buy. It led to me being consigned to the scrapheap of a National Health Service asylum.

Bank shareholders may be concerned that my plight was a result of their finance, but diagnoses of mental illnesses like schizophrenia are more than a way of disadvantaging family members or workmates. They have a real substance. As well as being a means of my consignment to the dregs of a Victorian-era asylum whilst my family lived on T-bone steaks, drove MGs and top of the range BMWs, and occupied four-bedroom homes, my diagnosis had a meaning. In the asylums, there was no hope of any life except being given debilitating and humiliating injections in the backside from all and sundry NHS employees, of living in a multiple-bed dormitory with other smelly patients, and of relying on IT work (industrial therapy) which paid £1.75 a week to buy tobacco. Choice and control? Hey that was 1975, who do you think mental patients were? Social model of illness, Recovery model? Do you want me to get on the phone and dial 333 for the restraint team?

In latter days I have come to have a discourse around diagnosis. Despite all the foregoing, it is not, in my opinion, a worthwhile exercise to deny the fact of mental illness. We may live in a dysfunctional society, and who are these people who set themselves up as psychiatrists and nurses to judge us? Society is mad anyway, so why do we need people like doctors to tell us we are mad? I think that there is philosophical currency in this point of view. It is the substance of books like *To Have or To Be?* by Erich Fromm, and the various works of Thomas Szasz and R.D. Laing, of the anti-psychiatry movement. Do we want, for example, to feel self-worth from what we own, or should we throw off the shackles of consumer society and live a life without regard to what our neighbour has? Shouldn't we look at ourselves and not be consumed by avarice and jealousy? What effect does this have on how we act as a society? I think that this is a valid critical stance.

However, there is no doubt about the presence of mental illness, as those who experience it testify. Yeah, sure for some it's cool to live in a therapeutic community where all you need is a couple of joints a day, I've heard that said, as a means of living with mental illness. For me, I'm more interested in the continuum between schizophrenia and bipolar disorder. There are such aspects as delusions and paranoia. These are not helpful to the sufferer; in my case they led to years of self-neglect in the absence of proper intervention. But now in the light of acceptable therapy, I am able to consider what went through my mind at my worst. When I was severely ill, not only did I think the Russians were coming, that people were signalling, that traffic was following me, but I would feel elated while off medication. I have spoken to others with a diagnosis of bipolar disorder who have felt elated and then depressed, but who also thought unhelpful thoughts such as the dog was speaking to them or that God was on the other end of the telephone. This is a useful way in which interaction can occur through narrative. I hold that narrative is a powerful tool; it's helped me. It's helped me to leave behind the days of neglect and abuse in the old asylums, and to connect with those of a like mind.

My dialogue with a diagnosis

3

Amanda Nicol

The madness, the craziness, all the textbook symptoms come to life. The seductive dreamlike internal logic of psychosis. Mania wasn't unpleasant, far from it. I'd been fast-tracked to a dazzling paradise armed with cosmic insights the like of which you wouldn't believe. And then it happened again. And again ... and again, but gradually with less force. Like some sort of gusher the pressure lessened and it settled into something familiar. It's made of the same stuff as creativity but now it's at a therapeutic level, without the delusions or loss of touch with grounded reality. These days the aftermath might mean a couple of days with my feet up enjoying some sort of work satisfaction or on a bad day, utterly exhausted and overwrought, but secure in the knowledge of what I need to do to stabilise, to get the balance back.

Twenty years ago its effects were cataclysmic; the mother of all post-party regret, the tattered life, another broken relationship, a head full of medication and scattered memories, as impossible to piece together as the contents of a china shop after a visit from the proverbial bull. Maybe when your head clears after a party you might remember, and unless you have done anything really extreme, it will be filed away by you and your mates as just a bit of fun. Not so with this. No one regards this as a bit of fun. In fact, it scares people to death. You can see it all over their faces. And as anyone who wakes up from a drunken night knows, the uncertainty of what you may have done or said is pure head-in-hands stomach-turning torment. Going mad blasts embarrassment into a new dimension. And that was the good bit.

What goes up must come down. Or in my case, what goes down must come up. The down came first. If there can

15

be an opposite of the extreme high of mania it is being suicidal: that unspeakable personal apocalypse, the excruciating state of being for which taking one's own life seems the only solution. How much more sympathy there would be for the suicidal if 'normal' people could experience for just five minutes what the suicide endures for months, or longer. But, like the dizzy heights of mania, the bottomless pit is not somewhere I visit these days. In fact these days I suffer less from even the ordinary blues than most people I know. Again, there was an easing over the years. And there is something else, a mixed state, to which I'm prone, but now I'm in the driving seat. I have my tendencies, proclivities, susceptibilities, sensitivities, whatever – I am an organism in an environment, in a predicament to which I, with my unique self, must adapt. Making the necessary adjustments, tweaking levels of this or that to thrive. It's only doing what every living thing does. Trying to get comfortable; looking after myself.

Things blur with medication. Large chunks of time disappear into black holes, parts of the story of your life, ripped out like censored pages of a book. The very part of the story you wish to read has gone, forever. Crippling side effects that scared the living daylights out of me – I had them all, and I couldn't handle it. Illness was scary, but not half as scary as its so-called cure. Others may tolerate medication, but for me, there had to be another way.

No one can help you with the decision to come off medication. My second psychosis occurred when I was on lithium, so as far as I was concerned it didn't work. Had it 'worked' up until then? Was I well because of lithium, or well in spite of lithium? There is no way of knowing. No one knows how lithium works. But then many things work without us really understanding how, like love, for example, or life itself. After all, human beings have been medicating themselves since the beginning of time without knowing how things work, only that they did work. Or in some cases, didn't. But until relatively recently the substances or treatments available were not industrial, and where there is industry there is vested interest, needing a persuasive orthodoxy to survive. Initially I could accept lithium; after all it was a natural substance, used for its calming effects since way back. So have lots of other things, some of them known to be very bad for your health long term, and some not. It looked to me like lithium fell into the first category. So, for the long haul I just couldn't comply. It might be OK for five years, ten, but what about fifty, sixty even? I was 22 years old. When I asked how long I would have to take it I was told with a shrug that they couldn't say for sure at this point, but, 'Maybe for life'.

Toxic. Toxicity levels. Blood tests. The shakes. The horrible metallic taste in the mouth that toothpaste can't touch. Weight gain. The thyroid issue. The toxic to a foetus issue. The leaden deadness. The extreme fatigue. The sapping of my creative flow. The inability to read. Suddenly it seemed that all the things I needed not just to feel good, but to be me, were prohibited. Vitality was to be a thing of the past, a preserve of the 'normal' people. Whose sort of health is that? Society's? The family's? I had been treated and dealt with; some unruly part of me had been tidied up and put away. Great if your idea of health is a repression of symptoms. It isn't mine.

And as for the drugs I was given for my acute symptoms, well, that they were poisonous was obvious to me and anyone who saw me on them. Tongue twisting and writhing uncontrollably. Eyes rolling. Memory in a centrifuge. The almighty crash as the tranquilliser kicked in. Suddenly perking up like some sort of robot, twitching, unable to sit still. Aching legs. Splitting lips. Lactation. Sunshine burning skin. Skin turning to wax. All the poor old girls together in the loos in the morning suffering audibly with their chronic constipation. A constant craving for sugar as the body desperately tries to pick itself up out of this toxic sludge. The inebriated feeling calling for endless cigarettes. No legislator who had been on antipsychotic tranquillisers could, in good conscience, ban smoking on a ward. And yet it has been. And all of this after being pinned down, trousers ripped off in front of a mixed ward and injected in my backside. I wasn't being violent, or endangering anyone. But I was as high as a kite, and at that point I most definitely needed sedation. But might there have been a gentler way? I'd like to think so.

Why didn't anyone tell me about side effects, or, let's tell it as it is, the impairment of brain and body function very possibly leading to long-term brain and other damage? Many trials on primates show this. That these drugs are tested on animals is in my view bad enough, but testing them on humans? Is this acceptable? Evidently yes, in a society that is willing to medicate children. No one told me about manic depression either, or even, for that matter, where I was. That was the healthcare that by coming off lithium I was potentially inviting on a regular basis (although I believe that things have improved since the late 80s, and even then I've no doubt this was done by good people with good intentions). That was my fear, and not an unrealistic one. It seems to me that once the initial crisis has abated, medication of this sort should be a last resort, when all else has failed. And those wishing to come off medication should have the option of doing this as an inpatient, or under supervision at home, in the care of a range of therapists, offering psychological, physical and nutritional care and advice for the inevitable, difficult and without a doubt frightening period of 'cold turkey' and beyond. I wonder what the results of a thorough and far-reaching cost–benefit analysis of this approach might be.

By staying on lithium I felt I could never really heal. Never move on or away from this experience. It filled me with despair that from this point onwards part of the definition of myself lay in a packet of Priadel. I refused to accept that my sanity was to be found in a bubble pack of pills that would damage my health long term. Proud, stubborn, maybe. A risk taker, probably. But I had assessed that risk. I had met long-term psychiatric patients and it seemed to me that many were being hospitalised on a regular basis despite medication. So they were not 'getting better'. They had a label, and it all became some sort of self-fulfilling prophecy. It was desperately sad to see. As my husband said the other night when we were talking about this, 'Maybe hospital did work for you!' Well, I'd never thought of it like that, but he had a point.

I think I suffer from 'survivor's guilt'. On seeing others still on medication and stuck in a revolving-door scenario, I could almost believe that I must have been a fake. A fraudulent lunatic, some sort of psychotic skiver. But a long-drawn-out clinical depression, two suicide attempts, two major psychotic episodes, three stays in hospitals, being held under Sections 4, 2 and 3 (although I was released before its end) of the Mental Health Act and a quick look at my old psychiatric notes remind me that I was, once upon a time, in a very bad way indeed. Recently I heard of a study which suggested that people on no medication whatsoever had an eight times higher rate of recovery from psychosis. Maybe I'm not such a fraud after all.

Have I struggled with mental illness? Or fought a battle with bipolar disorder? Not really. I called this piece 'a dialogue with a diagnosis' because in a sense it has been and is still that. Starting from a very low point in a very bleak place I began to explore what health was, what health meant to me. My health, and all of it, mental, physical, and spiritual. It meant taking responsibility for the decision I made. For the sake of my family and all those close to me, if I was to choose to do this another way then I had to get serious about it. But that makes it sound like some sort of regimen, which it wasn't. But it was a commitment. And I certainly didn't turn into a clean-living fitness fanatic overnight. With my self-esteem at an all-time low (having been sectioned is hardly a great selling point) the remainder of my twenties was a painful, often terribly lonely quest for any sort of oblivion, and preferably in any sort of company.

Stigma and shame are not the best building blocks for recovery. As with the stigma, which you, as a member of society, brought up with all that society's fears and prejudices, share, you have to fight hard with yourself against the shame of it; that belief that you are on the scrapheap, washed up forever. That is why I so desperately needed my faculties, physical, mental and creative, to keep boosting and bolstering that battered and bruised sense of self-worth.

I succeeded. But it was a gradual process. Things happened, life changes as it does, and slowly things reveal themselves. Things happen from the inside out. I got a dog. I had a dependant! I wasn't going to leave him in the lurch in a hurry. I didn't feel better therefore I got a dog; I got a dog and eventually I realised that walking him twice a day, rain or shine was making me feel good. It was fun, and he loved me. I met people and had something else to talk about, and without even noticing, all that drug weight just fell away, effortlessly. I was back in touch with nature, with the changing seasons, with nature's own mood swings. Walking remains the mainstay of my well-being – *solvitur ambulato*.

I started taking essential fatty acids and read up about diet and health. I still sought out ways of escape, but eventually in some way I got the better of myself, rediscovering the wellness that I had lost somewhere in an angst-ridden and confused pre-mad adolescence. I became fascinated by natural healthcare and the effects of body chemistry on the brain. I realised how sensitive I am to blood-sugar fluctuation, to hormonal changes, to the emotional consequences of the insomnia I seemed to suffer so often and to the effects of caffeine and alcohol. Moderation became my watchword. I came to realise that I didn't need the things I thought I needed. I didn't keel over without my props after all. Of course there were setbacks, lots in fact. Periods of deep anxiety and one terrifying spell of panic attacks. Again, my fear of medication sent me in search of a natural solution, learning about stress and what it can do to the body and therefore how to avoid it, and if not avoid, then anticipate, manage and develop strategies for coping – strategies whose side effects are beneficial.

This interest in my health soon broadened into an interest in and concern for the broader environment. Or maybe it was the other way round. An interest in the environment and ecology eventually came together into a holistic view of myself as part of nature, subject to its laws. We can see all too clearly what a toxic environment does to an ecosystem, what long-term damage can be inflicted, whether by misguided good intention or motivated by greed or profit. We don't know what we've got till it's gone. Whether that is sanity, health, or the wider world, we have to learn how to work with what we have got, with what we are, sustainably. In observing nature we can begin to understand healing and its timescale. The impulse of nature is to recover and be well. That is a mighty force on your side. I believe there is such a thing as a psychological immune system that can guide you if only you take time enough to listen. We all thrive in the right situations and circumstances. We all become unwell if this isn't the case. Pour in some chemicals for the quick fix, but know that there is no such thing as a free lunch. There is no pharmaceutical that we can put into our brain that will not affect the whole. Health has to be systemic, holistic, all encompassing. Of course modern medicine and surgery are incredible things, and many people I love wouldn't be here without them. But perhaps much illness and treatment could be avoided if more time was given to understanding the subtle mechanisms of our bodies, of which the mind is a part, not some separate fragment. We are not machines that we made and therefore know how to fix, we can only look at each case individually, and only really know through lived experience. So many aspects of modern life are patently crazy, and yet we capitulate willingly, handing over our personal power to doctors, as maybe we once did to priests. Personally, I'd always rather drive than be a passenger.

Now I live by the sea, and with every change in the weather I am reassured that mental weather is normal. And that extreme weather conditions are rare, they are special, they are frightening, and they cause havoc and destruction. They are natural and yet we can bring more of them about by our mismanagement of our planet's finite resources, and exactly the same goes for ourselves and the precious resource that is us. But at the end of the day, when that storm comes, that mighty power, the overriding thing to feel is awe. Isn't it amazing that that can happen? Amazing that your head can take you so far out? It is deserving of respect, that's for sure. Maybe one day a psychotic episode will be treated as just that, an episode, not a life sentence. It could be there will be many such episodes, with all their not totally crazy insights, notions and paranoia. Maybe in this altered state some doors of perception are opened. Perhaps there is an element of mysticism in there somewhere. After all, William Blake, considered to be our greatest visionary artist and yet thought of as mad by many in his day, liked to sit naked in his garden and saw angels in the trees. We need bows of burning gold and chariots of fire.

Maybe one day these things could be viewed as psycho-spiritual crises, as rites of passage even, with something important to tell us. Clinical depression we could all do without for sure, but even in that there was a lesson – it was a cry from the very deepest depths of myself telling me I was way, way off course. And my psychotic highs showed me in no uncertain terms the lavish beauty of the Earth, the connectedness of all things, gave me the courage to try things and fail (after all, what did I have to lose?), released an enormous amount of creative energy, and maybe most importantly gave me a non-judgemental compassion for people who are at rock bottom. I have always found people with mental health issues to be some of the most open and kind people around. Not the knife-wielding psychopath of popular mythology, but maybe in some way society's barometer; sensitive souls out there on the psychological front line, canaries down the mines of modern life.

STORIES OF EXPERIENCE

Flashbacks and more: My PTSD story

Richard Peacocke

4

Post-traumatic stress disorder (PTSD) is the development of symptoms following one's exposure to an extreme event of some sort. This event (or these events) will have either involved actual or threatened death or serious injury, or the person might have witnessed an event that involves death, injury, or 'a threat to the physical integrity of another person'. They may even have learned about an unexpected or violent death, serious harm, or threat of death or injury experienced by a family member or other close associate. One's response must involve intense fear, helplessness, or horror – or all of the above.

The symptoms one has resulting from this include constantly re-experiencing the traumatic event, often called 'flashbacks', avoiding situations that are associated with the event, a general numbing of feelings and emotions, and an increased arousal state. Rarely, a dissociative state can result that may last from a few seconds to several hours, or even days. During these dissociations, one might behave as though living through the event again.

Objects and situations that remind one of the events that caused the trauma are avoided because they cause psychic pain. This can also mean making deliberate efforts to avoid thoughts, feelings, or conversations about the event and to avoid activities, situations, or people who remind one of it. This may go so far as to include amnesia for an important aspect of the event. 'Psychic numbing' or 'emotional anaesthesia' also usually begins soon after the event. Enjoyment of previously enjoyed activities is reduced or extinguished, and one can feel detached or estranged from other people, or not able to feel emotions (especially those associated with intimacy, tenderness, and sexuality). One may even not expect to have a career, marriage, children, or a normal life span and this can turn into a self-fulfilling prophesy through dangerous or suicidal actions.

I suffer from these symptoms. Specifically, I re-experience traumatic situations – though I have learned how to avoid these by not thinking about the past (another symptom) and avoid memorials and getting together with people who remind me of the traumatic situations (more symptoms). For example, people often ask me to attend Remembrance Day functions or ex-military gatherings or parades, all of which I avoid like the plague – which is what PTSD is, a sickness of the soul. I am definitely psychically numb and this extends into all areas of my life. In fact, whenever I begin to feel emotions, my mind automatically dampens them down and tries to resume that grey flatness that is safe and comfortable for me, if not for others, and this has in the past led onto dissociative behaviour. My illness has resulted in my losing two wives and two girlfriends, my families, my house, my jobs, and so on. I wound up hospitalised for three weeks and have been seriously suicidal and self-harmed several times. There are still many days when I wish not to be here any more, but nowadays I find it easier than before to apply lessons learnt in the past to keeping myself safe until the feelings pass or are ameliorated in some way. This is no way for a grown man to live.

So how can I write about my PTSD experiences? As the sage said: 'With extreme difficulty.' I find it hard to recollect my PTSD experiences fully because my mind tries to shy away from them into that comfortable flatness again every time I approach them. The way through this for me is to write a bit at a time and edit at the end. This is how I have written what follows and I hope it offers some insight into my life.

Where are the sirens?

Mallorca in the sun. It is the end of September 2010 and I am sitting in the hotel grounds beside a cool blue pool, drinking OJ and sucking OP smoke (other people's smoke). People are all around me enjoying the warmth and sunshine, and music pumps continuously from a large black loudspeaker on the other side of the pool. I have been people-watching for the past hour or so, trying to avoid staring at the best examples of the finest England can offer, and soaking up some rays. Everything is mellow and melodious. I am relaxed. Calm. Collected. As I say, mellow.

The loud grey cloudy peppery thump in the distance draws my attention away from the cloying dampness of my swimming shorts and the stinging sun threatening my reddening body. Seconds earlier, I had been sitting here trying not to think about the onshore breeze cooling me beneath the blue-white Mediterranean sun, but now I am alert to all the small intrusions around me as I try to analyse the thump in the distance.

Visions of a colder greyer damper place wheedle their way unbidden across my mind. I hear the thump as the bomb goes off and the sky falls in. *'Felix is down'*, says the Battalion net radio and I feel fear hit my legs and shiver up my back. What do I do now? We are a bomb disposal unit creeping towards a bomb scene in a planned and ordered manner designed to minimise risk. The Boss, a 29-year old Sergeant, went ahead to organise the rendezvous, the RV, and now he is down which leaves me in charge, a 22-year old Corporal. What do I do? Sasquatch, the Royal Engineers Search Advisor, runs down the convoy. *'What do we do, Dick?'* The shock sinks in and the brain takes over. Could this be a come-on attack designed to hit the convoy as we overreact to the situation? *'Carry on the sweep as planned until we get to the RV.'* Sasquatch is happy with that. *'Okay. I'll organise it.'* He runs away, a camouflaged flurry of arms and legs and maroon beret among many others, all intent on getting this convoy of soldiers and policemen to the scene safely. A helicopter chases low overhead, rotor disc glistening in the winter sunlight, as the Brass react … I jerk myself back to the present day. This is not a sunny winter's day in 1970s Northern Ireland, this is a sunny autumn day in Mallorca in 2010. Get a grip!

The loud thump in the distance had sounded like an explosion, a powdery-grey cloud of an explosion, but where are the sirens? One would expect the constant music and the hum and buzz of the air conditioning to be drowned out by the banshee howl of sirens, had it been an explosion. Another thump interrupts the *Beatles* music droning out of the poolside speaker and now I am really alert, but still no sirens.

Were they 'two maroons for the lifeboat?' I don't know, but I don't think the Spanish use maroons. I remember destroying hundreds of maroons in Hereford, after they fell out of their *Use By* dates. We fired them off across waste ground and the thumps were very similar to those I have just heard. They flew well and exploded just above the ground the required distance away in a thump-flash and cloud of grey-white smoke. Maybe there will be a third thump? Still no sirens.

The two thumps might have been aircraft breaking the sound barrier – a sonic boom or two? Perhaps, but it would have to be military aircraft, members of the Ejército del Aire, as there are no more supersonic passenger planes that I know of, now Concorde and Concordski are no more, or does that show my age? But that might soon change. The music changes to Rod Stewart singing about going back to school, Maggie, and still no sirens. No one else has reacted either. I glance around. Bodies continue to broil about the place. Adrenaline continues to surge around inside my body, released by the thumps.

As no further thump is heard, and there are no sirens or flashing blue lights, my heartbeat lessens and I notice that the sun carries on burning me. My hormones are working overtime but I relax as the adrenaline and noradrenaline wear off. I sit up and wrap my beach towel about me, blocking off the rays and the breeze. I sip my orange juice and ice and look around me. My left foot itches across the instep so I scratch it with my right. My shorts are still cool and damp and continue to cling to my thighs. 'Night Fever' by the Bee Gees thumps and squeaks across the pool. And still there are no sirens. Relax! But I can't. My body wants to fight or flee or freeze but I do not allow any of these to happen. What about fright?

I sit and soak up the sun while sipping my OJ. I pull my towel up onto my head to ward off the sun and dampen down some of the cackling coming from several fat women wreathed in smoke on the other side of the pool as well as trying to block any more image-inducing input. Barry and Kim's 1969 Archies' hit 'Sugar Sugar' comes over to me, cooled by water and breeze, and I consider going for a swim.

Maybe the thumps were made by Spanish naval gunfire out in the bay, similar to the gunfire heard in the Falklands? But why would the Armada Española be firing guns in Palma Bay? Of course, they wouldn't! The problem with PTSD is that one's attention, one's alertness, once switched on takes a while to switch off again. What is needed is distraction but even Dean Martin's tones fail to soothe me. It doesn't help that the thumps are reinforced by other input jangling my memory strings. A jet liner takes off from Palma de Mallorca airport and crawls through the blue sky in front of me. The roar of the engines echoes off the hills across the bay and I see an Argentinean Douglas A-4C Skyhawk attack jet flying low over the steel blue-grey San Carlos Water in the Falklands. It is 1982 and I imagine the pilot's face as he is chased by tracer and rocket. The mottled grey and white jet skims the calm sea towards the ships parked in rows as they unload. A Westland Sea King HAR3 helicopter flies above the aircraft as it whips towards the warships and suddenly rises to the attack. Before it can loose its bomb onto HMS … who knows which, as they all look alike to me … an anti-aircraft rocket flies up it's exhaust and the neat little plane turns into a blossoming black, red, gold, and grey cloud thrusting forward between shining debris. The pilot, a small solid figure, is thrown away from the mess and drifts down under his parachute to splash into the chill waters of San Carlos. We cheer and whoop, and I switch back to the present.

Steve Harley and Cockney Rebel are singing their song about making him smile, and cooking smells and cigarette smoke waft across me. Sometimes it is like sunbathing in an ashtray. I still haven't figured out what the two thumps were, but their significance is diminished as I relax a bit more and lean back into my plastic chair. I sip my OJ with its melting ice. 'Why do fools fall in love …?' Sigh.

Still no sirens?

Good.

5

Pain: My despair

Richard Peacocke

I have been walking for three hours. My town clothes are warm and comfortable. It is summer and hot and dusty in the tracks and fields of Dorset. Skilfully outfitted ramblers look at me with curiosity, then turn back to their maps. I am reading Sylvia Plath's *The Bell Jar.*

All is deserted. Ripe crop and chemical tang, crushed comfrey and dry nettle, an abundance of different grasses in seed. Blackthorn hedges rise impermeably above a rock-strewn bank to my right and barley falls in great tablecloth folds into the valley to my left, to rise in breeze-shimmered sheets to a headboard of dark and brooding woodland. The noon sun beats down on my uncovered head and draws out my moisture in great gobletfuls, rinsing dust and seed in rivulets off my sore face. A pheasant calls from the edges of a dark wood.

My nose, overladen with toxic dust and no longer able to filter, allows further loads to deposit on my bronchial tubes, soft palette and tongue. I have no handkerchiefs, and the small number of nose tissues I find crumpled in my black winter jacket's pockets are already soaked with mucus and capillary blood from nasal passages raped by constant evacuation. My energy levels are rapidly failing, as is my aim – I had determined that I would die here among the fields of England beneath blue summer skies.

I find a crossroads – a right place, a meeting and parting place, a place of rest. An ancient place populated by streams of insects moving through hard-edged shadows thrown across sun-bleached path. Large bees thump past my ears and smaller creatures covertly buzz and zip about me. I place myself central, a traffic island for airborne insect life, and sit cross-legged with my head in my hands.

All is heat and dark and noise. I sit. Heat reduces but noise increases. The entomological rush-hour approaches. I sit. The World melts around me and symbolic representations upon which I have relied for my whole life are brought into question. I sit. I am no longer in a heliocentric orbit on a spinning rock; the World is orbiting me, my still form, and it is entirely noise and breeze-kissed cheeks and pain and eternal temporal pause-time – dreamtime.

Precious liquid, salt and warm, flows from my eyes. My cheek muscles jerk and my lungs stop their unnoticed slow rhythm, to suck air and blow waste in a jerky uncontrolled manner. My nose, so dry before, runs freely and my lips shake, and quieten, and dribble.

Sweat in my hair, neck, and forehead, I wipe the stinging liquor from my eyes as I open them. Sunlight streams blinding into my World, and much time has passed. Much much time has passed.

Dusk, and the insect traffic has given way to rabbits nibbling the few green shoots to survive the farmer's chemical holocaust. Unconcerned at my slowly unravelling presence beyond the odd cocked ear, they continue to hop and feed, hop and feed. Birds fly home across dusk-purpling skies. Sparkling, an as-yet finite number of stars peek through gaps in the curtain at tonight's audience.

I have been sobbing for some considerable time – though time has no meaning, and I have not realised that I am sobbing. My reality-symbols drift and sink into a symbiosis with the quiet nature-land about me. I feel drained. Degauzed. Unmanned. Energyless. Spirit-free. Shamanic. I spread my arms above my still-crossed form and tickle beneath God's beard. I give myself to nature. I have nothing left to live for, and want to be taken there and then, there and then. I wish for it and plead for it. I pray for it and beg for it. I plead, grovel and cajole for it. But Death eludes me, laughs in my face. I cross my arms and cry. My mind is clear and blank, black and empty. I have no thought beyond me. I am me am I. There is no other. I sob.

Then I stop. Everything stops. It all stops at once. All is silent and calm. I feel a gentle hand, a gentle enfolding warmth in the cold breeze still blowing against my cheek. I am lifted to my feet, yet not lifted. I am made to breathe my breath blown on the breeze into my upturned face. My tears dry. My pains recede. My eyes clear. Bats fly about me harvesting an airborne crop of late commuting insects. An owl calls. I look to see if there is anybody near, but I am alone. I feel her but she is not there. I do not feel loss. I take a deep breath and the spell is broken. I begin my long walk home.

Pain

Leaden
Dark shadows;
Endless corridors of pain
Screaming silently through time
To fall on ears deafened
And buffeted
By life.
To fall,
Quietly and unnoticed,
To smile,
To vanish into the past
And be forgotten
At last.

School: On panic, depression and suicidal thoughts

6

Thom

I can't pinpoint the exact moment things went bad. I guess I started getting anxious around September/October 2008. It started with small worries that I just ignored but over the months they grew and by Christmas things were getting pretty bad. I remember on New Year's Eve just as 2009 kicked in I got the worst sinking feeling, the feeling shit would hit the fan. It sounds stupid but as 2009 got worse I kept revisiting that night in my head.

The first panic attack I had was during an English lesson. I'd never had a problem with English before; though I didn't really mix with the other students, they were OK. The teacher was nice and I was good at the subject. I remember sitting there getting more and more wound up. During panic attacks my gut would churn, my palms would sweat and sound seemed to amplify, not sure why. After that, English became a lesson I dreaded; I would try and avoid it as much as possible by arriving late, leaving early and making all my Tutor Times clash with it.

As my anxiety got worse it spread to other lessons, The only ones I didn't dread were Art, because it was relaxed and you could move around and come and go, and History, because my teacher Mr Pring had lived a little more than the other teachers and he understood that there are bigger things in life than coursework deadlines.

I hated school. I was so full of fear I could hardly function. I remember walking into school feeling terrified, my head was just telling me to get out. The anxiety and depression began to show at this point. I was angry, short and aggressive with everyone. I was totally different from the chilled out happy-go-lucky boy I was.

Around March things had come to a head. My anxiety was in full swing and depression had set in. I avoided school as much as possible much to the annoyance of my sister. She gave me hell for skipping school and at the time I was pretty sure she hated me. The pressure was straining the family. Mum was fighting my corner against Alex. Dad agreed with Alex though he was rarely confrontational. Meanwhile I watched a rift form in the family and it was my fault; I felt guilty and mixed with the depression I thought a lot about suicide. Never attempted it though.

At first I thought the idea of a middle-class kid having depression was bollocks. On paper my life was great but over time I was unable to ignore the signs. I can remember sitting in Tech watching everyone talk and laugh with each other but it felt like I was on the other side of a one-sided window looking in. I wasn't there. I also had an out-of-body experience when I was walking down a corridor. A friend walked past and said hi and I said hi back but I saw it all happen from another person's perspective. Before then I'd always imagined an out-of-body experience would be weird and scary but for those few seconds I felt calm and relaxed.

In early April I went to the Doc and he arranged for me to do half days at school. This helped a lot. Now I can't understand why I didn't tell school how much I was struggling but I always viewed them as the enemy. I was sure they wouldn't help and I felt ashamed to have depression, I didn't tell anyone. Study leave began in late June and we got time off in the afternoon to say bye to our friends and teachers. I didn't turn up to mine, I've always regretted the fact I just disappeared one day but I wasn't up for it.

So that was school, There's a lot of stuff I've forgotten, and I'd rather keep it that way. That year really fucked me up and I went through a lot of pain, despair and fear. However I know there were good times as well, not many but they were there too and they must be remembered with the bad stuff.

Exams

Not much to say really, spent the month trying to revise. I don't know how I did the exams. Christ the courage it took.

Summer holidays

The summer holidays were shit. I was out of the places that made me anxious but the anxiety was still there and so was the depression. For the first month or so I did NOTHING, just sat I in my room. I didn't talk to anyone, didn't go out and only left my room to get something to eat, the depression was so bad. It's impossible to describe depression; it was like pain in my head that never stopped. Like an illness that ran through my whole body. I was sick. Nothing I did made it go away. Churchill described it as a black dog and I get that. Even when James and Connor came round and for a few hours I could have some distraction, the depression was always in the back of my mind like a dog following me.

Before all this, when I thought of depression I would think of it as something only celebs get, a kind of stylish flaw that gave the Paris Hiltons something to bitch about. But now I realise that the people who throw the word round every other sentence are full of shit. There's nothing glamorous or easy about it. If you've been through it you don't want to talk about it or broadcast it to all your friends. In my case I was too ashamed and too busy fighting a losing battle. Even to this day I still feel some weird sense of 'guilt'. Depression is hard and tough and it can fuck you up.

The depression was at its worst during the holidays. Suicide was on my mind constantly. Most people see suicide as a dark, nasty, tragedy you shouldn't talk about, but for me it wasn't a tragedy, it was a way out, a happy ending. If I was incurable, if the therapy didn't work then there was always suicide. It was a comfort. There's this great view in Cerne of a lake surrounded by hills and in summer it looks like something you'd see on a postcard. There's a tree at the top of the hill that overlooks all this. All my life I've walked to this view.

During that summer I thought if I were to kill myself that's where I'd do it. It was quiet and secluded; if it came to that I had it planned. I was in the grip of depression, I remember one night going to bed convinced that in a week I wouldn't be around. It's not that I wanted to die but if the choice was depression or death then death won every time. You must also remember this was at a time when I'd only just started therapy so no real goals or plans had been made and the antidepressants had yet to be given at an effective dose. I had no point, plan or hope at this point. Just depression.

During this time a boy who grew up in the village, and whose parents and younger siblings still did, killed himself. From what I know, Luke battled depression most his life and in his early 20s he'd had enough. Of course after this, suicide was at the front of our minds and things weren't looking so good. Alex and I had become pretty distant due to her inability to understand and the fact I'd pretty much closed myself off.

One night, she, James and Connor were round and after getting slightly drunk she started crying and begged me not to kill myself. I can't really describe how I felt but it hit me like a ton of bricks. At first I was angry. My back-up plan had been scrapped because she didn't want to lose me. In some twisted way it seemed selfish of her to keep me around just for her sake. Why should I suffer for someone else's happiness? After that night suicide was no longer an option. From then on I hoped for a freak accident or something.

Now I understand she was right to tell me not to kill myself and that of course she wasn't acting out of selfishness but love. Sometimes I wonder if she saved my life that night.

Of course just because suicide was out the window didn't mean I felt any better. Probably felt worse if anything. I found two ways to help relieve the pain. The first I found accidently, I'd had back pain for a few weeks and I was taking painkillers as often as I could; I found that they seemed to relax me a little and relieve the anxiety. Connor, who's going through a similar thing says he takes them a lot so perhaps there's something.

I realised after a while it was something I'd have to give up as I was getting kind of dependent on them and I'd read too much will do your liver and kidneys in. The second was self-harm. I got no thrill or kick out of blood or pain but apparently when you bleed your body releases endorphins and adrenaline which helped a lot. I'd be careful not to cut veins, muscles or tendons and I'd keep the cuts clean. If clicking your fingers gave the same effect I'd have done that.

By the end of summer it was obvious I wasn't going back to school and that was weird but also kind of a relief. The doctors were working on finding the right dose of antidepressants. September, October and November were difficult but I had hope for the first time in a year. By January 2010 things weren't fine but I was in a stable enough condition to start getting things together. It's taken a long time and I'm not finished yet but it's getting there.

The here and now

Here I am writing this. Are things OK now? No. Are things better? Yes. My depression is for the most part manageable. The memories are not as painful or as easy to recall as they once were. I'm still angry at the world and slightly jaded, but at least now I'll have the self-value to put myself first. If I'd done that two years ago things wouldn't have got so bad. Ghandi said whatever you do in life will be insignificant but it's very important you do it. You can't always know the meaning of your life, but know that it has one. I like this. I guess even bad things have a reason or at least an effect. Luke's death wasn't for nothing. It had an effect on Alex which had an effect on me. His death went some way towards my recovery and because of my recovery I can help someone else like Connor.

On a more personal level my future is uncertain. I've no qualifications to speak of and no desire to get any soon. But if I've learnt one thing it's that if your life can be fucked up in a couple of months then surely it can become great as well. As the Green Day lyric goes: 'I've been waiting a long time for this moment to come. I'm destined for anything at all.' As for suicide, I've worked too fucking hard to give up now.

7

Marianne

Amanda Nicol

That evening he had a game of pool with Tim, who said that he was going home soon. He said he needed to get his head together if he was going to go back to college in the autumn. The autumn, college, both these things seemed as remote as retirement to Dan. His college had granted him a year off, keeping his place open, having been informed of his 'breakdown' by his family. He didn't want to go back. In fact, the very thought of it filled him with dread. What good was a bad degree in French going to do him anyway? Tim, on the other hand, said that he couldn't wait to get back because his college was brilliant.

After a couple of games, Benny and a lanky bloke called George came in, demanding their turn. They said that something was happening in the main building – there was an ambulance and a police car over by Oak. Dan and Tim set off to find out what was going on. As they approached the side of the building that housed Oak, Dan felt a sense of foreboding – for once, the noise of the television wasn't blaring out of the ward window.

A policeman told them to stay back. The back doors of the ambulance were open and a paramedic was busy inside. After about five minutes there was quite a crowd gathered. No one seemed to know what had happened. Suddenly, a stretcher appeared with a body shaped lump under a white sheet. Dan saw part of a foot protruding from it, with traces of red nail varnish still clinging to a toenail.

'Fuck me, it's a stiff!' said Tim. Dan thought he was going to pass out. Whoever it was, was loaded into the ambulance

This chapter is an extract from Nicol, A. (2009) *The House of Bread.* Antony Rowe Publishing Services. Copyright © Amanda Nicol, 2009 which, after some scurrying about of doctors and nurses, drove off, with no sirens wailing and in no great hurry.

He'd always thought that when the sirens were silent, it meant that everything was OK, the ambulance was empty. Now he realised that it was when they were screaming for people to get out of the way that there was hope. He wanted someone to come out and say that the dead body had belonged to so-and-so, who'd died with a smile on their face at the age of 97.

Suddenly Krish and Spide appeared. 'What happened?' asked Tim. Dan wasn't sure if he wanted to know.

'A woman called Marianne topped herself. She'd only been here a few days. Yeah, managed to sneak some pills in and saved up the ones she got given ... Dead a few hours before anyone noticed,' said Krish, pulling his chewing gum out and winding it round his index finger.

Dan thought he was going to puke again. He told Tim he'd see him later and nodded at Krish and Spide. He saw Pamela sitting on a bench with her arms around herself, wailing. He stumbled across the grass, desperate to get away from the crowd that had gathered and its hushed murmurings. The news seemed to have spread pretty fast and people were making their way towards Oak like rubbernecks at a car crash. He could see Jack and Alec in the distance, heading for the bus stop. He couldn't face them either, so he dived into a side door of the old building and found himself in the corridor that led to the church.

The church! That was the place to be, surely. He ran the last ten yards or so, but the door was locked and the rose window's light was cold and dim. Just when he needed him most, God was out. He turned back. Call home – that's what he'd do. He ran to the phone. Typical, a piece of paper was taped to it that said, 'Out of Order'. He picked up the handset and it buzzed with life. Yes! He dialled his parents' number with trembling fingers. There was no reply. He tried Mat's number. A female voice answered. When he tried to push the money in, he found that he couldn't. The slot was blocked with what looked like a half-sucked boiled sweet. He dropped the receiver and stepped back, bashing into someone who was walking past.

There was a crash as a box fell to the floor. It was the man from the Games Room. Dan muttered his apologies, bending down to pick up cassette boxes that had scattered across the corridor. They slipped through his fingers and came to pieces. There was a crunch as he trod on one. The man told him not to worry and asked if he was OK. Dan blurted out what he had just witnessed and the man nodded, saying that he'd just heard about it himself. Leading Dan back into the deserted Games Room and into his office, he put down the box and offered him a seat. He cleared some papers off his desk, shut the door and sat down opposite him, taking his hands in his.

This time he really couldn't help it. Tears rolled down his cheeks as he gripped the man's hands. Eventually the flow lessened, leaving him gasping, his chest lurching spasmodically. He said sorry. The man said there was no need to be sorry, and that everyone was very upset. Dan said that he didn't understand – he wasn't really crying for the poor woman, he was crying for himself, which was stupid, because he was fine really, he was happy. The man looked at him and said that he didn't look very happy and would he like to talk about it? Dan looked around at the dusty little office, full of LPs, all labelled neatly. It reminded him of Mat's place. He said that he wouldn't mind – if he was sure he wasn't too busy. The man said that he wasn't, and to call him Bill. He made him a cup of tea, putting an ashtray in front of him in case he wanted to smoke.

He began to pour out his tale. The words came tumbling out, tripping each other up in their hurry. The details, he knew, were irrelevant now, but still, he told him how Fran had left, then come back, then left again, then reappeared, trying to be kind, but making matters worse, giving him hope, then saying that of course, she was still seeing Him. But it wasn't just that. He was frightened. He didn't really know what of, just everything. He didn't know what he wanted to do, what he wanted to be, and even if he did, he was pretty sure that he wouldn't be able to get it together. It all seemed so difficult, so pointless.

His desperate rebounding, the drunkenness, all the things he regretted. God, it made him cringe, thinking about it. Trying to get it together, to be positive about France, but when he got there, feeling totally lost and alone. He got ill, just a bug, but he couldn't shake it off. The people he was sharing the stark, ugly flat with got bored with him, so he lay on his half-collapsed camp bed, fretting, feverish. Anxiety set in, covering him like a pall. Anxiety wasn't a strong enough word for it. Terror more like.

He found it impossible to put it into words – it was as if he had a time bomb ticking inside of him. More and more it ate into his brain, panic, dread … He was desperate. Company didn't help, just intensified his feeling of isolation, of difference. Of failure. Why wasn't he coping? Other people were. They were making friends, speaking French, sending postcards home, casting aside heartache and homesickness, starting new romances. He was outside in the freezing cold, a beggar looking through the window of a happy home on Christmas morning.

And it got worse. From where he was, the beggarman started to look like a winner. Now he was trapped behind glass, like some sort of demented mime artist. He had to get away. He wanted England. He told everyone that the doctor said he should go home, that his bug was bad. People seemed to buy it. They were probably glad to get rid of him. He was cramping their style. On the train back to Boulogne he tried to be normal, to read and look out of the window, but his mind was racing, frantic, searching for somewhere to hide. It led him into what he thought was a ditch, where he could lie low until it passed, but found himself falling into a bottomless pit. He managed to reach out and grab the edge, and that's where he was when he got to Dover. Clinging on for dear life.

Home was no solution. His parents were dismayed, disappointed, exasperated. He said he couldn't face the flat. Anyway, he couldn't go there because he'd sublet it to his mate John. He told them he wanted to stay for a bit, just till he got his head together. They said he could, but that he'd have to get a job and pay his way.

He tried to explain to Bill, that although it might sound perfectly feasible now, at that point, well, they might as well have told him that he'd have to go and climb Mount Everest in bare feet. Which, come to think of it, wasn't unlike how it felt just getting through a day.

The unbearable days, the horrific nights, the endless weeks that turned into months. Pleasure became a memory, food turned to sawdust. The scampering upstairs to hide when the doorbell went, the agoraphobia, the claustrophobia, the terrible tension. Every fibre strung out like perishing rubber bands at breaking point. Then disintegration. A falling to ruin. No, a demolition. Slow and violent. God, his hair even started to fall out! The self-disgust that matured into loathing. The horrible taste of himself. At first sleep had offered some fleeting release, till the nightmares began. Night after night, strapped into a chair and wheeled into an arena. The audience, everyone that had ever featured in his life. Braying and pointing, laughing, their voices a piercing chant, wrenching him out of sleep and reducing him to knocking on his parents' door, once more a child with the heebie-jeebies.

It was unreal. He remembered looking at his hands, amazed that they'd once been useful. Staring out of the kitchen window for what seemed like hours, the task of making tea reducing him to tears. Until one day the tears just stopped. His humanity packed and left. The aged family cat staggered off to die and instead of grief, he felt envy.

He paused to light a fag, thinking of what Anna had said about how cutting herself was better than feeling nothing. Yeah, maybe she had a point.

'Go on,' said Bill. Dan told him how suicide appeared on the horizon like an oasis. It was logical. He needed to be put out of his misery. No one had told him that he could recover. No, that wasn't true, everyone did keep saying that it would pass – but what the hell did they know? They were getting sick of him. They'd be glad to get rid of him too – he could see it in their eyes, their faces set, their compassion supersaturated. He didn't blame them. God, what a relief – there was a way out! He was aching from the strain of hanging on. Down to his last few breaking fingernails. He was exhausted. He'd tried his best, done his bit. No one could expect him to bear it any longer. He kept thinking of that song in the *Messiah* that they'd done at school that went, *'Death, death, Where is thy sting?'*

He felt angry, thinking about it, that no one had taken him seriously. He'd begged for help, or felt as if he had. He'd even asked if he could see a psychiatrist – he knew he was crazy. He'd been to see a counsellor who suggested that he tidy himself up a bit and do some sport. He remembered it as the only time that he had laughed in months. The doctor gave him antidepressants, but they gave him a seriously bad trip. His bed turned into a slab of stone and his bedroom was a slimy dungeon. He couldn't get up, but knew he was a beast, half man, half woman. All he could do was raise his hands as far as he could to see them begin to sprout hair like a werewolf ...

He paused to look at Bill expecting to see him recoiling with horror – which he wasn't. When his parents had been at work, he'd spent hours on the phone to the Samaritans, who were kind, but only helped pass the time as he plucked up the courage to do the inevitable. Maybe he just couldn't face being a man. Maybe he was just too soft. He was impotent – totally. Mentally, physically, emotionally, the lot. How could he ever be a man? He couldn't even get out of bed.

If only someone had said that they knew how he felt. But how could they? If you're not suicidal the possibility of feeling suicidal is unthinkable, unknowable. To be alive is to wish to stay alive, the impulse, stronger than any other, is for survival. You might send a million people into the gas chamber because you feared for it. You might even resort to cannibalism.

He said he didn't think that it was the coward's way out and that he bet people were already saying that the woman had been selfish and weak and an egomaniac, but that actually he thought she was brave. The point was that you didn't have an ego. That was what made you want to die, because you're nothing without an ego. That doesn't mean you have to have a huge one. He looked at Bill, who nodded understandingly.

But how to finally let go? That was the sting. He knew it was never going to be easy. He knew that there was going to be that moment before oblivion, when the 0.0001% of himself that wanted another go would beg him to reconsider. But it would be too late, he'd be unable to respond, to undo the undoable. Everything that crossed his field of vision became a murder weapon. His mum's macramé plant-pot holder was a noose, the kitchen knives were daggers, the car a generator of carbon monoxide, his dad's razor … the medicine cabinet.

It was terrifying, like standing before a death squad. He could remember the taste of fear in his mouth, raw and black. Waiting for execution. Except that you couldn't just stand there and wait for it, because you were the executioner. You could say that it was different, because people waiting for execution generally want to live, whereas the suicide doesn't, but that's not true. He wanted to live – but this wasn't living, this was a living death. Anyone feeling like that would come to the same conclusion. As he said, it was logical.

He said he'd felt brave as he'd taken all the pills he could find – painkillers, most of them, which seemed to be the obvious choice, washing them down with brandy, writing his apologetic note to the world. Bizarrely, it seemed like the only positive action he'd taken in months. Hearing his parents' snores as his limbs went numb and his heart took on an unusual rhythm, which was the last thing he remembered.

He paused at this point and Bill put his arm round him, saying nothing. Dan told him about waking up in hospital, in a side room. Being told by a doctor that there was no way of knowing how much damage he'd done to his liver and kidneys, 'We'll just have to wait and see.' He'd asked if he was dying, the doctor said the same thing again, that 'We'll just have to wait and see.' A nurse came in and put some bread and jam on his locker. She said he had to eat it, and, 'What did you do that for, how could you be so selfish? What about your poor mother?' She didn't understand that at that point it seemed selfish to carry on living, since he was only a burden. His mum and dad at his bedside, looking so pale, his brother flying back from his travels to be with the family.

Where every other patient was a hero, he was a villain. Like a woman who'd had an abortion in a ward full of others having fertility treatment. A man with no legs wheeled himself over and when he'd told him what he'd done he'd spun away saying, 'Feeling sorry for yourself were you?' That was the point – the man with no legs was a hero, but depression takes away the capacity for heroism; you did feel sorry for yourself. Really sorry. People kept telling him that he was lucky to be alive, but he didn't agree. Looking back, he now knew how lucky he was and that when he saw that foot sticking out from under that sheet, he'd seen himself lying there. He did think about the overdose a lot, but that was because he could, unlike that woman. He told Bill that at least she had got what she wanted, even though it wasn't really what she wanted. It was the illness telling her it was, probably. He asked him if he thought people could kill themselves when they weren't mad. Bill said that he didn't know.

He finished his story, saying how amazing it had been to come back to life (sparing him the details of Cornwall and the speed), and how afterwards he'd levelled out and gone back to his flat. Now he was here, and he still wasn't sure why because, as he'd said, he was really happy.

He disconnected himself from the man's embrace and wiped his nose. Bill handed him a tissue and said, 'Blow!' He said that it was wonderful that he had lived to tell his tale and said that if he ever wanted to talk about it further, or anything else for that matter, he was more than welcome. As Dan was leaving, after saying thank you about a hundred times, Bill said that he looked forward to another tune on the piano.

He went back outside through the side door with his eyes puffy and swollen. It was raining softly, just enough to cool his face. There was a crowd of sombre people gathered at the bus stop. The Elf was there, her mum hadn't turned up, and she rushed over to him and hugged him, saying she'd been looking everywhere for him and wasn't it dreadful about poor Marianne. Dan held her, thanking her inwardly for bringing him back into the present tense, and he said that yeah, it was really, really dreadful, and he meant it, for her, Marianne Whoever-she-was, not for him, he was lucky, he was OK. It was history.

8

Can I ever be a good-enough mother?

Nicola Oliver

Is it possible to be a good parent if you suffer with a mental illness? Should a mother with schizophrenia, bipolar disorder or severe depression ever consider having a family? I never had the opportunity to make that decision. When I had my first son, Alex, in 2001 I never anticipated that one day I would have to parent him and his brother, Max, whilst suffering with bipolar disorder, an incurable mental illness.

Bipolar disorder causes a sufferer to fluctuate between abnormally elevated energy levels, cognition, and mood, and depressive episodes. During my manic periods I become out of control and during my depressive episodes I become incapacitated. My bipolar disorder was diagnosed in 2007 following a mental breakdown due to work stress.

Today Alex and Max live with an inconsistent mother. Sometimes I am the incapacitated mummy and they become my carer; often I am an irritable mummy and they avoid me; sometimes I am a good-enough mummy and they push boundaries like any normal child; occasionally, but rarely, I am a relaxed, fun mummy (but the fun times are increasing).

Before I started a family, I had had a good academic career and had excelled at my work. Right up until my mid-thirties there was no hint that I was going to be struck by a disabling mental illness.

When I decided to have a family I intended to be the 'best ever' mum. When Alex was born I was euphoric. Like most new mums, I fell in love with my newborn son and over the next three years I prided myself as being a besotted and devoted mother. When Max was born in 2004, Alex was three. I removed Alex from private nursery and enrolled him in state pre-school; I wanted Alex at home with me and Max.

Alex was an extremely bright and demanding child. However, his behaviour was challenging for both me and his teachers and I spent many days shattered, as I tried to be 'the perfect parent'. Over the school year I was called into pre-school on a regular basis to discuss Alex's behaviour. He had thrown a Lego model at the wall, he had pulled all the coats off the pegs, he was too rough, he was inconsiderate of other children's personal space .... Each day as I walked to collect Alex from school I began to dread being asked to stay behind to talk to the teacher about Alex's behaviour. I became detached from reality as I collected Alex from school and was unable to interact with the other mums. I felt as if I no longer lived in the real world.

Towards the end of the summer term, a close friend told me that she was concerned about Alex's behaviour and that she didn't want her son to play with him anymore. Her son taunted Alex, 'I don't like you, you're not coming to my birthday party; we don't want you as our friend.' Alex's behaviour worsened and I became increasingly depressed. By the end of the school year I felt suicidal.

I was exhausted by Alex's behaviour, guilty about the lack of time I spent with Max and unconvinced of my ability to parent. During the day, I hated Alex for being so difficult; whilst sleeping I would watch him tearfully and promise that tomorrow would be a better day. I continued to breastfeed Max in an attempt to compensate for his abandonment; my time was absorbed by Alex and his difficulties.

Over the 2005 summer holidays I finally sought help. A psychiatrist prescribed Prozac and provided counselling. Within months I felt back to my old self again. Later that year Alex was diagnosed with Asperger's syndrome and family life started to fit into place. Alex's diagnosis helped me understand that his behaviour was not necessarily my bad parenting. I was released from the psychiatrist with the warning to not get too stressed – after a person's first episode of depression, a relapse is probable.

A year later, in 2007, Alex was five and Max was two. Our family life was fairly stable and I decided to return to work. I got an exciting role as a management consultant in London. I worked 70 hours a week and Neil, my husband, became a househusband. Five months later I had a nervous breakdown and was diagnosed with bipolar disorder.

During the first few weeks of my breakdown I was highly anxious. I would sit rocking or pace around the kitchen counting the tiles on the floor to reduce the mental pain in my head. The mental health team doped me up with diazepam; I was oblivious to the children and their needs.

I then fell into the depths of despair. For six weeks I hardly left my room or my house. I was unable to look after myself or the boys – I didn't shower or brush my teeth – I just wanted to die. Occasionally Neil would bring the boys into the bedroom to see me. I couldn't bear any noise, light or touch. I'd scream at the children if they talked to me. Alex stood cowering in the corner. Max would cry and say to me, 'Don't worry Mummy, you will get better.'

After six weeks of severe depression I started to come downstairs occasionally. Neil and my mum cared for the children; I couldn't. I was unable to perform basic tasks like cooking or boiling a kettle. My mind just wouldn't work and I had to learn perfunctory activities all over again. I couldn't bear to be with my family and dreamed of running away. If I'd been a single mum, I would have handed my children over to social services.

Over the next two years I gradually became able to undertake necessary activities like feeding the boys and getting them to school. I still struggled to interact with the children; I had no instinct to do the emotional mothering stuff. Eventually I put post-it notes around the house to remind me how to be a mum. One would say 'offer the boys a drink', another 'tell them you love them' and another 'stroke their hair'. I was also unable to deal with non-routine and unpredictable behaviour. Whenever possible I avoided being with them; their squabbling, childishness, physical contact and laughter felt too painful for me to experience.

Today, three years into my recovery I am still not an ideal parent. Every day after the boys have gone to school I sleep, just to have the energy to cope when they get home. I still have periods of depression and chronic fatigue which incapacitate me; a childminder or friends look after my boys. I make numerous false promises to the boys because the promises are made when I am feeling OK but 30 minutes later I renege on them because of chronic fatigue.

When I am stressed my irritability is irrational (imagine full-time PMT). I become angry at my husband and the boys for no apparent reason. This is difficult enough for a mature adult to deal with, but for two young boys it is bewildering. The joke they told yesterday is offensive today. The cheekiness I should giggle at causes a rage. I have no ability to defuse squabbles or manage behaviour.

I am an inconsistent parent. The boundaries move in sync with my illness. When I am unwell I am unable to maintain boundaries. When I am well, my battle is twice as hard as the boys know sometimes they can and sometimes they can't.

Throughout my illness both boys have had to cope with:

- A sense of being ignored. Even on my well days I forget to hug, kiss and smile at my boys or talk about school and praise their achievements. On my bad days I'm hardly aware that they exist.
- The loss of close, intimate contact with me for short and long periods of time.
- Emotional neglect.
- Occasional verbal hostility.
- Ambiguous expectations/demands of their behaviour.
- Seeing me have episodes where they have been removed from the environment.
- Rejection, by other children and/or their parents at school who are ignorant about mental illness.
- A lower standard of living and financial hardship due to the lack of my income.
- The experience of different and potentially confusing care patterns.
- Taking responsibility for my behaviour when I am unwell.
- Confusion about how to interpret my behaviour, particularly my anger. Is it the illness that causes the anger, or is the anger a result of something they have done?
- Forced compliance due to my unpredictability.
- Loyalty to me, through guilt and fear about the situation.
- Withdrawal and isolation from social situations that I find overwhelming.
- Acceptance of their life situation.
- Learning and copying some of my symptoms and behaviour.

The ways the boys have coped with my illness have been very different. Alex is now nine and wears a mask to cope with my illness. He has turned into a lovely boy and excels at school and his hobbies. On the surface my illness does not appear to have affected Alex, however, like other children of mental health sufferers (Aldridge & Stuart, 1998), Alex endures a pressure to be good and a false maturity. He appears to readily accept the contradictory expectations of him – that is, that he is often a 'grown up' and 'a caregiver' at home, and a child at school. Unfortunately for Max this often means he is often a little dictatorial or bullying. I think because of my irritability, Alex fears for Neil's and my relationship and he often mediates between us.

The negative impact of my illness on Max has been more obvious. I had depression when he was one and have had bipolar disorder since he was three. At the time, a toddler needs his mummy to encourage him and help him explore the world and I was remote and inattentive. Today Max tends to dissociate from the problems at home and spends a lot of time in his own little world (normally hunting bugs). He happily defies adult authority and nonchalantly flouts any rules and regulations. At school he is defiant and perceived as the 'naughtiest' boy in the class. He is not doing very well academically either. At home he appreciates any attention given to him. Like me is quick to anger.

Research by the Department of Health has shown that the presence of mental illness in a parent has been shown to negatively affect the cognitive and language development, attention and concentration span, educational achievement, and the social, emotional, and behavioural development of a child (Falcov, 1998).

Despite the difficulties the boys have endured, we have survived these three years. We coped because:

- Neil worked from home for the year following my breakdown. Support from him and my Mum meant that I never had to really deal with the children alone.
- I built up the amount of time I spent with the children, slowly. Fixing a time limit, for example reading to them for only ten minutes, ensured I had an escape before it got too much for me.
- When I was able to spend more time with them, I avoided doing any of the highly stimulating activities, like rough and tumble, swimming or anything that might lead to a squabble.
- I am entitled to claim childcare fees for a child minder which provides the boys with a level of relatively consistent care.
- I fill up their afternoons with after-school activities so that I get additional adult support when I am with them (i.e., someone else is also responsible for them).
- We started family therapy. I decided to be very open with the boys about my mental illness and have tried to explain what I feel like when I suffer from the symptoms. I needed them to be able to think about the situation more objectively, and to have their questions answered honestly and openly. I needed them to understand why I avoided them and why I couldn't cope when they squabbled or became noisy. Not explaining mental illness can be confusing for children and increase the likelihood of them taking

personal blame and responsibility for the bad times.

- I use antidepressants and mood stabilisers to control my mood swings.
- I'm trying to teach myself to defuse difficult situations before they become unbearable. For example (when I remember) I tickle Max when he is cheeky instead of telling him off.
- I take regular weekends and weeks from the family. I find that the only time I really relax is when they are not there. I need this time to recharge.
- I allow the children to call me to account for irrational or inappropriate behaviour. Alex has learned to defuse emotional situations by reminding me to try and laugh when anger is inappropriate.
- I have developed an amazing network of friends who help with school runs when I am too unwell to leave the house.

When I was very ill I was unable to parent. However, my medication, my support network and my love for my children allows us to make the most of the good times and survive the difficult times. Would I recommend another woman with a mental illness to have children? … Hmmmmm, not sure about that – we have had a very difficult three years … BUT each month is getting easier and I love my children very much.

On schizophrenia

9

Andrew Voyce

About the middle of 1977 I was again admitted to a mental ward, in a hospital which was a former asylum in the south of England that had originally opened in 1903. I had been admitted to the acute ward twice before, and was to be admitted a further five or six times. I then had two final admissions in a similar hospital in Kent in 1981 and 1991, the last admission coming after five years as a homeless vagrant.

By the time of the 1977 admission, I had acquired a criminal record, having been first an inpatient with no offences recorded against me. This downward path from disabled student with a final examination failure, having been exploited by university drug dealers and family building firm alike, meant the extra burden of a criminal record to accompany my blemished occupational history on my CV.

So not only was the NHS unable to assist me as a young man with the classic circumstances of the onset of schizophrenia at my first admission in 1974, they were more than willing to understand me as someone with experience of living rough in my car and now with a criminal record, at my second and subsequent admissions.

So I had the guilt of criminality and the guilt of being unable to repay my new stepfather the money lent to buy a car for mini-cabbing on the plan advertised in classifieds in the *Evening News* and *Evening Standard*. It looked like easy money, almost too good to be true. It was indeed too good to be true, and I was left with this debt which we never spoke about again.

At the job I got at a relocated reinsurance firm in Edenbridge, I had one episode back in hospital. When I returned to the job, I was passed over for promotion up one measly rank when the office was reorganised. Inflation was 25% and my salary stayed static. As the first return to hospital had meant eviction from the flat I rented, I had been fixed up at Mrs K's cottage near Edenbridge. This was a house down a lane in the middle of a field. It was defended by a guarding goose. There was no central heating, not even an electric fire. Mrs K would say: 'It's not really cold; we'll light this paraffin heater to take the chill off.' There was no heat in the bedroom, or the bathroom that I used once a week. I could afford only an old banger, an old MG Midget and then an old Austin 1300 that failed its MOT. All my spare money went on running these bangers to get to work where my money was going less and less far. The food that Mrs K served up was disgusting. It made me retch, so I left most of it.

All of this came under the heading of 'not doing anything with pressure', a mantra from the psychiatrist and my parents. I tell you there is nothing like the pressure of freezing through the winter with inedible food and less and less money.

On top of that, there was the medical model. This meant I was coerced as a condition of the previous discharge to have injections of Depixol in my buttock every two weeks. These produced horrendous side effects of extreme restlessness and extreme sedation simultaneously. And it was all free from the NHS.

One day I packed my possessions into black sacks and put them in the boot of my banger. Mrs K saw me, and I told her I was going to the launderette. 'Oh you're not leaving really?' she said.

I had some Haloperidol pills and I drove into the Ashdown Forest and took them all with a carton of orange juice.

They didn't kill me but produced extreme shaking.

Come the evening and I wasn't dead.

I drove back to Mrs K's and vomited her meal all over the dining table cloth.

I drove around after that for a day or two before I had the next outpatient appointment with the psychiatrist. I told him I had had enough. He said did I want to go back in. I said yes.

So after no help with my personal academic and financial circumstances, after being treated with medication you would not give a dog, after acquiring a criminal record and a history as a mental patient to hide at work at lower status than a lackey, after spending a winter freezing in the middle of a Kentish field, it was back to the mental ward.

The bed in the male dormitory with just a curtain for privacy, the shared bath and laundry sack, the food in the communal dining room, the continued injections, they were all a relief to return to.

Such was the basic variation on the circumstances of my repeated admissions to mental wards.

Alcohol and the hotel bar

10

Henry Laxton

After I had finished my third, fourth, or was it fifth drink in this magnificent Surrey Garden of Eden, which doubled as a public house, I wandered back to my new car. It was a strange experience. On the one hand, I wanted to get back to the hotel room and just cry, it was just so overwhelming, too much for my mind to cope with. I was suffering with my alcohol problem, and in denial, and I could not accept defeat. I would not put the glass down, and there were a thousand good reasons to drink. Alcohol was my only friend in my world of aloneness. I had also been diagnosed with bipolar disorder and was at this time suffering from the manic side of the illness. This was wearing me down to exhaustion and causing me to make a lot of bad decisions. I was in no place to make good ones and the only friend I had to ask for advice was alcohol. I was at the jumping off place and completely alone.

Yet I somehow wanted to linger in this little village in which I spent my young childhood and early manhood. This is where all my difficulties were born and nurtured, and this is where I first started to run from my problems. It just seemed the easiest and best option at that time, although now I know better. I was to face my ghosts of the past and present full on. I could take no more reminiscing, it was far too painful to stay, and tomorrow was another day.

I drove my car back to a most wonderful country hotel, a short drive from my childhood village. The prices of this extravagant overnight stay were above my budget, but I did need spoiling a little at this time, and so quite easily justified the expense. I needed somewhere quiet to relax, and be able to think, without any distractions or interruptions. It was an idyllic situation, located in the heart of the Surrey borders, with beautiful and extensive gardens and water features, and vast and spacious rooms with sumptuous furniture and exquisite pictures. It was truly a world away from the mental institution I had spent a few weeks in before my journey here. My family still believed that's where I should be, or perhaps feared that's where I'd be going back to, if not today then sometime in the not-to-distant future.

In my hotel room, I ran myself a hot bath and considered all the ponderables and realities, but it was too much for me to take in so I did what I always did to escape. I had another drink from the mini bar. I had also switched on the television, and once out of the bath (which I used two or three times a day because of incontinence), I listened to the problems of the world on Sky News, and so forgot my own little world for a while.

I was only in the bath for ten minutes and then had a shave. I could not wait long as the restaurant and bar beckoned me, under the guise of a hot meal and a half bottle of French wine (half a bottle as it would look bad if I ordered a whole bottle just for myself). In reality, food was the furthest thing from my mind. It was alcohol calling me, and I would flirt and dance with it as long as I could stand upright and maintain my dignity.

I walked down the beautiful oak staircase dressed like a gentleman, in a new suit I had bought just for occasions like this, and made my way to the restaurant-cum-bar. The restaurant was very quiet; only two other tables were occupied and I sat as far from these as I could. I ordered the meal and asked for half a bottle of French red. I was not interested in the pedigree as long as it hit the spot, but I still went through the motions of sniffing the glass, after swilling it round, taking a small sip and nodding my approval. The waitress poured a good measure into the glass, smiled sweetly, and I was left to down a couple of glasses before slowing down a little, all done with great discretion.

I was feeling almost human again and when my meal came. I ate as much as my stomach would allow, then made my presence known to the waitress who was around the age of my two daughters and as bright as a button. I ordered a double brandy and coffee and discreetly gave her an over-generous tip. I was playing this game so well and nobody knew who I was. The sweet girl returned shortly with my order, and I talked freely, almost too freely, about my work, my family and my business. I was lonely and the conversation flowed almost as easily as the alcohol.

By this time, I was sitting in the bar which was a part of the restaurant. I ordered another double and a pot of coffee, and continued to make conversation until her boyfriend arrived. At this point, I made myself scarce as I was surplus to requirements. I sat in the great hall and sipped what was left of my brandy. I had had enough an hour ago and I felt my room calling. I didn't want to embarrass myself. A little later my thoughts were interrupted by a knock on my bedroom door. It was room service and I answered, accepting what was to be my last double brandy that night, and in fact for quite some time. I added some more hot water to the bath, disrobed and made myself comfortable with my drink. Now that I had my brandy with me I could relax, and I travelled back to Cyprus in my thoughts, and dwelt among the bars and clubs in the main street, where my fellow soldiers and I would spend our evenings.

I went into a blackout, and some time later when I came out of it, I found myself lying in a foetal position on my side, drinking in some of the bath water, and semi-conscious. The strange thing was that I did not realise just how serious it could have been if I had fallen into blackout again. I was oblivious to these dangers and it is only in hindsight that I now realise the severity of it all. I struggled to get out of the bath and noticed my brandy glass floating in the water as I pulled myself out. It took all my strength to lift myself up and out of the bath. I put on my bathrobe and struggled the short distance between the bathroom and my bed.

It was time for my medication, but I thought at first that this would not be a good idea because of the amount I had been drinking through the day. I sat there weighing up my life and then, without thought, I picked up my medications and began popping them out from the pack, one after the other, onto the bed. When I was satisfied that the amount would be sufficient to do the job, I stumbled to the mini bar to fetch a bottle of water (which was all that was left in there). I took a handful of tablets, opened the water and washed them down. I did this twice, then made myself comfortable on the bed. I did not think of the consequences, and did not take the time to write a suicide note to my dear sweet Ely or my two daughters, and within moments I was asleep. It was not a gentle fall into oblivion, more like a blackout. When I came round it was as abrupt an awakening as my falling into it. This was followed by another blackout like falling off a cliff. This happened three times in all.

During the third blackout, in my hallucinations, I saw my deceased father in his pinstriped demob suit. He just looked straight at me, and in my nightmare sleep of sudden awakenings said 'All the best son'. That was it. Just those words. But he smiled. He was at peace with me. I loved those words which he always gave to me whenever I left to go back to the army, or when on leave from Cyprus and Gibraltar. He would drop me at the railway station, and just before he walked away he would shake my hand and say those words I loved to hear: 'All the best son'.

The peace that came upon me out of my despair, confusion and fear, and of course extreme pain, was enough to keep me struggling, and fighting my way through that situation. The one thing that kept me fighting after I had pulled myself from the bed, then room and hotel, was my Dad's voice, so sweet the echo in my mind.

I stopped at every garage along the way, drinking coffee, buying coke, stopping whenever I started to lose consciousness. I was so weak after arriving at the hospital, I went straight to the accident and emergency department. A nurse came to me and said that I would have to go to the reception desk and give them my details. I told her that I had just taken an overdose and wanted to sleep. She took me into a cubicle and asked me a few questions about my self-disclosure. I could barely stay awake as I had used all my energy to keep myself from crashing my beautiful new car (not that I was that worried about it).

I answered a few simple questions about my identity, my doctor, and so on, and then as if by magic a trolley appeared and I was taken to another part of the hospital. The rest I don't remember as I fell into the beautiful sleep, during which I dreamed the dream of all dreams. I was so at peace and felt like I was floating, not flying but floating, hovering. There was soft music playing and I thought I was in heaven. I had made it at last. I woke up in Fairmile Ward some time later. After the usual formalities, I was asked not to wander about as they feared I would fall. I had a wheelchair and was told that if I wanted a cigarette there was a smoking room.

I didn't make it to the smoking room. I woke up in the main part of the hospital. It was very distressing but it made me start to think about my life in a different way. In fact I would never be the same again. A doctor explained to me that my left leg had swollen badly, and that I had poisoning of the blood and could have lost my left leg had this not been treated. I was given injections of antibiotics four times a day, and was on a constant drip which gently pumped antibiotics into me. I could not go for a cigarette now. I was going nowhere, and was there for the best part of a week, but managed to phone my dear sweet Ely. She, in turn, got in touch with my family to let them all know that I was safe and in good hands.

I was recalled to Fairmile Ward, taken there in a wheelchair. At last I managed to have a cigarette in the outpatients area before they took me up to the ward. For once I was actually glad to be there. This time we would get it right, and I would cooperate with them and find my way out of this mess. I was to stop drinking. It was not easy, but it was also not impossible. I found a self-help group, and within that group and others like it I was to make new friends and reacquaint myself with others I had known for years.

It's amazing just how far people will go to help you. Now, I am so happy. I married Ely and my family are pleased that I have turned from that dreadful life of slowly killing myself. I am stuck with my bipolar disorder, but I am learning each and every day how to order my life – to eat, sleep, rest, work, and all the things in between. I have to have discipline, a word I disliked intensely in my past, but now I love it as it keeps me well, along with the medication which has to be adjusted from time to time. Such was the impact of this journey of mine, in the way that events were to unfold, in changing my life forever.

11

Living rough, flying high

Roxanna Mullick

I had gone a bit 'high' at the age of 11, after being sleep deprived whilst in temporary foster care for three nights. That was four days of not sleeping and crying all night. I felt miserable, but quite elated at the same time. Then Mum came to collect my baby brother and me, and those feelings were pushed to the back of my mind, until the next time I was high. My next episode of mania was at the age of 17, following a period where I was diagnosed as depressed when I was 14. This was the start of a lifetime of severe mood swings, then known as manic-depression. Now my label is that of bipolar affective disorder, but I am so much more than this label. However, this is the story of my four months living on the streets when I was just 17!

I was working hard at school, studying biology, chemistry, physics and mathematics, with the view of fulfilling my parents' ambition for me to be a doctor. However, the constant pressure of going to school, doing homework all evening, then back studying all the next day, eventually took its toll on me. All work and no play meant that the good schoolgirl and dutiful daughter flipped. I could not stand the pressure anymore. The other big catalyst that led to me running away from home was the belief that my boyfriend at the time was actually my twin brother. Yes, I truly believed that my friend from sixth form, who was adopted and keen to locate his birth mother, and I actually shared the same mother. This perceived problem made me want to opt out of my life. So I ran away from home!

Luckily for me, I owned the most amazing coat. It was long, black and extremely heavy, with deep side pockets, and several internal pockets – it was a Bus Inspector's coat. This coat meant the world to me – it kept me warm, acting like a duvet at night, and even negated the need for carrying bags, because everything I owned was stored in the many pockets. I had a toothbrush and toothpaste in my left side pocket and some shampoo in the right pocket – so I did try to take care of my personal hygiene. My Mum and Dad's door key was kept safely in an internal pocket; and I used to use opportunities when I knew they would both be out of the house to return to their home, to shower and change my clothes. But a lot of the time I felt like a dirty tramp.

The 'tramps' living under the arches of Kingston Bridge took to me instantly, calling me their 'Princess'. They stroked my long brown hair whilst I slept behind their bonfire. I felt safe, and comfortable in the knowledge that if anyone came looking for me they would deny having seen me. But other nights were colder and lonelier. I spent several nights in the gardens next to the River Thames. My view when I woke up in the morning was spectacular – the posh houses on the other side of the river had long immaculate lawns that rolled right down to the riverbank. I dreamt that one day I would own my own house.

But I did own my own bicycle. This sturdy old bike, which I had painted blue, gave me so much freedom to travel. A fantastic location I frequented was Hampton Court Palace; I spent the summer roaming the beautiful grounds and befriending the guides. There were always people to stop and talk to, and I felt important, like a lady from the court of Henry VIII who was showing visitors from a future era around her home and gardens. Then, at half past five, when my visitors were all starting to leave, I would crawl under my favourite tree, with branches that reached the ground, and sleep until morning. Other nights I did not sleep at all. Too much energy and too much to do!

One other way I used to like spending my days, which really made me feel important, was to try on wedding dresses in the local bridal shop. What a diva! I would turn up day after day looking for the perfect dress, and enjoy the attention from the shop assistants as they zipped me in some of the most stunning outfits. I told them my imaginary 'fiancé' was extremely rich and money was no object. I wonder what other fanciful things I told them?

My alter-ego whilst I lived on the streets was that of bus inspector, called 'Inspector Clouseau of the Kingston Bus Garage'. I believed that because I owned an inspector's coat, I really was a bus inspector. One of the advantages of my perceived elevated status to the ranks of being employed by London Transport was access to their vending machine, and back then, in 1984, a cup of hot coffee would cost me just 8p. So, I would walk around the streets all day, keeping my eyes peeled for coppers, and eventually I had enough pennies to buy the most amazing plastic cup of hot liquid I have ever tasted.

One evening, whilst I was chatting with the genuine bus inspectors near my favourite vending machine at Kingston bus garage, one of the inspectors told me to 'get the next one!' Basically the bus conductor they were waiting for had a history of being late for work. So, I went upstairs to the top deck of the waiting bus and eventually the tardy conductor arrived for work, allowing the bus to set off. When he came to sell me my bus ticket, I told him 'you're late!' He asked me for my ID, prompting me to open my coat displaying my father's medals for careful bus driving and a beautiful, sparkling necklace around my neck. We both realised it was time I left. The grumpy bus conductor kicked me off the moving bus as it rounded the corner. By then it was raining, so I settled into a shop doorway for the night.

I had not been asleep very long in the charity shop doorway when I was rudely awakened by two youths kicking me in the stomach. They shouted at me and acted with bravado in front of their young girlfriends, when one of the accompanying girls recognised me from school. She yelled at the lads to stop their cruel beating, saying, 'That's Roxy, not some tramp!' They apologised to me and told me to go home, but I really felt at that moment in time that I had no home. That shop doorway was my home.

I avoided the 'Baddies' – the police and doctors and nurses from my local hospital, my Mum and Dad, and spent time with the 'Goodies' – people like postmen, milkmen, and even the man whose job it was to fill up vending machines. I told him that I did not have any money, but would love a Mars Bar; luckily for me, he was kind enough to grant my wish! Another kind person I befriended on the top deck of a London Routemaster bus wanted to buy me a present. Anything I wanted! I had my eye on some sweets in a jar I had often seen in a shop window at the bus terminus. They were the most beautiful, but expensive sweets – silver, sugared almonds. That little, white paper bag containing twelve sugared almonds became my most favourite possession, and those few silver sweets lasted me for weeks.

I was frightened as a startled rabbit one morning when three young men who had just tumbled out of a nightclub started to chase me. I remember running fast down the middle of the road with my black coat flapping open rather like Batman's cape, picking up so much speed that I thought I was going to take off. In contrast to my light-as-the-wind footfalls, their six heavy feet pounded the road behind me. My adrenaline was pumping, and I felt invincible!

I rounded the corner, and saw the most magnificent sight ahead of me – a milk float! I sped up and was able to catch up with the slow-moving vehicle. I jumped aboard, accompanied by the jangling of milk bottles. The milkman, whose name was Bob, put his foot down on the accelerator, and we zoomed around the corner, leaving the three thugs bent forward with their hands on their knees, trying to catch their breath. Mercifully, they had been unable to catch me. I felt free and 'high as a kite'!

I thanked Bob for rescuing me – my knight in a shining milk float. We chatted, or rather I talked 'nineteen to the dozen'. I had so much to say – so many ideas – I could not get them out quick enough. Eventually, we drove back to road where we had met and I helped him carry milk bottles up to the flats and delivered two pints here and three pints there, collecting the empties as I went. He rewarded me with a pint of milk and a bacon butty – what a feast for a starving, stick-thin teenager. I had not realised that I was so hungry.

The tipple that kept me alive for four months was a drink from the local pub – a glass of iced tap water with a slice of lemon that came with a swizzle-stick – into which I stirred a sachet of sugar and a little salt. (I had picked up the sachets of sugar and salt earlier in the day from the neighbouring coffee shop, when I had used their toilets to wash – I loved using the hand drier to dry my face and sometimes my long, brown hair.) Sadly, my toned, muscular body from the time when I used to row for England was starting to turn into a skeletal anorexic.

One evening, my Mum and Dad were driving around town looking for me, and Mum found me! I was outside the pub chatting away to my 'best friends' (people I had never met before that day), and sipping my drink. I felt 'cool' and important, but was mortified to have my mother make a scene. She demanded that I return home with her and Dad, pulling on my arm, but I was determined to stay put. She was curious to know what I was drinking, I guess she thought it was vodka and tonic, or maybe gin and tonic, but she definitely was not expecting the sugar and salt solution. She was so shocked at the taste that she spat my drink back into my glass. I wanted to die! Yes, the embarrassment of my mother's scene, and the culmination of weeks living on the streets made me want to kill myself.

I discarded my coat, and undressed to reveal my swimsuit. I dived into the Thames. But drowning was not so easy for this strong swimmer; it was a cry for help! I swam back to the river edge just as two young men were preparing to swim out and rescue me. However, when I emerged from the Thames as a cross between a mermaid and a drowned rat, I was aware of a searing pain in my right foot. I had gashed my foot open on some broken glass on the bottom of the river. An ambulance took me to Casualty, from where I was admitted to the psychiatric ward – a place of safety, and somewhere to rest and get strong again!

12

Recovery and rediscovery

Sarah Nayler

For me, recovery is an ongoing journey of acceptance and self-development. I feel that living with a mental illness is a huge learning curve. You need to find many things that can help you in your life and learn how and when to access them. My story has many aspects which have helped me along the way. I would like to share my story with you.

I have been told that I have a severe and enduring mental illness, which sounds very grim. I aim to share my ups and downs so that you can see the positive things that have helped me in my recovery.

About me – the teenage years

I first had signs and symptoms of mental illness when I was aged 15. Initially I was under the care of my GP and he blamed my changes in behaviour and mood on hormonal problems caused by puberty. At 16, I was diagnosed with manic depression (or bipolar as it is now named). It was a relief to have a diagnosis as finally my illness had been acknowledged.

I was hospitalised on an adult acute ward (as there were very few adolescent units back then). My early experiences of being admitted were extremely negative and distressing. I even went missing from the ward and was picked up by the police some 60 miles away from the hospital. This was extremely difficult and upsetting for my family. I was still very much a child at 16 but had now been placed in a very adult and potentially disturbing environment. Being unwell at such an impressionable age meant that I never fully gained my independence and confidence. I found it extremely difficult to develop into a young adult. I didn't feel listened to, I wasn't offered the appropriate support, there was a lack of information and I got fed up with trying so many different medications.

My instability, lack of real support and taking a cocktail of medications went on for roughly two years. In the end, my parents asked for a second opinion as I wasn't making any progress. I saw a different psychiatrist and for the first time I really felt listened to. Over a period of several months I built a trusting relationship with this doctor and we had a really good rapport.

My medications were reviewed and closely monitored and there were signs of real improvement. My mood swings were finally stabilising. I remember the terrible highs when I thought I was invincible, I loved myself, didn't need to sleep at all, would race around doing three things at a time and would speak very rapidly getting intolerant of those who couldn't keep up with me.

I also remember the painful lows when I hated myself and the world that I lived in, I felt guilty, unmotivated, and had no enjoyment or pleasure in absolutely anything. Sometimes I would have rapid mood swings where I would alternate between low and high in a matter of minutes.

When I was 19 I felt in a much better place, though my self-confidence remained shattered. I decided to look for work as I needed to find direction and my place in the world.

Getting work

I remember my interview for the job of sales assistant in a small department store. The gentleman that saw me had a lovely friendly face and put me at ease. It felt more like an informal chat than an interview and soon afterwards I heard that I had been successful.

I was extremely nervous on my first day and didn't know what to expect but luckily it wasn't too taxing and the people I met were really nice and friendly.

Six months after starting work in the department store, I unfortunately became unwell. I was starting to go high again. One symptom of going high is spending lots of money and wanting to buy loads of things. The department store was not the ideal place to work in this instance and everything became quick including my speech, my work and my ideas. I started choosing things to buy in my break and filled a huge box of goodies. When you are going high you gain an artificial confidence and you really don't care what you say and to whom! I remember walking into my Manager's office, flopping in the chair, calling him by his first name and telling him how tired I was. My parents were later called and I was sent home sick.

Getting another chance

In the six months that I had worked as a sales assistant I had proved that I was hard working, honest and reliable. When I became ill at work I wasn't sure what was going to happen to me. I had previously tried lots of jobs (even though most of them were just weekend jobs) and I had either left or been sacked due to my ill health. I was scared that this was going to happen again.

I was so lucky that my employer was sympathetic and gave me another chance. He even let me return to work gradually just doing part-time hours until I built my strength up again. This was a huge turning point in my life. I felt valued, worthwhile, liked and trusted. My confidence went from strength to strength.

To cut a very long story short, this job worked out very well for me and I stayed there for over seven years. I even got promotion to senior sales assistant. I made lots of friends, including one very special friend who later became my husband.

Leaving my comfort zone

At the age of 26, I left the department store to become a supervisor for a different company. I knew that I was leaving my comfort zone but decided that I wanted a change and to increase my chances of further promotions.

When I filled in my application form for the new job, I decided not to mention my mental health illness for fear of not being given a chance and also because I considered myself to be in a stable place. I was hopeful that what I had gone through in my teenage years was a thing of the past.

The new job worked out well to start with, but gradually the pressure of a new role, a lack of training and support and very much feeling that I had been thrown in the deep end initiated another relapse. Of course I was under added pressure because no one knew of my illness and I felt that I had to pretend that this was the first time this was happening to me. I became obsessed with my job, taking work home and discussing problems nonstop; I couldn't sleep, I was losing weight, I was very depressed. Eventually I was signed off by my doctor and this period of absence went on for over a year. I had several meetings with the personnel department but I remained in a state of depression and anxiety. In the end I lost my job due to my ill health.

Once again my confidence plummeted; I became scared of crowded places and experienced panic attacks. My marriage was going through a very difficult time. My husband found it impossible to understand my depression and mood swings. I had warned him about my illness when our relationship became serious, and told him how ill I had been in the past, but when it came to real-life experience there was nothing that could prepare him. After eight years of marriage, I was now on my own.

Being admitted for five months

I lost lots of things all at the same time: my relationship, my home, my health, my confidence, my financial stability and the sense of who I was. I was hospitalised on an adult acute psychiatric ward for five months. This time in my life was not pleasant, it was horrible and I felt I had lost the sense of who I was.

Supportive community mental health team

During my stay on the psychiatric ward, I was introduced to a mental health social worker who became my care co-ordinator. She was lovely and I built a really good working relationship with her. She didn't just help me on an emotional level but also in a practical way. She knew all about housing, benefits and rights etc. Anything she didn't know she would find out for me or signpost me to the relevant person. There was so much to deal with all at one time, but she helped me break things down into manageable chunks.

Supported accommodation

I was given supported accommodation through the community mental health team and was sent to live with an elderly couple who were mental health carers. Although the people were nice enough and I had the privacy of my own bedroom, it felt very strange sharing someone else's home. My meals were provided for me, my laundry was done for me, I was expected to get up at a certain time and go to sleep at a certain time. It was like all my independence had been taken away from me and I had previously been used to running a home. I stayed in this placement for six months, and at least it was a stepping stone and I was away from the psychiatric ward.

After six months, I got my own flat which was still supported. There was a number to phone in crisis and a key worker that I could see on a weekly basis. Although the flat was tiny, it felt more like home; at least I could come and go and I pleased. I had never lived alone before, as I went straight from living with my parents to getting married. I stayed there for a year until I was able to rent privately.

Self-help

When I was an inpatient for five months I saw a poster on the notice board advertising a self-help group for people with manic depression. I discussed this with my social worker and we agreed that I should try it. It was great, a place where I could completely be myself, could talk openly and honestly about how I was feeling and without fear of being judged. The meetings were only on a monthly basis but were of enormous help to me. It was run by two people who both had first-hand experience of living with the illness. There were no staff involved, which meant that everyone had freedom of speech and could discuss freely all aspects of the illness. The meetings were very informal and people got the chance to say a little about themselves and how they had been over the last month and raise any issues that they wanted to discuss. There was no pressure to speak; some people would just say their name and others wouldn't want to talk at all. Listening to others was equally important and very beneficial. Sometimes there would be a particular topic of interest to discuss and sometimes there were guest speakers giving talks about various subjects. Carers were also welcome to the meetings.

I attended the self-help group for four years, eventually becoming group facilitator with the support of my Mum (as carer).

Meaningful occupation

Meaningful occupation is very important to me as it really gives a sense of worth and satisfaction. When I was well enough, I completed a one-year course in office skills, and later progressed to do voluntary work in a small office. I also worked in a charity shop and undertook other administrative voluntary positions.

I found small talk with strangers difficult as the conversation always seemed to lead to what work I did, so at least now I had something to talk about.

Sharing experience

During my time as a group facilitator for the self-help group, I was asked if I would be interested in doing some work for the local university. This work would involve designing and delivering training sessions for student nurses about my experiences of living with a mental health illness. I was very interested and excited about this idea and went along for an informal discussion with a senior lecturer at the university. He was very approachable and friendly and explained more about the work.

I began doing ad-hoc work as a part-time lecturer, and was able to do this alongside other voluntary work for local charities.

I particularly enjoyed doing the lecturing at the university. The students were so interested and asked really inspiring questions. I really felt worthwhile and that I was helping people get the real picture of how it is to live with a severe and enduring mental health illness. I covered various subjects including self-help, self-management and medication. Somehow talking about my experiences and learning not to be ashamed of what had happened to me was of huge benefit. I undertook this role for six years.

Finding my soul mate

I had been in a few relationships but none had lasted for long. One day I was playing around on my phone and found a text chat room. It seemed pretty harmless, so I gave myself a nickname and signed in. After a few months I was texting a man who seemed really nice and was a similar age to me. After several text conversations we swapped details and became great friends. We decided to chat on the phone and this first chat lasted over three hours. We had so much in common and got on so well. After a month or so of chatting and emailing, we decided to meet up. He came to my home town to visit me and before long we were always on the train to each other's homes to see each other.

After six months we decided to move in together. As we lived 60 miles apart, one of us had to go for a life-changing move, and that person was me.

I was scared that the move might make me unstable, as I am not always good around life changes. However I adapted to my new life fairly well. I missed my friends and family but kept in touch by phone and regular visits.

Once again I was looking for occupation and started working in a charity shop. I also did some charity administrative work.

Changing teams

Once I was in my new home, I had to meet my new community mental health team. It is always daunting having to change health professionals, especially as you aren't sure if you are going to be able to communicate well with them.

Luckily, my new team were great. I had an occupational therapist and a community psychiatric nurse. The occupational therapist referred me to appropriate groups, for example, relaxation, walking groups, etc. We met regularly for one-to-one work and discussed my vocational skills.

Relaxation

I originally learnt about relaxation as an inpatient on the psychiatric ward, and at a later date when I was reintroduced to relaxation classes, I found ways to relax at home. This has been very beneficial.

Service user consultant

My occupational therapist informed me about the local trust that employ service users to be involved in various projects including staff training and interview panels. I was really excited as this was similar to the work I had been doing for the university. My occupational therapist got me the application forms that I needed, and also was my sponsor and referee for this work. I had an informal interview and was given the role of service user consultant. Again this work was only ad hoc, but really suited me. If you had said to me a few years ago that I would be sitting on interview panels for high-level NHS staff, I wouldn't have believed you.

My life now

My confidence has grown so much and I have been living with my soul mate for over three years. This is a relationship where I can really be myself, no matter how I am feeling.

My work as a service user consultant is great fun and a real challenge. Although it is only occasional work I hope that a part-time position may become available in the future.

I feel that my mental illness makes me more sensitive, which isn't always a bad thing. I feel that having experienced such lows and highs, I can really appreciate when things are on an even keel. I have learnt my limitations and accepted my illness but I will not let it dictate to me.

Family and friends

I would like to say a huge thank you to my family and friends who have supported me over the years through thick and thin. Although I have mentioned them last, family and friends are probably the most important part of my recovery. I consider myself to be extremely fortunate.

Summary of my recovery

Negatives
- Not feeling listened to by health professionals when I was a teenager
- Lack of information and support for my family
- Being given so many different medications
- Not disclosing my illness on my application form
- Having a husband who couldn't cope with my mental illness

Positives
- Family and friends being supportive and understanding
- Building good relationships with health professionals
- Working for an understanding employer
- Being given another chance when I became unwell at work
- Good support and resources offered from community mental health teams
- Supported accommodation (as a stepping stone)

- Self-help
- Medication
- Relaxation
- Sharing experiences
- Meaningful occupation
- Finding my soul mate, which means *I have the freedom to be me*

13

On rejection and acceptance

Hannah Walker

My name is Hannah Walker – I'm 54 and I live in Dorset. I'm separated from my husband and live in a cottage in a small village in quite a rural part of the county. I have a sister – both my parents are dead – and a wide circle of very good friends. I am the Chair of the Dorset Mental Health Forum, an independent charity run by and for people with lived experience of mental ill health. I was diagnosed with bipolar disorder and PTSD in 1991.

My childhood was spent in a supportive and loving environment on the Isle of Wight. I grew up with the feeling that I could achieve anything that I wanted to, and I went on to do just that. I excelled at sport, representing Hampshire at athletics and sailing, was captain of most of the school teams and was made Head Girl in the Upper Sixth. I was also self-harming quite badly, but no one picked up on that and I was merely labelled accident prone. I had a place at Warwick University to read philosophy and logic; instead, I applied and was accepted to be commissioned into the RAF as a personnel officer.

I won the Sash of Merit at Officer Training for being the most outstanding cadet and showing the greatest powers of leadership. I went on to have many postings, including Germany where I was the VIP visits officer, and ended up as the personal staff officer to a General in the Ministry of Defence. I was selected to go to the premier staff college at the age of 32 as a very young Squadron Leader.

I was working 16 hour days and had been for three years with very little leave. Additionally, I was having an affair with a married senior officer (which was not unusual for me) and was finding the secrecy of both my RAF job and my private life very difficult to handle. I began to feel stressed and started to lose sleep. Tony left his wife for me and we had to ride out the scandal – the RAF takes a dim view of affairs.

One morning I woke up and knew I had to go to the doctor very quickly as I could no longer cope with anything – a situation quite foreign to me as I had never felt that way before and had been able to cope with anything life threw at me. I made an appointment for that morning and knew if I had to stop and talk to anyone on the way I would just collapse. I managed to get through the door of the doctor's office and then collapsed – mentally. It was the start of a very, very long journey.

I was diagnosed with bipolar disorder and PTSD. However, the RAF decided that I was trying to work my ticket in order to get out – why, after an exemplary career, was beyond me. The services are not good at dealing with mental health issues and they are seen as a sign of weakness – indeed, there used to be a diagnosis of Lack of Moral Fibre in the RAF. I was alone in a flat in London – Tony was away – and feeling suicidal when I had a phone call from an officer telling me that I was to be 'thrown out under the same regulation that we use to throw out drug addicts and alcoholics'. When I explained that bipolar disorder was a mostly genetic illness, he replied that it was my fault I was ill because I had fallen in love with a married man. I realised that the RAF intended to punish me for that by discharging me without a pension – the Army couldn't punish Tony as he was too senior, so I was to take the rap. I won't bore you with the fight we had – suffice it to say that it took a year and I won. The price I had to pay was to be invalided from the RAF.

There followed a long period of depression. I spent weeks in bed crying and Tony didn't understand. Many times I reached breaking point and spiralled into despair. I felt ashamed and guilty and neglectful of Tony (we were now married) but I couldn't put one foot in front of the other. I felt empty and alone, but couldn't face friends. I gradually came out of a long year and regained what I thought was a normal life – but you're not normal if you have bipolar disorder.

I had one symptom-free year – then was put on Lithium and life became a drag; flat, emotionless and wearing. The psychiatrist who put me on the drug told me it was a last resort and that if it didn't work there was nothing else he could do for me – which I now know not to be true. I was also on antidepressants with all the attendant side effects – tremor, dry mouth, constipation and so on. Tony had an affair and I threw him out. My cats died – two were run over and one had leukaemia. I ended up in a psychiatric hospital with full-blown mania.

My heart raced; I felt euphoric and capable of achieving anything; my thoughts were unstoppable and frenzied and I was hallucinating wildly. My head was bursting with ideas and I wanted to talk all the time. I was put on a horrible cocktail of drugs including Librium and Haloperidol, which made me see double – I just thought I needed new glasses. My world was in turmoil. I walked madly round the ward all night and must have covered miles. I lost a stone in weight. Eventually I was discharged – not better, but better than I had been.

My moods started to cycle rapidly – one month up, the next down. When I was manic I decided that I was fine and didn't see what all the fuss was about – when I was depressed I couldn't conceive of ever being able to wash my hair again. Simple tasks were beyond me. Hospital admission followed hospital admission until I took an overdose to end the pain. When I woke up, I decided that I had to gain control of my life and stop living my diagnosis.

People with a mental health disorder often do that – they define themselves as 'bipolar' or 'borderline' rather than as someone who has a life outside illness. It's a societal thing – the stigma attached to mental illness is so strong that we are crushed into an undergrowth of ill health and embarrassment, too afraid to stand up for ourselves.

With hindsight, I realised that I had achieved everything in a state of hypomania whilst I was at school and in the RAF. At first, I was completely disoriented by this discovery – did it mean that I was some sort of fraud, achieving only because I was a freak? This thought threw me into a state of complete despair. It seemed to me that my friends only had the old Hannah back when I was hypomanic and could be the life and soul of the party. But then I realised that I was what I was – illness included – and that the ups and downs were merely more severe than those of 'normal' people. In fact I began to rejoice in my 'otherness' and it became an intrinsic part of me.

I decided to get a job and worked in a dementia care home – possibly the most depressing environment I have ever been in – run by a bully of a woman who cared nothing for the patients, merely for routines. I trained as a psychotherapist in my spare time for two years, left the nursing home and got a job at the local acute psychiatric unit. I had enormous fun with mad people and some of the best experiences of my life. I made new and lasting friendships which survive to this day.

However, depression was only round the corner and it struck in 2005. I went into hospital for a weekend and stayed 11 months. I was completely suicidal and could only think about death as a blessed release. I suffered irrational fears and dreadful nightmares which left me sweating and afraid.

I couldn't face the nights. I shall never know how I got up every morning, but get up I did and eventually it passed. I had a new, kind psychiatrist and a new CPN – I had sacked the previous one for incompetence. I lost my job – again – which brought back all my memories of being sacked from the RAF and I started to get flashbacks to traumatic times I had suffered whilst serving. So back into hospital I went.

This time, after countless antipsychotics and antidepressants I was put on aripiprazole and venlafaxine. After the initial side effects had passed I suddenly realised that, for the first time in years, I felt like myself again. Hooray! I thought, and promptly went high. Sensibly, my psychiatrist merely adjusted the doses of the drugs and the episode passed. Since then, I have only ever gone high and haven't had a depression – after all those years and all those drugs I finally found what I wanted; a cocktail that actually made me feel like Hannah – the real one.

I have had 24 hospital admissions since 1996. The first ward I went into was the most frightening and nevertheless companionable place I have ever experienced. I was attacked and the staff did nothing. I attacked another patient who had stolen my cigarettes and the staff did nothing. The night staff slept the evenings away, blissfully unaware of the carnage. However, I met people with the same diagnosis – homeless people, street people, alcoholics and just plain bad people and they all became friends in adversity. It was us versus them, and we usually won.

The second hospital was a completely different place – a small, seven-bedded unit in town, so I could walk out and pretend I was normal by going for a coffee. I was mainly manic by this time and must have run the staff ragged. I was up all night singing despite being on shed-loads of medication, which didn't touch me. Sleep – who needed it? Euphoria became my watchword. After I was put on my current drugs I never crashed and burned after a high, so they became quite addictive.

When I was working on the acute ward, the staff discovered the recovery principles and started to bring them onto the ward. Groups were introduced and people went for walks every day. Patients had cookery lessons and did occupational therapy regularly. After I was admitted, high, to the small unit, I decided that I would introduce the recovery principles to the staff. To be fair, they took it on the chin. I got all the paperwork from the ward I had worked on and gave it to the Team Leader; she embraced it wholeheartedly and the unit became a beacon of hope and meaning.

Recovery may be regarded as about leading a valued and valuable life, understanding problems and finding ways of coping with difficulties. Being in recovery does not mean that I am cured; there is no cure for bipolar disorder. Recovery is a philosophy, an approach, which requires individuals to discover hope, find acceptance, have control over their lives, find meaning in their experiences and enjoy empowerment and responsibility.

I think, thus, that I am in recovery. I popped out of my life for a few years and went down to hell and up to heaven; now I find joy in just managing my life. I can't put myself under too much stress and I have to have time to myself in order to clear my head, but I make sure I do just that. I no longer think I was a fraud to be such a high achiever – doing things well whether I am high or not is just part of me. I would not be without the illness, which may sound strange, but I have had some astonishing insights and have come to know myself extremely well. My friends tell me when I'm going high and make me take chlorpromazine and lorazepam to bring me down again. I overspend, but hey – it's only money and I now have a fishing rod for every occasion. I like myself.

I couldn't have achieved any of this without my sister and my friends – you know who you are – and my psychiatrist and CPN, who also know who they are. So thank you for reading this and I hope it's given you some insight into what mental illness means to one individual. Me.

Healthy body, healthy mind

14

Terry Bowyer

For the last 13 years, and ever since my first mental illness episode, I have been battling the debilitating and unwanted consequences of schizophrenia. In the early days my psychosis and mental distress were impossible to deal with, and it felt very much as though my life was over. All the things I cherished and enjoyed before slipped away only to be replaced with chaos, madness, and pain. I was transformed from a content and confident human being to a stranger in the throws of self-destruction.

It took many years for me to come to terms with this and I spent lots of time in a vicious circle of relapse as I constantly broke down under the many pressures of life. I developed a serious illicit drug problem and an aversion to antipsychotic medication which left me with little chance of getting better. After many hospital admissions and attempts from professionals to help me, I finally turned the corner in 2005 when I decided to accept my condition and take responsibility for dealing with it. I kicked the drugs and started to comply with treatment. I found the right meds, learnt to self-manage my illness, and turned things around. I gained stability and confidence and began to live my life again.

Looking back after a long period of reflection, the many different factors involved in a person's route to wellness fascinate me. There are many diverse reasons why people achieve stability and I suspect most people need to find the right mix and combination of these to unlock their recovery potential. For me reaching acceptance and compliance with treatment was a huge step. Finding the right meds and beating my addictions was another. But learning to self-manage my condition has been the lasting factor that I employ to maintain my wellness.

One of these management areas is physical health and how looking after my body is crucial to my recovery. The brain is, after all, part of the body so it makes sense that good body health will have a positive effect on the mind. Unfortunately, becoming unwell and the resulting lifestyle can be hugely damaging to the body, and in turn adversely affect the psyche.

Firstly, your diet changes as healthy eating goes out the window. I began binging on fast foods high in fat, sugar, and salt, and ate processed meals, fizzy drinks, sweets and anything easy to prepare. You are unwell, depressed, and in distress so you haven't got the motivation or presence of mind to cook. Quick calories are all you opt for. I spent years eating like this, not realising that all that junk food is highly damaging to the body and also good at making you feel low and sluggish.

Secondly, mental illness inevitably leads to medication and whilst the therapeutic benefit is not in question, the side effects have consequences for the body. My metabolic rate became very slowed by my antipsychotics so that any food I ate was not completely burned off and therefore became stored as fat. Meds can also vastly increase appetite and block the normal 'I am full' response of the brain so that massive overeating becomes the norm. I put on six stone and ballooned to an enormous size because of this, and losing this weight has been a constant battle for me in recent times.

Thirdly, lack of strenuous exercise becomes a real threat to your body's health. Illness brings apathy, lethargy, and low motivation – so staying fit becomes a very low priority indeed. For many years I avoided anything fitness-related, like sport or leisure interests, and would rather eat and sleep than get moving. But the body is very much like any machine – it needs to be worked and tested to stay in shape, otherwise it falls into disrepair.

Lastly, the allure of substances and illicit chemicals can become a real problem because you want a quick fix for the low and desperate mood you are feeling. I chased the highs of alcohol and amphetamines, cocaine and cannabis, and even heroin to lift myself out of the doldrums, but this is a poisoned chalice. You are constantly chasing that first high and I found that as I became addicted my life spun further and further out of control. I was also a heavy smoker so the cocktail of toxins invading me became truly scary – and it went on for years! The damage done to my body and brain must have been severe and I am surprised my excesses didn't kill me – I am sure many of my mental relapses were linked to my drug abuse.

As I stabilised and began to accept my mental health problem I could begin to think about my route to wellness. It became clear that the way I was treating my body had to change. I was 19 stone, surviving on takeaways, living like a couch potato, and drugged to the eyeballs most days. I had to ditch this lifestyle and make some drastic changes.

Altering the way you live and the way you manage your condition is not easy. In my twenties I simply refused to comply with anything aimed at my health and was basically in denial about my whole situation – I wasn't helping myself. This is true of many people, but I developed 'insight' and a keen internal understanding of my problems, even if I didn't employ it. With reaching 30 came the fear of a life in ruins and I realised that I had to take responsibility for my illness and take control of dealing with it.

So I began to use this insight as wisdom and a guide to learn from. What am I doing wrong? What mistakes am I making and how do I stop repeating them? What can I personally do to stay well? In the pursuit of recovery you either learn and adapt or repeat and relapse. I became sure I wanted to be the former and not the latter. Is there some happiness I can find in my life?

I gradually began to think about respecting my body's health and what steps I could take to live a more healthy lifestyle again. I ditched the crappy food and replaced it with a much more balanced diet. I now eat a lot more home-cooked food including fruit and veg, white meats, wholemeal carbs, and natural fibre. I still have the occasional burger or pizza, but just as a treat these days. I have found that by thinking about my food, and spending a bit more time preparing it, I can give my body some 'clean energy'. This lifts my mood and makes me feel lighter, and I am far less sluggish than I used to be. It is quite a change but I have found that living this way is easy to get used to.

Dealing with the side effects of medication like weight gain, increased appetite, or a slower metabolism takes a bit more effort – it requires a long-term commitment to strenuous exercise and increased body fitness. I have found three to five heavy sessions of activity per week can eventually shed the weight, boost the metabolism, and let you eat more food simply because you're burning more calories. I started with swimming, then added football, jogging, squash, cycling, and gym. It's become my fitness regime and weekly routine that I use to counteract the side effects. Exercise like this is also a great antidepressant and I get a real 'buzz' or 'high' out of pushing my body to the limit. I sleep better, have more energy, and generally feel healthier and more centred. I can now take my antipsychotics for their much-needed benefit without fearing their unwanted effects.

Another change I have made is cleaning right up. I've taken everything mind altering that had grown so close to me and thrown it in the bin. I stopped taking stimulants like coke and speed which burn your brain out. I've dropped downers like heroine, cannabis, and alcohol which wreck every part of you. Even cigarettes had to go because of the poisons and toxins they contain. I'm now clean, sober, in recovery and in control. I have more money in my pocket and my body isn't having to fight against all the harmful chemicals that were inside me. Beating addictions is not easy and requires lots of willpower, but for me it was a crucial step. Mental illness is hard enough to deal with on its own and you make it almost impossible if you throw in addictions as well.

For me total abstinence from all these corrupting substances is the only way. I still enjoy life without them. Sometimes I reminisce about the good old times spent whilst high on drugs, but when I look back they were few and far between and mostly artificial. You won't find happiness at the bottom of a bottle, chasing a line, or rolling a spliff. You find it inside and I live by this rule now.

So for several years now, my bodily health has gone hand in hand with my mental recovery. I will probably have my condition for life but that's not so bad. I have learned many ways to stay stable, control my psychosis, balance my mood, and avoid relapse. I want to give myself a fighting chance at remaining well and protecting my physical health has become a big part of this. By eating right, staying fit, and staying clean I can feel healthy, whole, and happy. I don't chase highs in dark places anymore – I find them naturally, for free, and in the life around me.

Up and down the mood scale

15

Maggie Walker

Wow! I was still so full of life and energy after cleaning the house from top to bottom that I dashed off for a quick run along the seafront. Wow! I thought, I must metabolise helium instead of oxygen like normal people, as I long-jumped my way along the prom, and maybe I could even be able to run across the water to France. Hey! I thought if I am going to France I am going to have to read the French Existentialists and quick! So I ran home and jumped in the car and set off for Brighton to look for second-hand philosophy books and when I got there I bought 43 of them and, for the joke of it, stole an additional one on ethics, after which I strode triumphantly back to the car laughing to myself and practically begging someone to ask me what I had done.

On the drive home I got up to 90 mph along the Lewes bypass, screeching round the bends with *Phantom of the Opera* at full volume and all the windows wide open for the benefit of any passersby. I had forgotten about the French Existentialists by then – except at half past four thinking that the time was *Sartre heures et demi* – but had some brilliant ideas about writing music using numbers instead of notes and putting the numbers onto a spreadsheet and making it into a graph! I tried to imagine a graph of *Phantom of the Opera.* Ha! I know what that would be like, I thought, in a flash of inspiration, as I put the track back to the beginning yet again at maximum volume, it would be like my annual book sales accounts! An initial upward trend – and then the financial *crunch* just as the music starts tumbling and cascading down like the chandelier crashing into the orchestra pit below!

Still giggling when I got home, I was having so many brilliant ideas about musical graphs that I decided I must write a book about it and immediately began researching the idea by collecting up all the relevant books I could find in the house, starting with music, then Artificial Intelligence, then practically everything else including, for some reason, a book called *Levels of Constituent Structure in New Testament Greek*.

Then I realised that I was going to have to get some sleep at some point if my inspired genius was to be maintained and I hadn't slept much the previous night because of all the cleaning. I took two Zimovane but thought I must start writing straight away rather than go to bed and waste time waiting for them to take effect. And then I was overcome by the most fantastic ideas for what were certainly going to be *the* most splendid and exciting money-making schemes ever devised! First, I would become a local drugs tsar, catering to the currently untapped but potentially lucrative middle-class market for Zimovane among Hastings housewives, and I wasted no time in starting on this brilliant new venture by typing into Google, 'Buy Zimovane online without prescription NOW'.

Meantime I had another fabulous wheeze! Since I had been having such a whale of a time cleaning my house – including using my toothbrush to make the plugholes sparkle – I would become a professional house-cleaner as I had so much physical energy to burn that cleaning all day would leave me able to sit still long enough to dash off my masterpiece about – whatever it was – in the evenings! So I phoned a number in the local newspaper for an agency that was looking for cleaners and left a message – since no one answered at five in the morning – telling them how jolly marvellous I was.

Astonishingly, someone phoned back the next day and a man came round later the same day to 'interview' me. He, however, was made to sit on the piano stool while I perched high up on the back of the sofa and interrogated him on – what exactly, I can't remember, but I do remember instructing him to play something on the piano, which he did with great gusto – with me beating time from the sofa back. I assured him that my cleaning abilities were second to none and that I was conscientious and reliable (certainly not the stealing type) and he would bitterly regret it if he didn't take me on.

Although I did calm down a bit after securing this job, I still felt unusually well and energetic for about a month. I took on eight to ten cleaning clients and attacked the work vigorously. I remember one client standing by looking on nervously as I emptied out the spice jars on the table – not separating them very carefully – and washed out the jars, not waiting for them to dry adequately but quickly replacing the spice, which then stuck to the sides. I looked triumphantly at the client periodically as though daring her to point out that there was about 50% less spice in jars in total, and they had largely turned to paste. 'You're very *thorough*', she murmured.

At another house, the client kept telling me that there was a perfectly good mop I could use, but no, I insisted on doing a 'proper' job by crawling round on my hands and knees, taking the washing-up cloth – not a floor cloth – into every nook and cranny. One lady said, before I had even lifted a duster, that she had been told I was the best cleaner in Hastings.

So the upshot of this period of excess was that I had been left with a job I didn't want any more after the first few days scrubbing people's floors and I owned fifteen blister packs of a medicine that may or may not have been Zimovane; I had no idea because the labelling was all in Chinese. Whatever it was, at a cost to me of £150, I was going to have my work cut out to make it *rich* as the local drug baron. I wasn't going to get rich polishing tables either, at minimum wage and having to travel all over East Sussex for a few hours a week.

Away from work, I also felt so great for a few weeks that I read, or skimmed through, literally dozens of books – though no French philosophy, and I can't say I finished much or can remember anything at all – and listened to a lot of extremely loud music through the earphones on my CD player. I had the most fantastic sensation that I was controlling the music that was reverberating round the inside of my skull, which I saw as rather like the Albert Hall, and everything else that was happening around me was happening in time to whatever music I was listening to/ directing.

I phoned and met up with all my friends and went out and about much more than usual, being uncommonly sociable and fascinating. I am not usually very sociable, and certainly not very fascinating, but I was aware at one stage, when some friends were round and I was cooking spaghetti, that I was holding court and waving the wooden spoon around like a magic wand. I felt like a spaghetti-magician until I noticed that they were looking at me oddly. My behaviours attracted a lot of comments like, 'Don't you look well!' and, 'You're on good form!' and – less gratifyingly – 'Blimey, what have you been drinking?'

I did work diligently at my cleaning for several months, so as not to let people down, although after the first few visits I certainly wasn't *quite* so enthusiastic about polishing every single light bulb and plug socket. Then I started to feel less energetic and got a bit more insight into what had been going on. Phoning people? Buying drugs on the internet? Stealing books? Furious cleaning? Cooking voluntarily? Cripes. What was I thinking?

And then, with almost no warning, I crashed right down, just as if a switch had suddenly been flicked, and the light was off. It was that sudden, like waking up after drinking too much and realising what ghastly things you have done that you had previously promised yourself never to do again. At first I felt deeply ashamed about stealing the book and grasped suddenly that a lot of my recent behaviour had been really quite ridiculous. Where I had felt so unaccountably light and energetic, I now felt leaden and lethargic. Where I had felt as though I was made of 'hee hee' helium I now felt like a mass of what Hamlet called *foul and pestilent vapours*. Where I had felt so buzzing with new and brilliant ideas, I now realised that if I had really been in possession of such a marvellous brain full of brilliant ideas I would not currently be hoovering other people's sofas for a living.

A constant stream of very loud thoughts ran through my head criticising me for my stupidity and selfishness. Instead of the loud music, I now couldn't tolerate any external noise at all, not people, not traffic, not the radio, certainly not any music. When I went to the shops, I was irritated by the noises of shoes squeaking, doors opening, fan heaters and the pathetic idle chatter of customers. I was annoyed with the shop assistants for taking too long to sort out my change and I thought angrily that people were either ignoring me, sneering at me or laughing at me. I hated everyone, most especially myself, and found it best to keep away from society by staying in my room. I had a TV in my room and thousands of books around the house to choose from, yet I could find nothing to interest me at all and the noise of the television annoyed me so it stayed off.

When I could no longer tolerate the thought of getting up, never mind cleaning, I resigned. Before the cleaning I was a self-employed seller of books on the internet, so, notionally, I went back to this. However, I actually did virtually nothing and earned virtually nothing for a while, as I stopped really thinking or feeling anything at all and spent a lot of time curled up in bed staring at the wall, rocking intermittently, neither reading, nor writing, nor thinking, nor feeling. This is *much* harder to describe than feeling wonderful, or even irritable, as it is nothing but a vacuum of sensation – almost nothing at all except a sense of pressure upon the head and the feeling that, whatever foul stuff I was made of, it was gradually congealing and I would end up setting hard like concrete. I thought that once I had set hard, only my eyes would work and I would look out on a world I could no longer engage with and had nothing to do with.

These events took place several years ago now. I remember quite a lot about the high period, since interesting, unusual and memorable things happened. However, I also did things I regret but I don't think I actually hurt anything or anyone, unlike other occasions when my behaviour has affected others in a very bad way. My memories of the subsequent period of depression are now very vague. There is not much to remember except the psychic pain and staring at walls. I did not keep a mood diary in those days and although I know I was miserable, immobile for long periods, and thought about death and that I was turning to stone, I have no idea how long it went on for. I do know that after the episode I have described I looked for a job, which I still have and enjoy and that, crucially, unlike self-employment, has a sick pay scheme.

This episode was not the first in my life by any means. I have been having periodic mood swings since I was 16. The first time I had no idea what was happening to me. It felt very good at first. I had a short period – maybe two weeks – of happy high and giddy feelings, staying up all night writing rubbish or intensively colouring patterns; one night hitchhiking across the county to meet a friend, (also possibly mad, certainly bad and very dangerous to know indeed). Another night I got the friend round to my house and we went out and set fire to the village notice board, caused a lot of criminal damage to people's property and, less horrifically but annoyingly for the residents, swapped all the garden gnomes about on a little close of bungalows 'for more socially equal distribution'.

This resulted in police action and I was expelled from school but then taken back, as a special favour, as really I was a nice sort of girl who didn't do that sort of thing as a rule. Unfortunately though, shortly after this brief high, during the long hot summer of 1976, I fell into my first severe depression, isolating myself from friends and trying to isolate myself from family. I lived in a tent in the garden. My memories of this time consist of lying on a camp bed looking at the canvas wall, hating the heat and hating the sun and finding comfort only in the radio which I hugged to me day and night. All the songs from the summer of '76 still make me sad at any time, but ever since then, when very depressed I can never listen to any music at all. I spent some time in hospital and saw my first psychiatrist. I also never went back to school again.

Highs have occurred infrequently. I am much more prone to depression and the depressions usually last a very great deal longer than the highs. Every high phase has been followed by depression but not every depression has been preceded by a high. Intervals between mood problems have been months occasionally, sometimes years have passed between episodes. Occasionally episodes of depression have lasted years, on and off, sometimes with hospital stays, sometimes with very lengthy periods of unremitting guilt or anxiety, and these episodes, like the highs, have frequently interrupted my life, both university and work.

I have never been able to determine what causes either highs or lows and I have no idea what changes my mood from one to the other. When I have been down, it has often taken weeks or months to get better. Nothing seems to help. All those suggestions in books like phone a friend, set yourself a small task for the day, do seem to work sometimes for some people, but I find they can often be impossible to follow, especially if you can't get out of bed and cannot bear to use the phone. In fact, rather than working at feeling better when low, it has more than once happened that I have started to recover seemingly completely spontaneously. Once I was mooching miserably along the seafront, when out of the blue a switch in my head seemed to flick on, and for no obvious reason I suddenly looked up and thought, 'Oh! The sky is so blue! And so is the sea! The grass is so green!' And somehow, suddenly the world is in colour again and all the people are smiling at me.

I have often read of people with bipolar disorder who are asked, 'If you could press a button and the bipolar would be gone, never to come back, would you do it?' Many people say no. They like and treasure the high feelings enough to want to keep these, despite the downside. Some people of course also become very creative and productive, as numerous artists, musicians and writers with bipolar disorder have done. My disorder is nowhere near as severe as many other peoples' so what would I do? For me personally, the high feelings, intense and pleasurable as they are, represent a very small part of my life. Apart from – once – a clean house with dustbins polished and lined up in order, nothing very productive has ever emanated from me during a high, despite my marvellous ideas. In fact, some very destructive and costly things have resulted. Depression, as much as hanging or torture, is something I could not wish on my worst enemy and is something I have had far too much of. I can't imagine having an enemy so vile that I would inflict a month of deep depression on them. I would be glad to be free of this disorder – until such time as research shows how the great bits of the highs can be retained while the depression can be eliminated!

When John met Anorexia **16**

John Evans

There are many emotions that have coursed through me during my 14-year, ongoing battle with anorexia nervosa: anger, fear, regret, happiness, sadness, even occasional bursts of laughter at the sheer preposterousness of my life. Above all, though, this second half of my life has been frustrating, for me, for my family, for the people paid to help me fight back. My Anorexia has experienced only happiness and constant, deafening laughter, and I have found myself incapable of frustrating it at every turn.

My aim in this snapshot of my life is to convey as accurately as I can what it is like to live within the world of Anorexia, how it feels to exist from day to day with the sole objective of going to sleep at night not one gram heavier than when you woke up in the morning. Truth is, I'm not sure whether years of study or listening to hundreds of sufferers describing their own battles could ever furnish anyone with this knowledge if they haven't themselves lived with Anorexia in their heads. You try to look for a comparison to make it easier to understand: alcoholism or drug addiction perhaps? But even this comparison falls down, because there are no magazines printing post-Christmas drinking plans or recommending drug programmes in order to shape up for the summer. For every family member or health professional saying that it's OK to sit down and that food is just fuel for the body, there are 10 or 20 magazine articles or television programmes or advertisements pushing the latest diet or the latest fitness regime or the latest government initiative in order to combat childhood obesity. Alcoholics and drug addicts are not fighting a foe that is crucial to life; as an anorexic I have to do the one thing that is most difficult for me in order to stay alive.

It's all my fault though isn't it? All I have to do is eat some food and exercise less and everything will be sorted. Why am I doing this to the people who love me? Why can I not see the damage I am doing to myself, to my relationships, why can't I see everything that I am missing out on? Before Anorexia smacked me in the face, this would have been my reaction too. Eating disorders make absolutely no sense, and I am not going to pretend that being under six stone in weight made me anything other than extremely unattractive, but I had become completely subsumed by fear of being overweight and the ostracism that would inevitably follow. This was the fear that Anorexia clung to, presenting itself initially as the ultimate guardian against my ultimate hell and in time as my only true friend in the world, my only support against everyone who wanted to ridicule me, to make me fail and, most critically, to make me fat.

An important part of recovery from an eating disorder is to discover why it developed, why among all the hundreds of thousands of men who were bullied and who wanted to get fit was I hit by the most fatal of all mental illnesses? I had a happy childhood, a typically sweet tooth and I was a particularly fussy eater, and I was outgoing enough to be told off for talking in class. The more I look back and try to identify the moment that the door opened to Anorexia, if such a moment exists, the focus falls more and more on my teacher in junior school. When I was eight, he asked me to write the names of anyone who talked when he was outside the classroom on the blackboard. As punishment, they would then be held back at break time. Having been brought up to do as I was told, I never questioned this instruction, and I was struck by how instantly unpopular this made me amongst my classmates. There was nothing more severe than a bit of name calling at this point, but I had a very definite sense of suddenly not being acceptable, of having to do something extra to counteract my lack of cool and my fatness. Doubt entered my life for the first time and my personality, at least away from home, shifted decisively.

When I recount this episode, ever more convinced that this was the point in which confidence left my life to be replaced, eventually, by Anorexia, the sense of security that this knowledge gives me is met by only scepticism and frustration from my family. They can't understand the link between the bullying, which got more intense and more physical when I entered secondary school, and my eating disorder, and they can't understand what happened to their happy, intelligent son. I don't blame them for this; I had done everything possible to hide the bullying from them and my schoolwork continued to hold up even as I was dreading the bus journey to and from school every day. Truth is I was overweight and together with my glasses, my 'swotty' reputation and the chronic lack of self-confidence that had its roots in the 'blackboard incident', I was an obvious target for anyone looking to demonstrate how hard they were. I knew I would have to do something to make things improve, and seeing as I couldn't cure my eyesight and didn't want to start deliberately acting stupid, losing weight seemed the obvious solution.

It started quite moderately, a bit more cycling here, a few less sweets there, and as the weight began going down, the bullying did begin to recede. I accept now that there was a direct causal link here – we were all growing up both physically and mentally and I had moved onto a group of friends who weren't complete idiots – but at the time there was no doubt in my mind that the bullying had stopped only because I was no longer the fattest boy in school. To my mind, the only way the bullies would stay away was if I never became fat again, and from that moment my life was directed towards the core principle of thinness. Walking was supplemented by cycling, then by dog walking and weights regimes, while sweets became a once a week treat. I would politely decline all offers of going out in the night, conscious as I was of the absolute necessity of running up and down the stairs before bed every night. I saw nothing wrong in this, nothing excessive in what I was doing, because I was convinced that I was a naturally fat person and therefore had to do more than a 'normal' person in order to stay thin. By the age of 18 Anorexia had me by the balls, but because my exercise and eating was still to a degree under my parents' control, it was only when I went to university that it ripped my life apart completely.

At this point in my relationship with Anorexia, I was so much the junior partner that the illness had complete freedom in which to embed itself in every aspect of my life. There was no frustration, only complete bewilderment at how I had got myself into the situation and also supreme confidence that a bit of rest and a bit more food would have me on my feet in no time. After all, that was all there was to it, wasn't it? I kept being reminded I was missing out on so much, the amazing student lifestyle that I was supposed to be living while I was down the gym and exercising in my room. In later years I would add family relationships, a career, playing football and girlfriends to a growing list of things I could be doing with my life if only I could get better, but Anorexia never gave me that choice. And I was comfortable with that situation because, although I knew my life would have been different without it, I was not convinced it would have been better. Anorexia made me secure, even happy at times, because I knew that if I could stay thin, no one would ever make fun of me for being overweight. Yeah I would have liked more money and it would have been nice to be able to make my parents happy, but if that got in the way of what I needed to do to satisfy the demands of my Anorexia, then they would have to be sacrificed. Even ten years on, the fear of being bullied again overrode anything, and Anorexia used this fear to secure itself so tightly that it came to influence every aspect of my life.

Whenever anyone tried to talk me out of my Anorexia, be they therapists, friends, family or work colleagues, they always emphasised the material things that the illness was impacting on – my poor health, my inability to play sport, my inability to keep warm in the winter – all of which were legitimate arguments and reasons to fight back. The thing is, you quickly learn to shape your life around your Anorexia, accepting the things you lose as the price for living the life you believe will make you happy and acceptable. I've never been ignorant of the compromised life I have led, but when you don't believe that there is any way things can be different, you give up fighting and try to live the life that Anorexia has constructed for you. And it's not the material things that hurt the most – like I say you adapt to those and learn to shut out the pain your illness is causing those close to you.

What really grinds you down is the stuff no one else can see, the things that never leave you until you go to sleep at night and then reappear as soon as you wake in the morning. The thoughts that Anorexia puts in your head get louder and louder until you do whatever it is that will satisfy the illness, be it exercise or putting food in the bin or deciding not to go out and expose yourself to a potentially risky social situation. And they stay away, maybe for five minutes, or even an hour, but they come back, and the more they are indulged and obeyed the louder and more frequent and more intense they become until almost nothing else seems to matter other than doing whatever you can to shut them up, even for a second. And all the time you can see the pain of those close to you and the damage you are doing to yourself and you become angrier and more despairing at your failure to resist, but still you don't feel angry enough to fight back, nor do you ever really hope to do so.

In the months after my diagnosis, I had no idea of what being anorexic meant and would mean for my future. Once I began receiving therapy, I began to discuss the fears that lay behind the eating disorder, the way it made me think and the actions I could begin to take to fight back. As my weight restored, I became convinced that I was winning, that all I had to do was to maintain a healthy weight and Anorexia would never darken my door again. Anorexia, however, has very little to do with what your weight is at any one time – my mood and my actions have varied little regardless of whether I was BMI12 or BMI 20, at least until I began to address those fears that underpinned the illness. The failure to tackle what was driving the Anorexia at an earlier stage meant that it stayed, sometimes waiting in the background, more often in the forefront of my mind commanding my every action.

By its very nature, as with all mental illnesses, Anorexia gets into your brain, controls your thoughts and never, never lets go. I'm not saying that I didn't think to the contrary, that the idea of acting against the Anorexia never occurred to me, because it almost always did. I almost never acted against it though, because of the guilt that I know would follow. It reaches a stage whereby every decision you make and every choice you take is directed by what your eating disorder dictates. Are you going to eat that food? *Only if you exercise to compensate later.* Do you need to walk before, during and after work? *You have to take every opportunity you have to exercise, because the guilt of not doing so will never leave you.* What's the best way to put out the washing? *Try taking each individual item of clothing from the washing machine outside to the line one by one. Don't worry about what the neighbours think, you are only doing what you need to do to stay thin.* And don't think for one second that I was ignorant of how ridiculous I looked, how much I was hurting the people who stuck by me, how much physical danger I was putting myself under. I knew all this, and I was frustrated at my inability to do anything to stop it, but that was just it, I felt like I had no choice.

I always clung to the hope that someday everything would change, that I would wake one morning with all the determination and strength I would need to move on from my Anorexia and to embrace the life that was waiting for me. That day never came, however, and while I waited I resolved to do all I could to keep my Anorexia as quiet as possible, to satisfy it in each and every way because I knew I could not handle the guilt of going against its orders. This wasn't guilt about letting someone down or carrying out some petty crime, this was gut-wrenching, ever-present guilt mixed with fear that until you compensated for what you had done would never leave your mind. If I missed my early morning walk, that would be all that occupied my mind all day until I either skipped a meal or did extra exercise later on to make up for it.

Obviously my work suffered accordingly, but whatever dressing down I received was nothing compared to the deafening catcalls of my Anorexia whenever I acted against instinct. My life became a rigid routine, less a life in fact than an existence, where I ate exactly the same food at exactly the same time and did as little sitting down as possible, all with the no-compromise aim of not putting on weight. After the age of 18 I never expressly intended to lose weight – it seemed to happen with little or no direction from me – and thus I managed to convince myself that I wasn't a proper anorexic. The less I subsequently did to fight the illness, the stronger it became, the more its voice merged with mine until they became indistinguishable.

In those early years, when I was trying to find an explanation for what had happened to me and why all that exercise and dieting had not turned me into the rippled Adonis I had been expecting, I became frustrated by the apparent impossibility of a man becoming anorexic. Every textbook I read and every first-person account I scanned spoke back to me in terms of 'her Anorexia' and the ways in which 'she' was affected. I was never affected by any kind of male reluctance to admit I had a female illness, not least because I was diagnosed before I really knew there was anything seriously wrong. I knew I'd lost some weight, but I was actually more concerned with how tired I was. I can, however, see how the emphasis in eating disorder information on how it is predominantly a female issue could dissuade a male sufferer from coming forward, especially as it is often those people with low self-esteem who are most vulnerable. I was fortunate – if that is the word – to be diagnosed at university, as I doubt I would have received such a sympathetic hearing from my peers at school.

Nevertheless, I have never felt disadvantaged as compared with the female sufferers I have encountered. This is certainly true of my two inpatient admissions, where if anything I found it easier to integrate myself and to remain above the inevitable tensions that such an environment engenders primarily because I was the only male on the ward. In my opinion, it is Anorexia that has set me apart from other members of my own sex, rather than my gender distinguishing me greatly from other anorexics. When my friends were out getting drunk and chasing girls I was at home, running up and down the stairs. When I deigned to join them and they went for a takeaway, I would politely decline all offers of a chip, pretending I wasn't hungry. And when I went to the gym, whilst other men would look at their reflections face to face, checking out their pecs and biceps, I would always look side-on, just to check that the packet of crisps I had eaten earlier had not turned me into a blimp.

I've never met an anorexic with precisely my back story or a list of behaviours and rituals that exactly mirrors my own, though general themes do seem to exist. Fear of being fat is a virtual given, though this can be to do with fears of ridicule from others or more intertwined with feelings of self-worth and what the sufferer feels they deserve. I do consider myself fortunate in that I am 'just' anorexic – I have never been bulimic nor have I resorted to self-harm or drugs as a release from the pain. Indeed, the lack of real regret serves to highlight the extent to which Anorexia had taken over. Yes, I was sorry that this was how my life had turned out, but there was nothing I could do to change things so why bother worrying about it – just get your head down and concentrate on living the best anorexic life possible, while continuing to cling to the hope that one day that switch in your head would click and everything would resolve itself. Whatever anger I could summon up was directed squarely at myself for being so, so stupid. I had no anger left for my Anorexia.

After 13 years of hoping, I gave up. There was no way that I would ever be able to live without Anorexia so I might as well accept its presence and move on as best I could. I'd got through university, moved three times, had five career changes, one hospital admission lasting three months and sworn hundreds of times that I was 'really trying, honestly', and still nothing had changed. Sure I'd had times of being a healthy weight, but the thoughts and behaviours never went away and my priorities never changed. I got tired of fighting and lying and pretending that everything was OK, so I just gave up and accepted my life as an anorexic. I truly believed that if I gave up hoping and stopped fighting back then things would get easier, that the voice would occasionally go away and the guilty feelings would stop as long as I did everything I could to satisfy my Anorexia. The feelings remained though, as strong as ever, and every time my weight fell an extra 100g (I was back to weighing myself before and after every meal), I dismissed it in the belief that things would sort themselves out.

And I believe giving up was the crucial stage in what I hope and believe will be my eventual recovery from Anorexia. As it turned out, giving up hope had not made me any happier, it did not make my friends or family any less worried about me and it certainly did not do anything to quieten the voice in my head or make it any less omnipresent. After a few months I came into contact with a recovered person who, despite my scepticism, was adamant that they had left the illness behind. And something inside me wondered what if? If they could fight back, what if I gave it one last try? The hope had kept me bubbling along in my own little anorexic world, confident that everything would work itself out. Once I stopped hoping, it made me realise how empty my life had become and quite how unhappy I really was, but I also knew that I could not fight back alone. The decision to ask for help again, despite the history of failed attempts and broken promises, is perhaps the strongest thing I have ever done. My first hospital admission had happened without a great deal of input from me. I ruled it out completely because of my job and hoped that my therapist would drop the idea. Even when work agreed to grant me three months leave, I never really believed I would be cured nor really worked to achieving this end. I restored to a healthy weight before discharge, but this only allowed me to establish a new basis for my self-esteem as the 'One-Admission Man'.

Ever since the bullying began and I became painfully aware of my lack of acceptability amongst my peers, I had constantly sought reassurance that I was likable, funny or clever. I continued to act in accordance with my own values and those of my parents, who never withheld compliments when they felt they were deserved, but that wasn't enough anymore. I had been conforming to what my parents and I believed was right when I wrote the names on the blackboard, but that still didn't stop the hostility from my classmates. I was never sure of anything from that point, and even when I received reassurance doubts remained which were later seized upon by Anorexia. The only thing I knew for certain was that I knew more about football than anyone else, and thus I played up to my 'Statto' image because I knew no one could beat me in that single area. Later, when I began to be complimented for my new, slim-line physique, I felt that I had to be the slimmest, fittest person at school, and all my efforts went towards that goal to the detriment of all other aspects of my life. And when I left hospital for the first time, I could no longer claim to be the thinnest person in my world. I had been sustained in my upward momentum by constant praise over my progress and how well I was fighting my Anorexia, and I began to shift the basis of my self-esteem from being the best anorexic to being the best, one-time only, anorexic hospital patient.

And that is OK, up to a point, as long as you continue working on your eating disorder once you have been discharged. For me, however, discharge merely allowed me the freedom to get right back into my anorexic life, albeit with the buffer of a few extra pounds. My therapist saw the danger signs a long way off, but I just deflected her concerns until we both got frustrated with each other and called it quits. Discharge as an outpatient just bolstered my belief that I had been cured, even though my weight had begun to recede once more. As my self-esteem was based not on me being healthy but merely on my staying out of hospital, I managed to convince myself that I had recovered, even when everyone around me could see things had gone backwards. And even when I did give up hope of recovery, that knowledge that I had 'beaten' Anorexia in one hospital admission was the one thing I could cling to, my one piece of sure-fire evidence that I was a success.

So the day I agreed to a second hospital admission, I not only handed control of my life away from my eating disorder, I also took the risk of destroying what remained of my self-esteem. This time I knew I had to go into hospital with a clean slate, willing to start my life and my value system from scratch if I was truly to recover. This time I confessed all to my boss in the hope they would let me have the time off, instead of almost pleading with them to say no as I had four years previously. Once I had made the decision to fight back, other things came more easily, and I found help within the hospital to support me on my new path. Crucially, I also had the self-pride of knowing I had decided to go one more time, which galvanised me for the battle ahead.

Even then, however, progress was not up and up. I kept a daily diary throughout my second admission, recording my thoughts as each day brought new challenges, fresh achievements and ever-increasing weights. My mood could swing from day to day from optimism to despondency, as detailed in the following extract. Anorexia was not as dominant in hospital, but neither did it stay at the door, and every move against it, whilst easier to attempt, still brought it screaming back into my mind.

Saturday 9 January: Day 27

Days like today are the reason I have to keep fighting – unless I give up my Anorexia, I cannot meet Hannah for coffee, walking leisurely around the shops and not worrying about how far or how fast we go. I've had a great afternoon, precisely because I felt able to spend time with my best mate, and that is what life is about. What would be better: a happy, fit guy or a sad, lonely, thin guy? There is no competition.

Good snack out. Tried a milkshake for the first time ever (toffee caramel fudge) then, having missed my bus I paid £7 for a taxi rather than walking around for 45 minutes in the cold. Those are the type of decisions I have to make, the type that sensible, healthy people make every day of their sensible, healthy lives. I certainly feel more relaxed and if there's only one thing that has come out of this then it's that my friendship with Hannah has been reinforced. She has been more of a friend to me than I can say and the only blessing this illness has given me is that it has brought her into my life. Thing is, I feel as if recovery would actually be good for ME. I want to do it not just for Hannah, my family, my health, my job and my mates, but actually for ME. Days like today are what it's all about, it's why I came back and it's why this time I will get there. It will be the hardest thing I have EVER done to beat this but, hell, if it was easy I would have done it before now. I might never run a marathon, play up front for Everton or win any body-building contests, but if I can just learn to love myself, to recognise the qualities I have instead of looking to portray myself as some kind of health freak, I will be more healthy and less freaky. I can do this and I will do this.

Sunday 10 January: Day 28

Emotions all over the shop again. If I'm honest, what Mum said about me at Christmas was absolutely true – I have always run away, always tried to outpace the Anorexia instead of meeting it head on. If I never challenge the Anorexia, how can I hope to beat it? Just waiting and hoping it will go away has never worked. Pushing the illness only as far as *it* would allow only provided temporary relief. I just feel like I need to keep pushing, maintain the momentum that I have built up. At the same time I'm wary of going too quickly and creating false hopes and expectations, especially when I see my parents. Can I really let them down again? I'd love them to share the excitement and optimism that I have at the moment, but can I really expect them to be anything other than sceptical. Even the staff here clearly have their doubts – maybe they think I'm hiding something – but it's not a 'sod them' proving point with them, I simply want to repay them for all the help they have given to me by proving that this can work. I can never hope to repay my parents for everything they've done for me; all I can do is try to make them happy.

At the end of the day (literally) I feel positive. Another day without exercise, and we'll just have to see what the scales say tomorrow. They definitely still hold some fears for me, and my default setting is still against weight gain, but again today was so positive that it all seems worth it. This remains a very scary thing that I am undertaking, but is also exciting and filled with such potential that it would be criminal to give up without giving everything I have.

Good stuff – snack out, meeting Karl, making people smile.

There were a number of things that got me through my second hospital admission and set me on the path to recovery which I continue on today. Support from staff, family and friends was crucial, especially at the times when Anorexia reacted to being challenged by extra food or less exercise. As I had no choice over eating the food I was presented with and no chance to exercise to excess, much of the guilt that Anorexia routinely piled on top of me was removed, as indeed was any pride I could take in being the thinnest person in my world.

By giving me a break from 'Anorexic John', hospital allowed 'John' to emerge from a 14-year hibernation and, much to my surprise, people seemed to like me when I wasn't desperately seeking their approval! I began to take positives from every friendly text message I received and every board game I played, because this all allowed me to rebuild my self-esteem from scratch and to base it on something more substantial than being the best at something. Above all, I now had belief in myself, belief that I could beat this, that I was something more than the illness and that, actually, Anorexia did not have to be my life.

And I continue to fight, my mood continues to go up and down and I am still coming to terms with a future about which I am uncertain. Anorexia lends you that certainty, a feeling of safety and security when you have failed to find it elsewhere. Anorexia, though, does not make you happy or relaxed or indeed lend you the safety and security that you believe it does. And Anorexia never, ever leaves you alone, until you fight back and choose to live.

17

Shit happens

Ali Quant

Intruder

Check behind sofa. Go into kitchen. Try to dodge the entrance to the loft above my head, because the man up there is watching me through the crack. Back into the lounge, check behind sofa to make sure no one got in in the two minutes I was out of the room. Into bathroom, stay away from extractor fan in ceiling because man in attic can see me through that too. (Please note this prevents all showering, can't stay in there that long. Not good for someone with cleanliness issues.) Back into lounge via hallway which is a gauntlet to be run – the stairwell behind me, the cupboard to my right, the bedroom at the other end all serving as perfect hiding places for the predator. Check behind sofa again, oops didn't pull it out quite enough so have to do it all over again. Try to ignore the lumpy carpet where the sofa's been moved so many times. Repeat until shoulder hurts from moving furniture so many times a day and downstairs neighbour thinks I'm in training for a marathon. Then repeat some more.

I can't wait to move to a flat that feels safe.

Shit happens

Today we shall be talking about *actual* crap. Poo. Shit. Faeces (or feces, I guess, for our friends across the pond). Take warning here and now, you might not want to continue reading if you're eating or have a dodgy constitution, or if you get triggered or upset by talking about the icky stuff that comes out of butts. Sure? OK then, here we go.

For a long time, I've dealt with a little extra poo in my life than most people deal with (unless they're in the colonic irrigation business, I suppose). Not from me, you understand – from one of my voices.

One of my voices is a kind of Dog, the closest I'd be able to describe him here is he's kind of halfway between a normal dog and Anubis. And one of the things he does is transform things into dog shit. Up to now it's always been food, I will be cooking a meal and suddenly the Dog starts laughing and there I am staring at a pan full of shit instead of pasta or whatever it started off as. Then I get told all kinds of unpleasant things, usually on a theme of 'eat shit, dirty bitch!', taunting me and telling me that's what I should eat because that's all I'm worth eating. So the pan and its contents get whipped off the cooker and straight into the bin, leaving me somewhat distressed and scared to attempt to eat for a day or two. I do have a mental list of 'safe' foods which have never been transformed, and there are some foods I just can't eat anymore because without fail they always get transformed whenever I attempt to prepare them.

But I work around it, not that it's particularly easy to deal with, but it is a known territory. I know that as long as I get rid of everything the muck touched (i.e. usually a pan and utensil of some kind) as soon as possible then I can generally cope with it, despite the unpleasantness. And thankfully it's not something that happens every day.

However for a day or two he's been trying out variations which have been incredibly unpleasant and not so easy to deal with. Anyone who knows me knows I spend an inordinate amount of time washing or otherwise cleaning my hands; that's part of a different set of issues entirely. The Dog has for some reason decided to use this against me in a very direct way: he has started transforming soap and cleaning things into poo. So I take a handwipe from the tub, start rubbing it over my hands with the intention of getting clean, only to look down and see my own hands are covered in shit. Or I go to wash my hands, press down on the soap dispenser, and instead of soap out comes shit. He's done it in the shower too, with shower gel and shampoo.

I can't stop it happening, I have no way of knowing when it will happen and all I've been able to do is hold my hands under running water for as long as possible to try to get all the crap off and do my utmost to not go to clean them so often. As a temporary measure I've taken to wearing disposable gloves for as long as possible because these can be changed as often as I need to and they do reduce the amount of hand washing I do. I feel incredibly dirty wearing them, I've always hated wearing gloves, but at the moment I'd rather feel dirty from a relatively clean box of medical gloves than have shit on my hands all the time. But that is only going to work for a while. It has to stop soon because I can't go around wearing gloves forever.

I know why he's doing it. He knows I've been more stressed than usual recently so he knows he can get away with it; he knows I'm less able to find ways around things and avoid his tricks. He always tells me I'm dirty, bad, rubbish, and by changing soap into muck he knows he's getting to me in one of the most disgusting and distressing ways he can. It means he's got an excuse to taunt me and laugh at me and call me names. It means I'm losing that bit of control that cleaning gives me. It's dirty and unpredictable and I'm not in charge of it anymore – *he* is.

I hate how it's always aimed at things I can't avoid. Well yes, you can avoid eating for a while, but it's not as if you can give up for good. Same with washing. If when I went to bed there was a pile of crap on my pillow, I'd be able to avoid it completely; I'd just sleep on the sofa. But when it's things like food and my own hands, it can't be avoided, it has to be dealt with face-on. I hate that he knows that. I hate that he knows precisely how to get at me, and that he knows when my defences are right down like they are now.

EXPERIENCING THE SYSTEM

Surviving: From silence to speaking out

18

Helen Leigh-Phippard

The story of my 12-year journey through mental health services can be split into four broad stages. First is my breakdown into illness. This is followed by what I think of as 'the silent years', a period of four or five years of feeling completely oppressed by mental health services. Then came a year when the diagnosis of a brain tumour pushed mental health problems somewhat into the background, but also offered the first sign of hope of possible recovery. Finally comes a period of slow painstaking recovery, of coming to terms with my mental health problems, of taking back control over my life, and of learning to manage my symptoms.

My initial breakdown was astonishingly fast and absolutely terrifying. Suffering from anxiety and stress as I tried to juggle a demanding job with being the mother of a toddler, my GP prescribed a course of antidepressants. Within a day of starting these I was hallucinating and within 48 hours I was in Accident and Emergency (A&E) having overdosed on paracetamol. The overdose was the outcome of a bargain I had made with the swarm of hundreds of huge metallic hallucinatory spiders that had filled my house for two days, my life in exchange for them not hurting my daughter. In A&E I was treated for the overdose and seen by a consultant psychiatrist, who concluded that the hallucinations were due to the medication and discharged me to the care of my GP.

My GP changed my medication and reduced the dose, but the damage was done. The hallucinations didn't stop, although they did become less severe and less frightening over time. I have now been hallucinating daily for around 12 years and have become so used to them that they rarely bother me at all, but in the first months and years they often left me paralysed with fear. Not surprisingly, my mental health deteriorated rapidly. At the same time I began to suffer a range of neurological symptoms, apparently side effects to psychiatric medication, and I really had no idea what was happening to me or how to deal with it. A referral to a psychiatrist offered no answers: the only help he could offer was a diagnosis (severe psychotic depression) and more medication.

After three months of worsening hallucinations and constant problems from the apparent side effects of medication I became convinced that the medication was poisoning me and cut the soles of my feet to let the poison out. At this stage my GP suggested a short stay in a psychiatric hospital might help me and give my husband some respite. The admission was handled over the phone: I spoke with the ward manager and agreed to a voluntary admission on the understanding that I could come home at any point if I wanted to.

I was admitted to hospital on a Friday evening. Although I was very scared, the staff were friendly, I had a room to myself and everything seemed OK at first. However, I soon realised that I had made a mistake in agreeing to admission: who I was, and who I would be forever after, was changed dramatically by the apparently simple act of agreeing to a voluntary admission to a psychiatric hospital. It was very quickly obvious that what I said or wanted no longer mattered; I was a psychiatric patient and that meant that my opinion, my own wishes, everything I said now had very little value.

One particular incident stands out. When I was queuing for medication on my second evening in hospital an incident occurred somewhere on the ward. Alarms sounded and staff all converged on one of the corridors. I was given my meds and sent to my room. I was already having problems with the medication because the dose had been increased on my admission to hospital, despite my protests, and I was experiencing worsening side effects. By the middle of that evening my arm was burning as though it was on fire. I called a nurse and asked for an ice pack to relieve the burning sensation. The nurse left and came back a few minutes later to tell me that I couldn't have any ice and I couldn't be experiencing side effects of the meds, because I hadn't taken them. They hadn't been signed off in the medication record book and so I couldn't have had them. I insisted that I had and explained that the alarms had gone off as I was given my meds and that must be why the book hadn't been signed – but no one believed me. Moreover, the nurse wanted me to take a dose of the medication now since she didn't believe that I had already had it. I refused and decided that I wasn't prepared to stay there any more. I asked to be discharged but was told that I couldn't leave – I had to stay until a doctor decided I was fit to leave.

This was the moment that changed my life forever. As a working professional I had been treated with respect throughout my adult life and as far as I was aware no one had ever doubted the veracity of anything I said. Yet here I was telling the truth but no one would believe me. I had also been told that I could leave when I wanted, but now I was being effectively held against my will. I felt as though I had been sent to prison for a crime I hadn't committed.

I had to stay for another 36 hours, until Monday morning when a meeting was held to determine if I should be held under section. I lied throughout the meeting and everyone present knew I was lying. I was asked if I was hallucinating and I said no. We all knew that wasn't true but I didn't trust any of the mental health professionals present with the truth any more. Fortunately my husband wouldn't agree to a section and I was allowed to leave.

For the next five years I was trapped in a mental health system in which I felt utterly powerless. I was transformed completely by my short stay in hospital and in particular by the way I was treated while I was there. I felt angry, frustrated and helpless, but I was also determined never to go back. The next five years were devoted to doing what I had to do to survive my mental health problems and to stay in some control of my life. This meant becoming a silent patient, but also often a non-compliant one.

On my release from hospital I was prescribed sulpiride, an antipsychotic that caused a tremor similar to that of a Parkinson's sufferer (I was also given procylcidine, a medication usually prescribed for Parkinson's to counter some of the tremor). Taken in combination with the antidepressants and sleeping pills I was also prescribed, I was nothing short of a trembling zombie. I knew that if I continued to take the medication I would not be able to look after my daughter, and I was very afraid that I would lose everything if I became the compliant patient that the mental health professionals wanted. So I refused to take any medication other than antidepressants and eventually I stopped taking those too.

For the next five years I was both a difficult and a largely silent patient. These years were characterised for me by distrust in mental health services and an overwhelming sense of disempowerment. For five years I saw a psychiatrist once a month for ten or so minutes. I quickly learned to say as little as possible. The loss of control over my life meant that I was constantly feeling suicidal, but my fear of readmission to hospital also meant that I was learning to manage those suicidal feelings in order to avoid that outcome. I reported this to the psychiatrist on one occasion, but the next time I saw him he said that the fact I had mentioned feeling suicidal during our previous meeting meant that he was considering a section again in order to administer ECT. He made no mention of the fact that I had said I was managing the suicidal impulses, and I was reminded that I had no control over what was written in my notes. Over a period of several months I came to realise that I wasn't going to get the help I wanted from mental health services and that, if I said too much, I might find myself sectioned. So, as an act of self-preservation, I learned to be silent, to give only monosyllabic answers to questions.

Antidepressants didn't improve my symptoms and caused so many side effects that I eventually stopped taking them (I was prescribed more than half a dozen different antidepressants one after the other, some in combination with lithium, over a period of about three years), initially without the knowledge of my psychiatrist, although when it was obvious that my symptoms had neither improved nor worsened since I'd stopped taking them, I did eventually tell him that I had done so. All this time I was also continuing to suffer neurological symptoms, which were dismissed by medical professionals as side effects of the psychiatric medication. I lost my sight briefly on a couple of occasions, had recurring numbness and tingling in my hands and feet and across the back of my head, burning sensations all over my body and urinary problems. I also started to lose my hearing and was fitted with hearing aids.

A year or so after my hearing problems began I developed problems with my balance and was sent for a brain scan by my ENT consultant. The scan revealed a small meningioma brain tumour. I was more relieved than scared. I thought I now had an explanation for my continuing hallucinations and the neurological symptoms I was suffering from. My neurologist and neurosurgeon both insisted that none of my symptoms could be due to the meningioma, but I didn't believe them, and was hugely hopeful of a cure. I was scared of neurosurgery, but I also had hope for the first time in five years.

I eventually had a craniotomy to remove the tumour. This was a turning point for me for several reasons. For around a week I thought the neurosurgery had cured me. I had no hallucinations and, although I did have some new neurological symptoms, I put those down to the surgery. I was very depressed while in the hospital after my surgery, but once I was discharged I felt euphoric at having survived the surgery and at being home once again. However, after a couple of weeks the hallucinations returned, followed more slowly by the symptoms of depression and the familiar neurological problems and I had to accept that I had not been cured. Although this was difficult, it heralded the start of a long, slow but transformative process of coming to terms with my mental health problems.

At the same time, following the surgery my psychiatric care was transferred to a community mental health team; I later understood that this should have happened on my discharge from the psychiatric hospital some years earlier but hadn't, for reasons that have never been satisfactorily explained. This transfer proved hugely helpful, not least because for the next three years or so I had a fantastic community psychiatric nurse (CPN). I was hugely distrustful of her at first: for most of the first year I was largely silent during our hour-long meetings, giving only my usual monosyllabic answers to questions, but her patience proved infinite and her listening skills were profound. For the first time in more than five years I had met someone who wanted to listen to what I had to say (even when that was very little), who respected what I said and appeared to think my opinions about my illness and my treatment were worth listening to, and who actually tried to help me understand what was happening to me.

Looking back, I am always astonished that no one apparently saw the need to explain what was happening to me during the first five years of my illness. I was terrified because I didn't understand what was happening, but mental health professionals simply gave me a diagnosis, told me that my life had now changed and I had to accept that they knew what was best for me; yet once I had a better understanding of what was happening to me that sense of terror lessened and I was much more able to manage my symptoms. Of course, there was more time for those kinds of explanations in community care, but I also felt for the first time that I was in the care of someone who was focused on helping me, rather than simply managing me.

This was the beginning of my long, complex and difficult process of recovery. Key to that process was a CPN who understood recovery as a philosophy, and who worked in a recovery-oriented way from the outset (although it was two years into that process before I understood that that was what she was doing). In our long conversations she always focused on me, what I thought I needed, what I believed my biggest problems were, and how together we might find solutions to those problems.

I had been more or less pushed into taking medical retirement from my career as a university lecturer some years earlier, and my CPN quickly realised that I still hadn't come to terms with that career loss and that this was contributing to my continued mental health problems. She suggested that I consider volunteering locally as a service user consultant, and this was probably the most important thing she did for me. I joined a mental health service user project run by the local branch of MIND, which worked with the local NHS Trust and other service providers to involve service users in the development of mental health services and in staff selection and training.

Over a number of years this work became central to my recovery for four key reasons. First and most importantly, I began to meet and talk to other service users. Up until this point I had never had a proper conversation with another service user about mental health problems or services, or indeed about anything else. As I heard their stories and worked with fellow service users, I very quickly came to admire and respect them and this attitude had a profound effect on my views about my own mental health problems. I began to appreciate the resilience and courage that so many mental health service users share in the face of a largely unsympathetic and stigmatising society, and in the space of a few months I went from being ashamed of having a mental health problem, to being proud to be a member of the mental health service user community.

Second, I found a use for my teaching skills that gave me a sense of purpose while at the same time potentially contributing to the improvement of service provision. I began to get involved in the training of NHS and other staff in mental health awareness, recovery, risk assessment and understanding suicide. This was difficult work, but I soon realised that I was good at it and that I could often change peoples' attitudes towards those with mental health problems simply by telling my story. A couple of years later I began to work with the carer and service user group in a local school of nursing, contributing to the mental health team's teaching on various modules of the different nursing courses. I also became involved in the development of research in the local NHS Trust and in an advising scheme for DPhil psychology students on placement locally. All of this work has allowed me to use my teaching and research skills once again, to do something worthwhile and that I can feel proud of, and this has been invaluable in helping me to recover some self-esteem and self-confidence.

Third, having the opportunity to tell and retell the story of my journey through mental health services has enabled me to gain a rich personal understanding of my own experiences. I have tried to gain access to therapy a number of times over the years but, until recently, had been deemed 'unsuitable' and 'too vulnerable' for therapy. That meant that I had little opportunity to talk about and gain an understanding of my breakdown and subsequent mental health problems. Telling my story as a service user in a training environment proved enormously useful in allowing me to explore what had happened and to think about it again and again. As I did that, I began to understand my experiences and explore them in conversation with students. The more I did this, the more I took ownership of my own story and the more my story began to change from being a very negative story to, at least in parts, a positive one.

Fourth, it is a cliché to say that information is power, but it is also true. Developing mental health problems and in particular entering the mental health system is a profoundly disempowering experience. In my first five or so years in the system I felt that I was often treated as a child, I was very much the object of a process, told what to do, when and how to do it and labelled as being non-compliant if I asked questions or rejected particular treatments. In contrast, becoming part of an active service user community was an incredibly empowering experience. Suddenly I had access to information – about my rights, about how the system should work, about what I should be told and the choices I should be able to make, and, most importantly, I had access to managers and policy-makers. I began to understand that there is often a huge gap between what should happen in services and what does happen and that making my own decisions about my treatment is being assertive, not non-compliant, and is a crucial key to recovery.

This final stage represents the past six years of my life, and takes me to where I am now, managing, living my life, not recovered but definitely in recovery. My symptoms are little changed from the first years of my illness, but the difference now is that I feel in control of them, able to manage them most of the time. I don't expect ever to be free of them, but I am also confident that, on the whole, I can cope with them on a day-to-day basis. I still need help to do that, but I can often find that help from servicer user and other colleagues rather than from statutory services. Perhaps most importantly, I can look back at my own experiences and know that, having survived so much, there is no reason to believe that I can't continue to survive whatever life and my own mental health problems have yet to throw at me.

19

Life is like a game
of snakes and ladders

Diana Byrne

I went to University and I gained an Honours degree in Psychology, Philosophy and Physiology. My first glimpses of mental illness were apparent during this time, however I did not realise I was ill then. So I never got help. One 'high' episode was when I decided it would be a wonderful image to present myself as a living demonstration of Freud's Id/Ego. Half of me was the Id – one half of my hair was bright pink, with a sexy revealing top, pink fishnet stockings and red high heels. The other half of me was boring normal. As you can imagine it caused quite a stir!

Then 29 years ago I was stopped from jumping off a bridge. I was taken to a police station where I had my hands handcuffed behind my back, my feet tied together with a belt. I was flung into a police van and sat on. I was put in a cell and was there for eight hours, without being given a drink or told what was happening. I was sectioned and spent the next two years in an asylum.

I was put on the locked ward and heavily medicated, later on, finally being diagnosed as having manic depression. I will never forget my fear that my family had had me sectioned and I would have to stay there for the rest of my life.

Even now, when I hear or see the police I feel terrified.

Another memory was the sounds of the keys in the door, reminding me that I was incarcerated and unable to see the sky or feel the air on my face.

I spent the next 20 years as a revolving-door patient. Being heavily medicated in a ward for six to eight months, discharged, not complying with medication, back in. I have been sectioned several times, being subjected to horrendous treatments such as the barbaric control and restraint (being jumped on by nurses, restrained and heavily medicated).

My freedom taken away, no choice as to which medication, no activities, no say in what time I went to bed or what food I ate.

Only drinks at specific times, nothing in between.

Having day clothes taken away (given a man's nightshirt with a split up the back), not allowed out. Having visitors turned away. They even padlocked the fridge. I called it 'sectioning the fridge'.

When I talk about excessive medication, I mean it was a chemical kosh – I became like a zombie, shuffling and dribbling. I call it 'Toxic Care'.

I used to have dreadful side effects caused by excessive medication which no one explained to me and I was not offered any procycladine. The long-term use of multiple medications – for example, two antipsychotics and two mood stabilisers over the years, led to an increase in appetite, felt like legs full of cement, weight gain, locked joints, slowing down of my metabolism, thyroid problems, lithium tremor, kidney problems, excessive drowsiness, and fatigue and sedation, and finally I am now diabetic caused by meds.

I have gone from being totally against medication and non-compliant, but now I realise that I need medication to keep me alive. I do not function without it. I learnt this over 20 years (I must be a slow learner), since my life has been a rollercoaster or a bit like a game of snakes and ladders. Before I realised that the medication was essential to my well-being, I would experiment with it and would end up in hospital.

My mood swings in the early years were severe and profound. When I was high I would often think I was wealthy, buying lots of things I could not afford, or need. I never opened bank statements or answered letters from my bank manager and ran up excessive debts. I believed that double yellow lines were for me to park on, so got loads of parking tickets and had my car towed away. I felt there was an aura of sun shining through me. One time, I drove my car fast just to see what would happen, believing I was immortal. Once, walking along a cliff, I lent out with my coat open, leaning into the wind and out over the edge of the cliff. Everyone should try it! My husband managed to pull me back.

I would also have so much energy that I did not need to sleep, becoming argumentative, irritable and annoyed with people who were not as fast as me, who couldn't keep up with my thoughts. I was also highly sexually active, with no inhibitions.

For me my lows are horrendous. The crashing lows are to very dark places, with terrible emotional pain, loss of hope, fear of life and the future. It feels like it's never going to end, and can last between three months to two years. I duvet dive, withdraw, become isolated, self-neglect, have dark thoughts, and become psychotic, believing I shouldn't be alive, that it's too painful. The asylum had a cemetery and on a cold dark day in February I thought I should be in the grave. I tried to dig it up.

Sometimes when I have a depressive psychosis I have seen and smelt decomposing bodies (I even took up the carpet looking for it). To avoid the smell I wear perfume and light joss-sticks. I believed I would be dead by 30 so I never took out a pension or insurance or a mortgage.

I have attempted suicide several times, and once an overdose and cut wrists left me in a coma. I have also attempted to use car exhaust fumes and once I tried to kill myself by crashing my car on purpose.

Some of the things that led up to a suicide attempt were:

a. A total loss of hope, despair, seeing no future and not seeing an end to things

b. Terrible emotional pain: utter despair

c. No coping strategies or problem-solving ideas

d. Not being able to ask for help

Even though I hated how I was treated, being sectioned and locked up saved my life (I never thought I would say that).

I only wish there were more therapeutic ways of caring for a suicidal person. My early experiences led me to fear the Mental Health Service and its punitive treatment, which echoed my persecutory mind. My experiences were horrific and often led me to not getting help early on, consequently resulting in a suicide attempt.

Sadly my mother and sister did not get help. My mother attempted suicide when she was pregnant with me, again when I was aged 16, and finally committed suicide a few years ago. My sister also committed suicide.

Stigma was most destructive in my family. We were not allowed to talk about how we felt or thought. As an example, when I was in the asylum my father sat in the car (too ashamed to accept I had a mental illness), while my mother came to visit me. Another time I heard him say 'it's not on my side of the family. The madness is all on yours (my mother's).'

My husband and I tried for eight years to have a baby. The general practitioner and the psychiatrist knew, but never told me, that the medication was making me infertile, I went ballistic when I found out. However I did finally get pregnant. My unborn son was put on the at-risk register. I was put in a mother and baby unit, where I was yet again over-sedated so much that I could not look after my son. I remember using the buggy as a zimmer frame!

Finally when I was allowed home, I pleaded with my psychiatrist to reduce my meds, which were changed and three weeks later I could care for my baby.

My journey has been long and painful, up and down. I treasure each morning I wake up that I am well. It is so precious and I am constantly learning new ways to keep well. Some of the things that keep me well include my husband who is my soul mate and who I can always talk to and who has seen me through dark times. My son I love to infinity and beyond and is my reason to be alive, to hold on in stormy seas.

Another positive thing is gradually gaining insight over the years, which has been helped by three really good community psychiatric nurses (CPNs) (over 29 years, not that many). When I have lost hope, which took me to really scary places, the CPNs and my husband held the hope for me. They believed I could survive and did not give up on me. A CPN once asked me 'If you were to die tomorrow what would you regret not having done?' I gave it a lot of thought and realised I wanted to travel the world. Gradually I got better and did travel. What amazing experiences!

An important phase was going from denial that I had a mental illness (for 20 years) to reaching acceptance. This was helped when I went to the Manic Depression Fellowship self-help group, and I realised I had similar experiences to the others. I also learnt a lot through trial and error over years with being on and off medication, and when a rather good psychiatrist took the time to explain why I needed to take the medication and how it worked on my brain. I am at present in a well phase (for the last eight months). The medication is helping to keep me stable and long may it last.

Some of the qualities of CPNs that have helped me are: genuine caring; trying to understand my experience; working empathically and in collaboration with me to help me maintain wellness; empowering me to maintain control of my life; holding the hope for me in dark times even when I have lost it.

At one point I was sent to a sheltered workshop where I was paid a pound a day to paint wooden toys. I was demoralised and felt I had fallen off the ladder of life. I was often crying all the way there and all the way home. Is this how low my life had come?

Eventually, I was sent to a day centre. Here the staff were very supportive, always available to talk to. I enjoyed the art and pottery classes, which I found incredibly therapeutic and the pottery was always fun. The tutor had a wonderful sense of humour. I also did gardening and cooking – I had not done that for over a year. They really helped me through the darkest days of my life.

Now, my meaningful activity that gives me a reason to live and get up is the training of mental health nurses at a local university. I have been training nurses for 11 years as I wanted to try to contribute to their training to improve the quality of nurses overall.

My experiences of the disgraceful way some nurses treated people was so bad that I felt compelled to try to change attitudes. All this has a tremendous *positive influence* on my stable *mental health*.

Finally, I was one of 40 service users offered a place on a recovery training course in the USA. This was to have a profound effect on me; it was life changing and immensely life enhancing. The trainer was an inspiration to us all. We looked at 'what was strong/not what's wrong'. It has enabled me to take back control of my life when in the past I have felt mentally paralysed. To start to really live life; it gave me hope for the future and life, not just to exist but to dare to have dreams and go out and get them.

Important lessons I have learnt on my journey of the past 29 years include learning to be my own best friend who needs gentle care and love, not punishment (whereas in the past I would blame myself and feel unforgiving and punish myself). I have also learnt through all these years that I can help myself, whereas in the past mental paralysis would turn me to frozen ice. I now search out ways that help me cope and feel better. Most of all I have forgiven myself.

I am constantly learning. I am not cured but I am on my *Journey of Recovery*.

20

My involvement with mental health services

Andrew Voyce

Akathisia. Antipsychotic therapy. These are the key words which are mutually exclusive and which tell the story of my treatment for schizophrenia.

Akathisia is derived from the Greek for 'not to sit' or 'without sitting' and was the side effect that I had from a psychiatric injection called flupenthixol. Antipsychotic therapy is the effect I have had from the oral medication I have been prescribed since 1991. Since the implementation of community care I have had antipsychotic medication by tablet, and after a few years on 'typical' tablets called chlorpromazine and trifluoperazine. I am now prescribed an 'atypical' or modern tablet called olanzapine which gives me very few side effects. The old typical tablets did not give me akathisia but did have quite a sedative effect and also had an effect on my skin on exposure to sunlight. Nevertheless I took them every day and did not become unwell. Indeed I have not been an inpatient for 20 years now, and the offending which accompanied my revolving-door years has not been repeated either.

During the time under community care I was together enough to finish an honours degree and an MA. For the last ten years or so I have taken atypical antipsychotic tablets and have continued to feel well compared to my days in the asylums. For me it's great that I don't think unhelpful thoughts such as that Morse code signalling is going on to my enemies, and I find that the subduing effect of the tablets is not overly intrusive.

'Side effect' is such an innocuous term. But what akathisia meant to me was hell that endured day and night for seven days. The seven days after an injection, in particular of Depixol, were long hours when I was continually driven to move, but when I suffered extreme tiredness simultaneously. Hence 'not to sit' – an overwhelming compulsion to move, but at the same time for me there was a desire to crash out, to sit down or lie down. This consumed all my waking hours. It beats me how the nurses could be said to be on observation duty. I would explicitly tell the staff of my discomfort and they would have witnessed me going to the dormitory at four o'clock each afternoon for a week. Yet on the few occasions when I was present at ward rounds to discuss my welfare (as was then the norm), the only suggestion was that they increase the dose. When they tried this the akathisia would be even more unbearable. You can look up akathisia on Wikipedia.

My revolving-door pattern would be to not challenge the regime of the authoritarian NHS, which was enforced by the likes of a nurse in a white coat with green epaulettes, who trained in a special hospital. So I avoided confrontation with the likes of that guy, and would do all that the ward required, including packing soap in IT (Industrial Therapy, not Information Technology), making baskets in OT (Occupational Therapy), and residing in the multiple bed male dormitory.

This compliance would lead to me being discharged after a period of months, and then I could escape the injection regime. The temptation to maybe save £25 from a menial job or to cash in the balance on an Access credit card would win out, and I would be blissfully happy with no injections. Then I would usually descend into vagrancy and a particular bugbear for me at that juncture would be the presence of traffic wherever I went. This would give me paranoia and I might start to believe that people were conspiring against me. So after a brush with the law, usually, I would end up in a ward again and the same failed treatment would begin over again. I would have to endure the humiliation of dropping my trousers for a young girl nurse or complete stranger to inject my backside – this was what the NHS insisted on. I would then become a model patient again, be obliged to take injections, and get discharged, with the certainty of being readmitted in due course.

On my last admission to psychiatric hospital, they tried to put me back on injections. I told them this was using the British State to abuse me and that I would do property damage if they injected me. So they went ahead and gave me an injection. After seven days, when I felt OK again, I got out at night and put a paper around a brick. On the paper were all the details of the injection and the nurses involved. I threw the brick through a church window. The next day the doctor told me I was going to be put back on tablets.

That was 1991, and I have taken a tablet every day since then. I have not felt paranoid or deluded and my carers have supported me to keep up this therapeutic regime.

Electroconvulsive therapy

21

Judith Haire

I was 37 when I experienced an acute psychotic episode and I was hospitalised for six months. My childhood had been dysfunctional and I'd been depressed in my teens. I went on to marry and after three years of abuse, rape and domestic violence I found the courage to walk away. Keeping my emotions hidden I tried to start again but the past slowly crept up on me and mounting and debilitating anxiety changed to agitation and then to psychosis.

After a terrifying week hallucinating alone in my house I was admitted to the psychiatric ward on a Saturday night. I was extremely confused. I had little idea what was going on but I felt abandoned and I curled up into the foetal position on the bed and tried my hardest to shut everything out.

For the first 11 days I refused all food and drink because I believed myself to be dead or in some kind of metamorphosis. My life was perceived to be in danger and the psychiatrist told my family he was saving my life rather than my sanity. I was sectioned for 28 days under the 1983 Mental Health Act and ironically I did start to eat and drink voluntarily almost immediately afterwards. I was still catatonic and mute. The section was later extended to six months.

In the hospital I was given a variety of antipsychotic medications but none brought me back to reality. After four months of treatment I seemed to have become stuck. I'd come to a halt and stayed there. My head felt full of fog and I moved and thought in slow motion. Fires and flames featured a lot in my hallucinations and I've since wondered if this was a symbolic representation of all the anger I'd suppressed in my life.

The energy rush of the psychosis was quite incredible and almost orgasmic in a sinister kind of way.

My psychiatrist said he had no option but to send me for electroconvulsive therapy (ECT). I was sectioned and had no say in the matter. I did not want to have ECT but there was nothing I could do, so I became resigned to it. ECT has been in use since 1938 and involves passing an electrical current through the patient's brain to produce an epileptic fit, hence electroconvulsive. No one is certain how it works but it causes the release of brain chemicals and makes the chemicals more likely to work and aid recovery. Also it stimulates the growth of new blood vessels in the brain. At the time I felt powerless and more unhappy as the time drew nearer.

I was weighed and had an EEG (electroencephalogram) to see if there were any problems with my brain. Years later I was reading my medical notes and discovered they'd found a cerebral insult in my brain during this EEG. A cerebral insult is a kind of lesion which heals in time. I asked the psychiatrist if it could have been caused by my first husband's violence but he thought instead it could have been caused by stress or by the medication I was taking at the time.

On the morning of my first treatment I was woken very early to shower, wash my hair and dress. I was then taken by a nurse to another part of the hospital. I felt quite numb.

I had to lie on my back on a table and a needle was put into the back of my hand to deliver a short-acting general anaesthetic, and I was also given a muscle relaxant. The next thing I knew I was coming round.

In the interim, electrodes had been placed on either side of my head. This is known as bilateral ECT. These electrodes delivered an electrical stimulus. The stimulus levels recommended for ECT are in excess of an individual's seizure threshold. For bilateral ECT this is between one and one and a half times the seizure threshold. The electrical stimulus is 800 milliamps and lasts between one and six seconds.

The headache I suffered after the first treatment was relentless and the worst I have ever experienced. To make things worse, I knew I had to undergo the treatment another five times. I had two treatments each week.

The ECT did not work immediately but it did work in time. A friend who visited me on the day I'd had my first treatment said how distressed I was to have the headache, how I was convinced my mother was on fire in another part of the hospital, and how my description of this made her think it was a reflection of very deeply felt emotions.

I did return to reality. The brain fog lifted. The chattering in my head stopped. Gone were the hallucinations. I was back in the real world. I felt very angry and I really resented having the ECT treatment; I thought it was barbaric.

I have to concede it was helpful. Of course had the antipsychotic medication olanzapine/Zyprexa been available at that time perhaps I could have avoided the ECT. I was to discover later that olanzapine was very effective.

I went on to leave hospital and eventually gave up my medication to lead a full and interesting life once more. If I'd had any say in the matter I don't believe I would have agreed to the ECT treatment and I am glad it is now used less and less. It is well documented that brain damage occurs in every case. That knowledge upsets and angers me and I firmly believe it should never be given without the patient's consent.

I was fortunate enough to recover from my psychotic illness and really feel I had to lose my mind to find it again.

My descent into psychosis 22

Judith Haire

I was 37 when I experienced my first acute psychotic episode. The illness had crept up on me slowly after years of stress, firstly in my dysfunctional upbringing and then in an abusive marriage. I was admitted to hospital in July 1993 after being alone in my house for a week experiencing terrifying hallucinations.

I was curled up on the back seat of the car as we drove into the spacious grounds of the hospital, a red brick Victorian building, We went inside the building which was very dark and dingy and were led into a nurse's office. My mother spoke at length and I sat very quietly. I was hallucinating and experiencing delusions. On the day of my admission I'd thought there were bombs in my back garden and that I was part of a plot to assassinate the Queen. I did not know what the date was or who the prime minister was.

Eventually I was taken to a dormitory and I got on to the bed, curled myself into the foetal position and tried to shut everything out. I didn't look at my mother and sister again and they left. Although I didn't really know what was happening to me, I felt alone and abandoned.

Years later when I read my medical notes I was astounded to read the report made at the time I was admitted and there in spidery handwriting was the comment 'binge drinking' and 'two bottles of spirits a day'. To this day I have no idea where this information had come from. It was simply untrue. I had not drunk alcohol for almost two years.

The next morning I awoke somewhere else – I'd slept on the floor of a large room. I'd taken my bedclothes with me and I had no clue where I was. I was hallucinating that I was back at school and this was the assembly hall. I was taken to the dining hall where there were other patients. I was scared of everyone and very confused. My parents came to see me that morning although I have no memory of their visit, as I was catatonic and mute. My father wanted to take me home but I was too confused to understand. My mother realised how very ill I was and told my father I must stay where I was so I could get better.

I was terrified. I was seen by nurses, doctors and social workers. The diagnosis was that I was having an acute psychotic episode. Apparently 25 per cent of rape victims go on to develop depression and or other mental illness, a shocking statistic.

Flames and fires featured a lot in my hallucinations. The energy rush of the psychosis was quite incredible – almost orgasmic. Some of the imagery will stay in my mind forever, of distorted bodies trapped in a huge net at the bottom of the sea, of the collapse of an oil rig, of Siamese twins and severed limbs. I was travelling at speed on a huge rollercoaster, I was being hurled from the rollercoaster. I was pregnant too. I was lying in a field which was being ploughed by a huge agricultural machine and the huge blades came sweeping across me slicing off my head. But I was an observer; it seemed to happen in front of me on a huge cinema screen. I would see brightly coloured pictures in the room and hear music playing in my mind and all over my body. I would visualise extravagant Busby Berkeley musicals and sometimes the chattering of nonsense words in my mind became exhausting,

The voices I heard in my head were sometimes female and sometimes male. The voice would usually make a running commentary on what I was doing or summarise what I had just done.

I would sleep in all my clothes, always ready to get up and go if I needed to; I had this constant fear I would be attacked; I was frightened that I was being observed through the mirror on the bathroom wall; I was overwhelmed with terror, imagining all my family had been wiped out in a nuclear holocaust.

For the first 11 days in the psychiatric hospital I refused all food and drink. I believed myself to be dead or thought I might be in metamorphosis. My mother tried to feed me from a spoon and my friend brought me my favourite bananas to try and tempt me into eating. She said my lips were cracked and dry.

My life was perceived to be in danger and the psychiatrist told my family that I should be sectioned. He said he was saving my life rather than my sanity. The social worker did not agree with the psychiatrist and refused to sign the forms. She told my parents she was worried I would lose my job. My parents begged her to sign the forms saying they were not worried about my job. They wanted me to be well. And so I was sectioned under the 1983 Mental Health Act. Although ironically I did start to eat and drink voluntarily almost immediately after I was sectioned.

My sister who had come to visit me was shocked when she looked into my eyes. She said they were 'dead'; there was no light in them. She felt she had lost me and was very upset. My work colleague told my friend Caroline that I was in hospital and she came straight to see me, I remember her visit vaguely. She said I looked very thin, almost skeletal and that I was sitting up in bed with my arms outstretched and my fingers clawed. This I can remember doing. My hair was unwashed and I was quite calm, obviously drugged, and puzzled and confused as to where I was.

She came to see me again and the nurse came out to her before she found me and told her that I had the right to challenge being sectioned. She said it was important someone I knew and trusted explained that to me before it was too late, as there was a time limit. The nurse insisted Caroline spoke to me about it. Caroline was already unhappy about what was happening to me and was also very anti electroconvulsive therapy and she feared that would be given to me if I was sectioned. I was very distressed that day and very tearful. I was frightened of everyone and Caroline observed I had lost all my confidence. I did not want to do anything to upset anyone and really did not know what to do. I did not manage to appeal so Caroline appealed to the Mental Health Board on my behalf by fax five minutes before the midnight deadline.

On the day of my appeal I do remember being helped to walk along the corridor by my mother. I was physically very weak and found walking difficult. I was very drowsy from all the medication I was taking. I was absolutely terrified of the doctors on the appeal panel. The result of the interview was that I was too ill to be released from the section and indeed it was increased to up to six months. So my fate was sealed and I had to stay in hospital whether I liked it or not.

I was still too frightened to sit with the other patients and would want to wait until everyone had finished so that I could eat alone. My behaviour was misinterpreted by the staff as my own inability to care for myself and they said I needed prompting to eat. What they failed to understand was my fear of sitting with the other patients. I was too nervous to go to the toilet on my own or to bathe on my own. I was terrified of switches, knobs, machines, fire bells, fire exits. I was overwhelmed with terror, imagining all my family had been wiped out in a nuclear explosion.

I spent hours and hours sitting alone on my hospital bed, clutching my bedclothes and often crying for help but nobody came. I often took bedclothes from other patients' beds and would wander round clutching sheets. I was still terrified of the other patients and of the staff. Many of the staff seemed unapproachable. I remember being very tearful very late at night and the nurse said she was too busy to talk to me and I would have to wait until the morning – the sense of rejection was overwhelming.

I was given a cocktail of antipsychotic drugs to try and find one that would ease my symptoms of hallucinations and delusions. I remember most of these were given to me in liquid form and tasted foul. It would take ages to get me to swallow the liquid. It was lonely in the psychiatric unit and often little attention was given to me by the staff. Some staff I got on with and some I was positively frightened of. I was taken to different departments of the hospital for scans and tests and one day a male nurse dragged me along a corridor by one arm; I was still trying to put my clothes back on again. I was terrified and felt my wishes and needs were being dismissed by this nurse who showed no understanding or empathy. Another nurse was reading her book and said she wanted to finish reading it before she could talk to me.

Everything was made more difficult as I was in the company of people often more ill than I was, which added to my sense of persecution and fear. For weeks I was too terrified to go into the psychiatrist's office and would only go to the door or sit on the chair for a few seconds. I could not verbalise what was wrong. I was puzzling and puzzling to understand what was happening to me.

I found the interior of the hospital ward unwelcoming and drab. Sharing a dormitory was frightening and there was little to do in the daytime. The door to the staff room was usually shut and it was difficult to find staff to talk to. At the same time we were discouraged from talking to other patients about our illness. I did meet one woman and we became close friends but the staff then moved her to another ward as it was felt we were becoming too dependent on one another.

Halfway through my stay in the Victorian hospital we were all moved 20 miles to a new mental health unit near where I lived. At last I had my own bedroom. From my window I could see the buses and realised how near I was to my home. This lifted my spirits considerably even though the move itself was very unsettling for me and I relapsed a little initially. During my time in the unit I continued to feel isolated and frightened and forgotten about. Many of the staff did not have any understanding of what I was going through and seemed reluctant to stop and talk to me. They paid little attention to me or to my anxieties about being there, about being separated from my loved ones and friends.

I was asked to go to groups in the daytime but I found these very unhelpful so refused to go. I could not see the point of sitting in a circle with depressed people and talking about depression. I did not need that. I wanted to hear music; I had to ask for the radio to be put on.

One day I was feeling particularly anxious just before lunch and the male nurse insisted I take a diazepam. I hated to do this as it made me feel very woozy and detached from everything. He later apologised for giving me the drug saying he had since realised I became anxious when hungry so he had given me the diazepam needlessly.

During my six months in the psychiatric unit my weight fell by two stone to eight stone twelve pounds and it hurt me to sit on a chair because I had lost so much fat and muscle tone. I was fed on extra meal replacements to try to increase my weight.

I became tremendously constipated from the medication. My stomach protruded like a football but the staff were slow to notice and to take action.

Many of my clothes went missing from the ward.

I would like to say that the help I received from the staff was constructive or comforting but I cannot. I can only say that the sense of isolation I felt was not helpful. Resources may be stretched but when one is psychotic it is important to receive reassurance and to know that staff can give of their time.

At one point in the overall experience, a psychiatrist was very taken aback when I asked her if she had taken the antipsychotic medication she had prescribed me, herself. I asked because I was so fed up with the many debilitating side effects: weight gain, craving for carbohydrates, hunger, dry mouth.

After five months in hospital I'd reached some kind of plateau and had some way to go in my recovery. I felt very foggy, and moved and thought in slow motion and the psychiatrist said he had no choice but to send me for electroconvulsive therapy (ECT). I was still sectioned and had no say at all. Though I hated the treatments and thought it barbaric the ECT did work and did bring me back to reality.

By January 1994 I was considerably better and very anxious to get home. Eventually the psychiatrist released me from the sectioning and I was free to go. He said I was too well to stay in the hospital or the halfway house but not quite well enough to live on my own, so with his agreement I went to stay with my father and his partner for a month before returning home to live my life again.

23

Performing the room: Four days on an acute ward

Alec Grant

The room

A room with a bed. A man on the bed. Levi's on the man. Half-dried piss on the Levi's. Man's hands on damp Levi's. Man wakes up. Massive hangover. Mouth caked and crusted. Feels his face. Stubble on face. No recollection. How he got here. On this bed. Where he is. Still half drunk. Checks hair. Checks face. Checks tee shirt. Checks jeans. On his body. All his.

Sits up. Looks around. Small room. Nine by six feet. Hospital bed. Hospital duvet. Plastic chair. Mirror. Institutional paint. Beige. One thing. One thought. At a time. Nothing more. Possible.

Where? How? No recollection. Panic. Voices. Outside. Who?

The nurses

From their voice tones, the nurses are probably mostly young: mid- to late-20s through to early 40s? The nurse in charge is a sincere and personable man of about 40. He has just completed a BSc at a local university, in a health-related subject, having qualified as a mental health nurse about ten years before. At some point he greets the man after coming into the room to explain the ward layout and routine. The man cannot retain this information, however, and is soon just as confused as he was before the conversation with the nurse in charge.

The other nurses are always in the periphery of the man's awareness. He hears their voices, and this evokes panic in him. They never come into the room.

The man

The man in the room is 52. Tall. Grey. Bearded. He is an academic in a local university. His teaching and writing is generally in the area of mental health, and related research. He is a manic depressive and an alcoholic. He likes the first label better than the second, but will, as the years pass, come to view his alcoholic tag positively. Recently, for the first time, he has had a prolonged episode of hearing voices and false beliefs.

The voices appear to come from outside of him and are loud. They shout:

'Kill yourself, you bastard', and
'Die, you fucking cunt', and
'You worthless heap of shit', and
'You fucking cunt, shit, bastard, cunt …'

Sometimes, frequently, he wants to kill himself, partly to silence the voices and also because he begins to believe what they say of him. A few years later, he will attempt suicide twice, before giving up alcohol and becoming an alcoholic in recovery, enthusiastically and willingly attending AA, and before being prescribed helpful medication for manic depression.

His false beliefs included owning a small plane and having a private pilot's licence. He believed he had both. He believed that he had hidden his plane on the South Downs because of people who were conspiring against him. He did not know who these people were and trusted few individuals apart from his wife. Before finding himself in the room, he spent weeks agonizing about where he might have hidden the plane. At the time, he was too paranoid to leave his house, looking at ordinance survey maps instead, to try to figure out, from memory, likely spots where the plane might be.

He couldn't remember where or when he passed his pilot's examination. But he knew he did. He did not know for sure what he would do if or when he found his plane, but thought that selling it might be an option.

He also believed he could talk with God. Before he started to talk with Him, Her or It, he would have described himself as an agnostic. Being suddenly able to talk with God didn't change his position in this regard, as he didn't have any spare energy to work on this metaphysical issue.

But he could only talk with God on the phone. One day, the first day that it happened, his wife came home and walked into the living room. 'Who are you on the phone to?' she asked. 'God', he replied. Kind of used to his craziness over the preceding few months, she didn't make much of this. After allowing a few minutes to elapse, she casually and quietly said 'And what does God sound like, if you don't mind me asking?' 'He sounds like a middle-aged, middle-class Englishman.' 'Oh', she commented. 'And what did you and God talk about?' 'I can't tell you,' the man replied, 'because it's top secret, you see. I'll be in very serious trouble if I give away any information.'

Message in a bottle

The police weren't involved at first, but years later he would lose his licence for a year. At the end of that year, which also marks 365 days dry, he climbs into his newly serviced and MOT'd car and opens the glove compartment. An empty half bottle of vodka stares back at him accusingly, there since August 2007. Although he doesn't have to do this any more, he throws the bottle over a nearby fence, a well-rehearsed strategy.

Bottles used to inhabit his pine desk, in various degrees full or empty. One day, having been off sick from work for several months, he helped himself to his first drink of the day. It was dawn and, living near the beach, the seagulls chanted their calls in unison. A nice tumbler of vodka, with a little orange juice to ensure that vitamin C levels weren't depleted! Staying drunk all day also meant that if the voices happened they had little potency. They could fuck off. Staying drunk all day also meant that the rushing thoughts, with him more or less constantly, were dulled.

He turns away from his desk, noticing for the first time as it were, a pile of work on the floor of his home office (nine by six feet): mainly writing jobs, long past their deadline. He spots his wife in the corridor. 'How long has this stuff been here?' he asks with some alarm in his voice. 'Over six months', she replies. He sees his reflection in the vodka bottle in front of him, on the desk. Grey pallor, dirty dressing gown. The face on top stared back at him accusingly, sending out an SOS: 'How much more?' 'How much more?'

The Punch and Judy show

The nurse in charge goes, leaving the man alone in the room. Gradually, the events of the last few days come back to him. With things closing in on him, he threatened suicide. His rushing thoughts, voices, false beliefs and paranoia had become increasingly worse, and he did not feel he could cope any more. He started to express the wish to kill himself publicly and his wife made him see his GP who, in turn, made the psychiatric referral. Hence the room, the nurse in charge and the nurses.

He was there to dry out and be medicated. The role of the nurses? This wasn't specified, but he began to notice a pattern. Every half hour or so, one would pop her or his head through the door, then leave again. He wasn't not sure if they explained that this would happen. Maybe they did.

Sometimes they pop their heads round and smile, then go away. Sometimes it's a head without a smile. After a while, the man asks one of them why they're doing this. He finds out that it's because he's considered a suicide risk. Fair enough.

But he begins to become irritated by the fact that they don't talk with him. Now you see them, now you don't, like a mad and boring Punch and Judy show. The fact that they don't seem to want to talk with him, yet want to look at him at regular intervals, fuels his paranoia. Is there something else going on? Something that God might know about? Or want to know about?

He decides to observe *them* at regular intervals, in between them observing him. So, the next nurse pops her head around at 1pm, and the man opens his door at 1.15pm on his hands and knees (in the interest of subterfuge) and looks up at the nurses' station. He is secure in the knowledge that the nurses can't see him looking at them, and he is initially enthusiastic about keeping up his half hourly observational schedule.

He observes some interesting things. During one observation, a young male nurse, called Colin apparently, has just bought a puppy for his family and is telling the other nurses about the fun he and his family are having with it. They haven't decided on a name for it yet.

During another observation, a young African woman is talking about her career development with the other nurses. The man doesn't catch her name, but hears enough to know that she wants to become a community psychiatric nurse. Apparently this will give her more contact time with her clients. The other nurses agree that this is a good thing.

I'm not hungry

The man stays in the room for four days. His hangover wears off eventually, but he remains desperate for another drink. He does not leave the room. None of the nurses seem particularly bothered about this. Psychiatrists, or maybe the same psychiatrist, visit him and prescribe him new medication. The nurses keep up their half-hourly brief observations even though the man tired of observing them after the first day. The man refused meals as he was too scared to leave the room. Friends brought food in for him.

A room with a view

All of the above more or less happened to me – I was the man – although I have disguised some details in the interests of anonymity. I occupy multiple stakeholder positions in relation to my mental health and addiction difficulties: the fact that my original training was in mental health nursing, later psychotherapy and cognitive behavioural psychotherapy, that I'm a mental health nurse educator, and that I write about mental health and, ironically, communication and interpersonal skills issues.

The curriculum for mental health nurse training has, for decades, been populated by notions and constructs from counselling models. Specific aspects of humanistic psychology are elevated as essential for the mental health nurse's toolbox. In particular, Carl Rogers' core conditions, including warmth, genuineness and unconditional positive regard, are seen as qualities that no self-respecting mental health nurse should be seen without.

Universities might like to think that they turn out nurses in their Sunday-best interpersonal gear. However, it seems likely that over time many newly qualified nurses will be gradually socialised into forms of organisational custom and practice that work to the detriment of empathic engagement with clients. Throughout the years, according to information from the national audit office, a disproportionate number of complaints about NHS treatment are related to communication problems. Equally, studies of acute psychiatric inpatient wards in the UK in recent times have consistently found them to be generally anti-therapeutic. Contemporary data from local studies in the south of England suggest that some newly qualified mental health nurses were dismayed by the fact that organisational, management and related bureaucratic work used up the time available to interact with acute ward patients. In order to cope with this dilemma, some nurses in those studies simple reconciled themselves to an administrative/managerial rather than a therapeutic future. Others still, it would seem, leave acute ward work to become community psychiatric nurses or to work in some other specialism. Of course, this leaves acute mental health nursing as the perpetual 'poor relation'.

From a wider perspective, bureaucratic organisations in any part of the service sector – in, for example, health, education, policing – tend to have their own operating rules and procedures. Such rules and procedures are likely to often trump the things that well-intentioned, enthusiastic and idealistic trainees or students are taught in their universities, colleges or training schools, and we should never be surprised about this.

However, there's always room for improvement where human decency's concerned. My last 'rock bottom', pre-alcoholic recovery, was when I was arrested for drunk driving. I spent the night in a police cell, a room quite similar in area and colour to my room on the acute ward. Although banged up, a nice police officer came to check on me occasionally, and make sure I was OK. I found out her name, Catherine, and she called me by mine. She brought me extra blankets because I was cold. She said goodbye to me when I left in the morning. I will never forget her.

24

Freeze-frame: Reflections on being in hospital

Nigel Short

Early January – hospital

The room is quiet. I can hear the muffled drone of a vacuum cleaner beyond the closed door. Big Ben is chiming 11 a.m. across the river. It's wet and miserable. I think it's Thursday. I am lying still. The single wooden bed feels solid beneath me. The cream-coloured duvet lies crumpled under my unexercised body. My unwashed matted hair stinks. My right ear and clammy right cheek rest against a pillow, a pillow that's thin, synthetic and uncomfortable. The stale starched cotton is cool. My nose breathing is shallow. Sticky discoloured saliva is leaking slowly from the corner of my mouth. My tracksuit bottoms, smelly Mambo tee shirt and black ankle socks are warm. I am shivering. I can smell the sweet sickly smell of a rotting banana. Its decomposing shape rests on the pillar-box red quarry-tiled windowsill.

The unwanted white bread coronation chicken sandwich sits untouched on top of a cheap paper plate: another reminder that I am worthless. I am off my food. A white plastic cup is full of tea. I didn't want it when it was warm. I don't want it now it's cold. I am tired. The sleeping tablets are working at last. I am slipping in and out of much-needed drug-induced sleep. Somebody I do not immediately recognise suddenly bursts into the room. He hasn't knocked. He is now standing at the foot of the bed. His sudden appearance startles me. My heart rate increases.

'Are you getting up?' he shouts. 'You have been in bed all day.' 'I'm tired', I whisper. I feel afraid again. He has power. 'Don't you want to get better?' he says. He finishes his verbal interaction aggressively by saying, through gritted teeth, 'Get up you *cunt.*'

He turns round and briskly walks out. The door slams shut! The room returns to a comforting peace. It envelops me. It protects. I am frightened. I have been in hospital for about a week. I know the room very well. The walls are sky blue, the ceiling magnolia. The door has a small window about head height: 12 inches by 12 inches. I remain imperial. A floral curtain covers the glass on the outside. Anybody can look in: unseen. I lie here for a little. I feel like a child. I feel almost like I did when my parents had told me off. What had I done wrong? I hadn't been out of this room on my own during the day, since my admission. My heart is racing. It feels like it will burst through the walls of my chest. I am over-breathing.

I am worried about saying anything. I eventually get up. I make my way to the nurses' office. The walk down the corridor is long and deliberate. I am walking in slow motion. Other people are staring at me. There are two nurses in the office. One of them is the man who swore at me. I ask him if he has a problem with me. I want to try and repair and resolve this difficulty. He says 'What are you talking about?' I repeat what he said to me. He denies the incident and particularly denies using the word 'cunt'. I walk slowly back to the room, chastised. I lie down on the bed. I cover my body with the duvet and stare at the wall. I am feeling *very* vulnerable now.

I know that there is possibly a disruption in how my autobiographical events are recalled, and I know that I may recall singular events yet summarise categories of events. My over-general memory, when I am 'flat', is often associated with poor problem-solving skills and the accompanying difficulty of me trying to imagine future events, both of which contribute to the maintenance of this awful misery.

Early January

I am extremely nervous. 'I'm going into hospital for a while. I need a break.' I tell a friend. I remember standing in the garden using a phone. What I don't remember is how this happened. I didn't have a mobile phone. Maybe we had a wireless phone?

A suitcase is packed. I wait for a hospital driver. I get into the car. The driver owns a handmade brick company. I try and talk about bricks. I run out of things to talk about. I pretend to be asleep.

My mental health had been deteriorating very slowly for about six months. My sleep had been progressively getting worse and I had started self-medicating with alcohol each evening.

In the months leading up to my hospital admission I had been living in a one-room flat. It was near the old house. I could continue to see my children. I was also spending most evenings in a local public house, The Clown. It was usually full up with people like me; people who were disenfranchised for some reason or other. The juke box contained many of my favourites and the Guinness was good.

I often think of the irony of the pub's name. Perhaps all along I was being a clown?

January – hospital

I regularly ruminate about my inability to sort myself out. I am a psychotherapist for goodness sake! I know that my anxiety and depression difficulties often place me in a vulnerable place. I become gloomy about the future. I remind myself of all my errors and mistakes. This experience then results in restrictions that often conflict with the self that I previously experienced. For me there was a severe reduction in my confidence, my enthusiasm, my adventurousness and my generally happy-go-lucky perspectives.

It was early morning, seven o'clock maybe. The ward domestic came into the room unannounced and started hoovering the carpet. How dirty can a room become overnight? The nursing staff had the unenviable task of getting me to eat and drink. Hearing their different tactics was interesting. I tried to imagine what each one would say as they came into the room.

'You won't be able to go home if you don't eat and drink.' 'C'mon it will make you feel better.' I went for about ten days without eating. I had been making small marks on the wall behind the small wooden locker in the side room with a pencil to help me keep track of the days. I had seen Gene Hackman do this in the film *The French Connection 2*.

I had no appetite. I was able to drink however; I had remembered liking cold Ovaltine when I had been in hospital at the age of ten. I asked the staff and was offered this drink several times a day. I was also drinking the warm cold water from the sink in the room, making a cup with my hands like Marlon Brando does when we first see him in the film *Apocalypse Now.*

Interestingly and curiously, when I did want to drink, particularly during the night, I was told I couldn't have one. 'If we give you one then everyone will want one. We don't have enough milk.' I would then shuffle back down the long corridor to my room. On the way I would pass several nurses who were sat outside the rooms of people who needed special watching. They would look up from the books they were reading. I saw one nurse reading a book about therapeutic relationships. It felt like they all knew that my request for a drink had been met with refusal. Humiliation and more shame.

By the time I got to hospital I had used up all my narratives. I had run out of things to say and as far as I was concerned had so far been unsuccessful in trying to explain what I was thinking and feeling. I had resorted to self-damaging ways of communicating. My difficulties had separated me from people; people I knew and loved. Now I was in a hospital about 60 miles from home; even further separation. The friends who visited me would have seen a very quiet withdrawn person. I wanted to see them but felt ashamed. I thought I had a personality disorder and this perception was confirmed by my clinical nursing notes (I was shown my nursing notes by a nurse). In spite of what seemed like reasonable internal dialogues, I felt like a failure.

February – hospital
My enthusiasm for life has drained away. I am unmotivated and I lack energy. The prospect of work is daunting and I am aware at the end of each day how much I am confabulating. I seem to be permanently hot, sweaty and cold. My creative edge has abandoned me and I feel worthless and hopeless. At the moment I am unable to see a way through the sticky treacle path that lies ahead of me.

May
Found some notes I had made in hospital. I have tried to replicate the way I now see them written on the hospital notepaper.

… up the river on each side
the immense confusion of greenery tumbling
down to the river's edge
The jungle, every inch of it slithering with life.

The designated smoking area is adjacent to the hospital respiratory unit. The hustle and bustle of the main hospital corridor reminds me of the main souk in Fez, Morocco.

March
One of the nurses on the ward tells me that I am going to be given some time off of the ward unaccompanied. I make my way up to Soho in the west end of London. There is a takeaway cafe in Charing Cross Road that sells what I think are the best falafels in the city. (A falafel is a fried ball or patty made from ground chick peas and/or fava beans.) I first tried falafels on a visit to Jerusalem in 1976. I brought a falafel and some pita bread and made my way to Tower Records in Piccadilly.

On the walk I munched my way through my snack. For a short period all seemed well. I was anonymous and content. At Tower Records I brought myself two compact discs: *Pieces in a Modern Style* (2000) by William Orbit and *Painted From Memory* (1998) by Elvis Costello and Burt Bacharach.

I also brought a small personal compact disc player. Interesting how songs seemed to fit into where we are at that time. A crystallising. One of the songs on the Costello and Bacharach compact disc, *This House Is Empty Now*, was particularly poignant and painful. It is a song about a couple breaking up. The protagonist is sat in their empty house. The partner has taken their belongings. I interpreted this song literally and metaphorically. My house was empty now. Where did I belong? I also thought that my life, my brain, my whole being was 'empty now'.

I was keen to try and resolve any difficulties with the young nurse who had called me a 'cunt'. I wanted my stay in this hospital to offer me a helpful and productive therapeutic experience. Having spent many years as a charge nurse in a busy inpatient unit I did not want to become, however innocently, 'The Unpopular Patient'. Staff morale and service user's dissatisfaction is evidenced in literature and I did not want to be treated unfairly or become a 'non-identity' or 'non-person'. Stockwell (1984) describes how some nurses could, perhaps unknowingly, become prejudiced towards some patients. She suggests that an unpopular patient is one who is seen, for example, as being non-compliant, resisting the treatment being offered, or one who the staff think should not be on the ward. I was trying very hard to improve my distress.

I often think about this incident, particularly when I visit London and see the hospital. It is not so upsetting now. Maybe this young nurse was stressed, maybe he had been told to 'get me out of my room'.

February – hospital

Thoughts drop in unannounced
My awareness is grabbed
I have to attend
Dialogues percolating through and
Then the sparks begin to fly
The tinder is crisp and vulnerable
It's destroying me again
Their continuous streams
Their continuous screams
Blue linen trousers

Take away the edge
Ease the burden
Bringing smiles all round
Temporal tyrants attack every core
Sacred, secular sources
Invade my very being
Press the escape button
The gala melon changes shape
Bananas begin to spread and shed
Their skin
Innocent oranges change and
Turn mouldy
Neglected in their burial bowl
Arab songs keep me entertained
White clouds have lifted my soul
A phone call interrupted
A mundane evening tape after tape after tape
Would I lie to you?
Tomorrow will find me peeling off the label
Another gift
Another token
Rubber plants
Growing more dark shiny leaves
My life needs re-potting.

March – hospital

I am lying flat in my bed. I am feeling anxious again. Seems like a permanent experience. I think I am improving however. For weeks I haven't cared about my feelings. I want to relax. I am tired of feeling agitated. I am usually a relaxed type of person. I remember the Jacobson (1938) progressive muscle (PMR) relaxation method. Progressive relaxation involves alternately tensing and relaxing the muscles. PMR may start by sitting or lying down in a comfortable position. With the eyes closed, the muscles are tensed (10 seconds) and relaxed (20 seconds) in sequence. I try it. I start at my toes, and slowly working my way up to my head, I relax the major muscle groups in my body. It works. I am just left with my mind. I hold this experience for what seems like just a few seconds. The clock tells me it has been several minutes. I become very frightened. I cannot feel my body. I have to move my hands. How else do I know I exist? I gingerly touch my left thigh with my left hand. I have to, I need to. What a wonderful sense of relief. I am still here. Who can I tell? I go to the nurses' office. I tell one of the two nurses what I have just experienced. The nurse I have spoken to looks towards the other nurse. He looks bored. The more I try to explain my experience to the nurses the more bored they both appear to become with me and my story. I apologise to them and retire to my room and feel worthless and vulnerable again.

March – hospital

Following my unsuccessful relaxation explanation to the two nurses I am now lying in my room, alone, again. The nurse I wasn't speaking to knocks on my side room door. She slowly, quietly and sensitively opens the door and asks if she can come in.

I nod. She comes closer and sits on the floor; her back against the wall. She draws her legs up towards her chest and rests her arms on her knees. She says: 'That sounds like an interesting and frightening experience you just had, you know, when you were relaxing.' I reply with a 'Yes.' She then says 'Can you tell me more about it?' I tell her that I had found the experience very worrying and yet strangely comforting. I have spent many months not really paying any attention to my feelings. My experiences of sadness are both typical and untypical of how other people might have experienced sadness. I wasn't sleeping or eating well and sometimes I had some very strange ideas; some I acted upon. I spent many evenings trying to cut my left thumb off. I thought at the time that this would make me feel better; for short periods it did make me feel better. How could I begin to explain to someone that trying to cut my thumb off made me feel better? How would this action be appraised by people?

How do I now, ten years later, make sense of this experience? Many conversations in hospital were short and contain many exclamations. Careful! Get up! Oh dear! I don't remember having many conversations with the staff. Tuesday mornings would guarantee some natter; it was ward round time. A member of the nursing staff would come to my room to presumably gather a summary of 'How my week had been?' The interaction was often very brief. Closed questions ensured brevity.

I am now able to see that my difficulties were not the whole Nigel, but for many months the black dog or pig or cloud insisted on its pre-eminence. One relies so much on mental material, voices and internal monologues and dialogues, that the whole morphs to become just the mind!

I was unsure then how to reconcile the continuous, conscious, indiscriminate, cognitive plate spinning. Like an extremely enthusiastic excitable silver ball in a pinball machine, my thoughts and feelings would often be uncontrollable. I was mirthless. I regularly felt like a square peg in a round hole. Nothing fitted.

Now however I feel more in control, I am able to see my experiences for what they were. In Arthur Frank's terms, I embarked, when I was able, on a quest, a journey. I did not want to remain stuck in a story which had been mostly made up on my behalf.

25

Bad and mad: Mental health problems and the criminal justice system

Andrew Voyce

My first admission to a mental hospital was before Christmas 1974. I was 23 years of age. I had no criminal record.

I had several trigger episodes that led to the onset of schizophrenia in the context of a biological predisposition. I accept this version of how schizophrenia develops. I now recognise that certain patterns of behaviour that occurred at my worst periods had occurred immediately prior to my first contact with the NHS asylum system. In particular this unhelpful behaviour consisted in very unwise financial transactions leading to homelessness.

My periods of vagrancy were very unhappy times. They quite often included contact with the criminal justice system before a return to an asylum – this was the revolving door for me.

As I said, when I first had contact with a National Health Service asylum I had a clean record. There were at that time three main issues to resolve in my life, as well as addressing clear mental health issues – I believe I had surely shown psychotic behaviour. The asylum could have got me an honorary degree called an 'aegrotat' as I had recently sat but failed my finals; there could have been action to recover a good sum of money withheld from me by my parents' building firm and which I never saw; and I could have cooperated with Reading police to name all the drug dealers in that town who had exploited me – I would have been happy to do that.

Instead I was discharged just before Christmas 1974 and was told there was nothing wrong with me. Then I duly had a confrontation with my family which led to me living rough in my car after that Christmas. I ran out of money and filled up with petrol, driving off without paying, multiple times. They got you for that even in 1975 and I was sent to hospital as a condition of a probation order. The knife edge of living on my wits had been no good for my mental health, and I became very paranoid around my offending, and was distressed by traffic that I felt was tracking me.

So, back to hospital for a second time, this time with a criminal record. Now I got a diagnosis of schizophrenia. So it was like: 'what, been to university and need some help, wasted a lump sum you've had, feeling paranoid, your family think there's something wrong, can we salvage something from this young unblemished life? – Nah, go away!' But when it's: 'what, been living rough, stealing milk bottles from doorsteps, got a criminal record? Yeah, bring him on! We know that!'

After that second admission, I was put on medication that caused horrendous side effects. There then followed, until 1991, a pattern of me being discharged on medication by injection in the backside that they knew I would discontinue on discharge, my return to vagrancy (usually with offending), and the readmission to the asylum for the same failed treatment to be repeated. I wonder, did the nurses take bets each time on how long it would be before the police returned me to hospital? I was admitted about a dozen times to the asylums in Sussex and Kent, and each time after that first occasion there was an element of contact with the criminal justice system. My offending was not acquisitive, it was not to feed a drug or alcohol addiction, it was not part of a gang culture. It was connected with survival without a home as a destitute vagrant.

I frequently found that police custody or spells in prison, usually on remand, were preferable to asylum life as I was given no medication, in particular no injections, and so I could spend my time happily deluded. I would listen to the jailers' keys and interpret signals from them and the radios playing, I would think all sorts of unhelpful things and not get bail or ask for help. I neglected myself and was deluded. If prison is for the bad, the sad and the mad, I was of the mad.

What saved me from this spiral of misfortune? It was Mrs Thatcher's community care. She is not associated with social justice, but I have her to thank for the closure of the asylums that were at the heart of my revolving-door time. Since my last admission in 1991, I have not been an inpatient and, crucially, I have not reoffended. Thank you Mrs T.

How did that happen?
Service versus personal needs

Jamie James

I look back and wonder, 'How did that happen?' My life has fallen apart, I have fallen apart, I hang on by a thread. But it hasn't always been like this.

I am the adult who has lost her way and needs someone to hold her hand and be there for her when the pain of living gets too much. The pain of living today. The pain of accepting my yesterdays.

Without warning my world became dark. I could no longer do all the things that marked me out as me. I couldn't work, I couldn't socialise, my world was dismantled. I could do nothing about it. By the time I realised what was happening it was already too late.

My world closed in on me. I was consumed in darkness. A darkness without edges. There was a long way to fall. A deep, scary black void full of strange voices, strange bodies, all of whom hated me. They surrounded and closed me in. Distorted faces, distorted voices. All the while getting louder and bigger. All the while I became more scared and a cocktail of alcohol and prescribed drugs became my only solace in this world full of danger and fear.

The bodies dance wildly across the walls of any room that I am in. I cannot escape. The voices shout loudly all day and all night. Many voices all shouting at me. All pointing and laughing at me. Planning my end.

I feel a hatred of self. A feeling stronger than any feeling that I've felt before. So powerful. An infinite hatred.

The voices want me to hurt, they want me to die. It used to be just me but now they taunt me with images of other people. If I don't hurt myself, if I don't kill myself then it is my duty to hurt and kill those selected for me. I don't want these thoughts. I want the feelings to go away. But no one wants to listen. No one wants to help. And all the while the images, the urges, the taunts get worse. I am left alone with them in a dark world that is strangling me.

Snapshots of my past, real images play over and over again both in my mind and outside of me. They're everywhere I look. They're in every thought. Nowhere is safe. Nowhere is free. I am surrounded by a continuous replay of childhood traumatic scenes. It's not just the images. I get the emotional pains. I get the physical pains. Pains I blocked out as a child surge through me now as an adult. And I find it hard to cope. It feels dangerous. I feel scared. Scared they will take me over and I will never live again.

In my childhood I hoped for help. None came. I am an adult now asking for help. I am met with the same response.

'Distraction', they say when I ring the 'Duty' number. Do 'they' not realise that all of my waking hours, all of my life has been one big distraction? For I can't cope with being me. With living in the now. It hurts too much. My sleeping hours don't count. I don't sleep. Sometimes medication knocks me out so I have a few hours of being not awake. But, it's not sleep. Don't talk about 'distractions'. I have done all of that before I ring. I need you to be there. Be that person who sits with me in the midst of my 'madness'. Don't tell me what to do, don't walk away, don't pass me on, don't put me on hold, don't cut me off. Just be there. Respect me. I so easily could be you, and you – with chances of fate – you could so easily have been me.

Have I felt respected? Have I felt listened to? Have you been there when you said you would be?

I went to my GP. He didn't know me but he listened to me, he read my notes, he listened to me again and he offered a referral to the mental health team. I didn't know what I needed but I knew that I needed help so I went along with the referral and the system clunked into gear and my life took a different turn.

My community psychiatric nurse (CPN) said he'd be there for as long as I needed. He said that he offered a safe space for me to talk. To share. So I saw him, the same time, the same place each week and my life unfolded. I began to talk of my past and of my present. I trusted him. I even thanked him for being there.

My weekly meetings kept me sane. I felt like a pressure cooker. My head hurt so much it was as if I was going to explode. And still is. Physical pains, mental pains, emotional pains, spiritual torment. My weekly sessions meant the pressure was alleviated and I could cope. Sometimes

– just. I made it from one week to the next. The support was crucial. I was lost in a world with angry shouting voices in me, in a world of evil images and constant play and replay of flashbacks. My past had tumbled into my present. My present was shattered. Just breathing at times was a painful and most difficult thing to do.

I was given labels, borderline personality disorder and post-traumatic stress disorder. I was obviously disordered! These labels might have helped those who were dealing with me. But the labels have strangled me and suffocated my voice. All feelings negated. I am no longer upset because I have a right to be upset – I am only upset because of my 'disorder'. Professionals pull back – they surround me in a thick brick wall of labels and diagnosis. They don't look for the door in the wall that they have created. They don't open the door, walk through it. They don't risk meeting 'me'. The whole person. The person not defined by textbook behaviours. I am here. I am hidden behind your jargon. Look and you will find 'me'.

My experience is that 'me' doesn't count. A shame. Your loss. I count.

I survived the last 18 months, nearly 2 years, with the support of my CPN. The one who promised he would be there. Then one day I had a phone call telling me he was 'unavailable'. Without warning, a faceless new manager exerting their new-found power and authority decided to pull the plug on my support. No reasons were given, no warning, no ending. I begged for help – no one listened. In this review, no one asked me what I needed. 'I' didn't count. The mental health team replayed all the negative lessons I had internalized throughout my life. Lessons which they were meant to be helping me to get over.

I am lost with the world blackening around me and swallowing me up on the inside. I hear voices, I see faces, I ask for help. But there is no one there. All I ask is that you see me. Just me. Acknowledge I exist. Acknowledge my pain. My pain of now and of the past and then … and then help me. Give me my once-a-week slot to alleviate the pressure. Be available when times get just too hard. See me, notice when I'm drowning. Don't turn away. Respect me.

When you work with people, treat people with the regard and respect that you would hope to be treated with. None of us want to be lost in our maddening, cut-off, angry worlds. Be real. Be human and you might just connect with 'us'. We have become lost in ourselves and with that connection perhaps we could journey forward together and on our journeys we will alight at a point of wellness and you will have helped.

You will have used your skills but more importantly you will have allowed yourself in your scientific world to access your humanity and through empathy you can give hope to others and a freedom in life – a freedom of mind for which we all strive.

I am lost in my mad, 'dis-ordered' world. How did that happen? Remember I could be you. And you, you so easily could have been me.

27

SEX

Richard Peacocke

Counsellors and doctors know loads about everything, but sometimes because of that they feel they should know everything about everything else, too. On the subject of sex, they seem to have one tune. Sometimes I feel completely *robotised*, but at other times I could do with a damn good fuck to take the world away for a few shattered moments and make me feel lovely and loved again. However, when I broach the subject on the side (as it were) I am told that my sex drive is knackered – and, of course, I believe them so don't even try to make contact. And anyway, who should I try to connect with? Nobody wants to be near an ugly fat smelly wart of a loser like me – and a shag would certainly be well out of the question! But I still feel that grinding ache in my organs …

'You know, one of the first things which disappears is the sex drive, so don't worry – it's only temporary. It'll come back.' But this sage piece of bollocks misses the mark almost completely. The sex drive does not go, it is sublimated beneath a vast ocean of undeservedness. You don't deserve a cuddle, so you don't ask for one. As you have not been cuddled, you cannot be worthy of one. But of course you know that already, so what's new? You are obviously unlovable, otherwise someone would love you. You know that you are fat-or-thin-or-ugly-or-unspeakable-or-dirty-or-smelly-or-untouchable-or-not.fit.to.be.seen.out.of.the.house-or-a.total.disgrace.in.every. department, or some or all of these, and so anything which seems in the very least to agree with your view of yourself is grabbed and held on to – because you have to believe in some-damn-thing and you have to be right about some-bloody-thing! Even if it is about how utterly fucking disgusting and fucked up you are!

'You know, one of the first things which disappears is the sex drive, so don't worry – it's only temporary. It'll come back.' It never went anywhere! It has always been there. I am a man and I enjoy looking at women, and I'm sure you ladies enjoy the sight of a man. And then there are you who prefer the sight of another man or woman. Whatever, and I don't really give a toss what you like, it does not go away. But I just clearly knew that I was too ugly and disgusting, that my clothes were too shabby and that I smelt too bad for even the remotest chance of the other party feeling the way I did. I knew that, so I repressed my feelings. It might have been nice to have been proved wrong once in a while, instead of having my belief reinforced!

'You know, one of the first things which disappears is the sex drive, so don't worry – it's only temporary. It'll come back.' But you get into a habit of not bothering anyone else for sex. If the feelings get too much then you take yourself in hand and relieve them – but, of course, that is selfish and dirty as well! You know your partner is suffering in silence – and probably doing the same as you – because you are poorly, so you feel guilty. I mean, I should have waited until she came home and then stretched her out and given her a good seeing to instead of partaking of autoerotic fruit. But she would not want me; she only stays here out of charity: you can't desert a sick man because that would make you look a right bastard – and we can't have that. Nope, must stay and see it through. Anyway, that is how I think she thinks.

'You know, one of the first things which disappears is the sex drive, so don't worry – it's only temporary. It'll come back.' Yes, but whose? Some partners are so distressed about this illness, this invisible ailment that they lose all sex drive themselves. They never try to be sexy or excite that lump of crying meat who used to be their partner in bed next to them – I mean, why should they? There is no sex drive, is there? It's the first thing to go. And there I lie, wide awake and thinking, thinking, thinking. No one cares a shit for me. The person I love the most, my bestest pal in the whole world, doesn't fancy me anymore. Mind you, that's no surprise, is it? And I have seen how people glance at me in the street, glance and look away. They also obviously wonder at how I have been let out alone. Everybody knows I'm a nutcase. They all know that I am mad – if not yet raving, it won't be long! This stands out clearly in the way I walk – the *Nuthouse Shuffle* – even though I try very hard to walk properly, it's the drugs they give you. It is obvious in the places I go – the surgery, and always hanging out with a nurse. And everyone at work knows as well, and are laughing at me behind my back: 'Couldn't hack it!' 'Fucked up, big time!' 'That's the end of a promising career!'

'Not see his face around here again! And good riddance to bad rubbish – he was crap at his job anyway. We'll all be better off without him!' And my family – it is better not to talk about my family! I have never been so patronised in my whole life. For crying out loud, can't I get treated a bit more like a human being?

Do you know, sex might well initially be a very low priority on the agenda, but human contact is all about sex. And contact is high on the agenda. Without contact, we're lost. So, okay, I can't raise a smile because I have been coshed by all the bloody tablets I take. That does not mean I don't feel the need. That does not mean I don't want you. That does not mean that I don't love you – even if I find it hard (very bloody hard) to understand what you see in me.

Maybe a massage? Or some encouragement? Don't just piss off to bed and leave me downstairs, night after night. Don't imagine that is what I want to do. Perhaps I am frightened to come upstairs before you are asleep, in case you laugh at me. Perhaps that would be just that little bit too much for me to bear.

ON BEING A CARER

28

Dementia: The end remains inevitable but the journey can be improved

John Major

Introduction

I would like you to accompany me along the road that I have already walked caring for my wife Helen. Before setting off however, I feel that it is important to share a few statistics about dementia with you so that you have a better idea just how many other people are also walking with us.

In the United Kingdom at the moment there are around 750,000 people with dementia with that number rising all the time. This is due not just to an ageing population but also to increased awareness of dementia, with the result that many more people of working age are being recognised with some form of dementia. It is estimated that one in three people who die over 65 will have a dementia of some form although many will not have received a diagnosis. If you add to all these figures the carers and family members for each person recognised, we have indeed a very crowded pathway. Yet at the same time we have a condition for which there is no solution, only a limited range of drugs that help to slow the progression for some people with Alzheimer's, not all forms of dementia.

Governments around the world have only recently raised the priority given to dementia, but I would suggest that they are motivated by the belated awareness of the cost of care rather than the quality of life of all those involved.

It is therefore this aspect, the quality of life, that I would like to talk about as we walk along, based upon the very personal experience I gained looking after my wife.

Early stages

You will often hear people say in light-hearted conversation, for example, after going into a room and forgetting what they were looking for, that they'd had a 'senior moment' or 'it must be dementia'. If only it could be so simple. In my wife's case the first signs were not forgetfulness but confusion with decision making, handling sudden changes, and answering the telephone when she did not know who it was – basic aspects in her working life and many other people's as well. As someone with responsibilities, it was a dramatic awareness of the problem she faced and was to stay with her for many years. I should add that in the early stages, awareness of what is happening is emotionally draining for the person with dementia; it recedes as the condition progresses, but not for the carer – that emotional strain stays with you throughout.

I strongly urge anyone in this position to take positive action: see your GP, do not delay and, I regret to say this, do not let the GP delay things by saying things like 'You're just getting old, come back and see me in a year's time if you are still worried'. Dementia is not a natural part of the ageing process and, although there may indeed by very little a GP can do in terms of medication, it is better to be referred for a more detailed assessment. It is also important for the carer to go along to all meetings with the GP to make sure nothing is missed or misunderstood. It is also up to the carer to explain some of the difficulties that brought you there in the first place. In other words, you are already speaking for two people.

The early stage is the time to plan for what lies ahead. Do not ignore that. Too many carers I have met tend to have a form of denial either because the person they are caring for can manage quite well or that they are able to lead an ordinary life. Do not lose the opportunity to start planning, to recognise what is ahead of you.

For example, this is the time to review all your finances, mortgages, wills – in fact anything that requires decisions to be taken when all parties are, in legal terms, of sound mind.

This is also the time to find out a little more about the form of dementia you are faced with. After all, each person presents differently and each person progresses differently. One word of warning, a visit to a website and downloading too much information will either frighten you or overwhelm you. Make sure you study for the circumstances you are facing at the time. Start to ask the right questions.

In the meantime lead as normal a life as possible. If you are used to going out, then keep going out. Do not feel there is a stigma to dementia and do not be afraid to explain to your friends and others what is happening. Your social circumstances will change later so make the most of what you can do when you can do things – and please do them together. There will come a time when you really miss the shared experiences of life.

This is also the time to make a few adjustments that will allow the person to lead as full a life as possible and help them to maintain a level of independence. For example, you know how frustrating it is when you cannot find some everyday item, something that has been put in the wrong cupboard. Avoid the frustration by putting labels on your cupboard doors and kitchen drawers that says just what is where. This can be in words or a simple picture. Leave toilet and bathroom doors open so that they know where to go. Helen used to like reading a newspaper so I made sure she had one each day but I also gave her a task – cut out and put into a scrap book articles from the paper that she found interesting. This not only maintained her interest in reading but gave an additional purpose of selecting and recording. To give a structure to her day, I prepared a daily job list of things to do and ticked them off as she completed them. This was helpful for quite some time until eventually the 'job' became the ticking and not actually doing the task!

During the early stages there is no reason to stop people going out by themselves but do give them a little extra protection. I was able to find a necklace-style locket for Helen which opened up to contain her contact details as well as an outline of her medical condition. I ensured that she had a card in her handbag with her address and always had a small amount of money in her purse. She understood at that stage that if she got into difficulties when she was by herself (I still had to go to work at that stage), she should get a taxi and show the driver the card. Those of you looking after a man however do have a problem. Men are somewhat reluctant to have things attached to them such as wrist bands with details or will put something in one jacket pocket and go out next day in another jacket. My tip therefore would be an attachment on the house key ring.

Other things in the home are memory books and family photograph albums, music (a great survivor that will accompany many people all the way along the pathway) and jigsaws. I was able to find special jigsaws that have adult pictures but child-size pieces.

Television did cease being a form of entertainment and stimulation, becoming instead an uncontrolled irritant in the corner of the room, a talking head that did not respond and raised voices leading to an increase in Helen's anxiety levels. Radio however can be very helpful; it can almost become a friend. Choose your radio station with care and use it with some of your own music to maintain a balance – a constant drone of sameness soon becomes 'wallpaper' and is of no real help to you.

One final note of caution as we come to the end of the Early Stages. Once your cared-for person loses the ability to do any of the things I have listed, do not persist. The ability will have gone; there is nothing to be gained by saying 'Well you did this yesterday' as that will only upset you both. Just move on, accept that there is one thing less they can do for themselves and start being creative about what they can do. Some of the first things that Helen, almost overnight, was unable to do included telling the time and writing a cheque. The last point is understandable as none of us like writing cheques, but it rather helpful to know what time it is!

Mid-stages and possibly dealing with secondary conditions

Let me first of all repeat something I said earlier, that people do present with dementia differently and that they also progress differently. These points are particularly important in this section as I will be sharing with you some of things that happened with Helen which may not apply to you, the reader.

There are periods of stability and other times when just everything is changing rapidly. This of course will be all part of what is happening in the brain and I will leave the explanation of that process to others more suitably qualified. What I must emphasise is that the changes you see and experience are not intentional on the part of the person you are caring for. They do not wish theses changes, and indeed would be extremely concerned about what they were doing. The only consolation for them is that by this stage they themselves may not be quite as aware.

As we moved along to the mid-stages, Helen lost the ability to read. My solution was to do the reading for her. We would go together to the library and jointly 'choose' books to read. It is important to involve the person in as many things as possible even when their involvement is rather passive. The books that were most helpful contained humour which allowed me to take a break from the reading and share the 'funny bits' before resuming the story.

Another difficulty was that Helen progressively lost her mobility, moving from a walking stick, to Zimmer frame, to wheelchair. This also required adjustments to equipment and the provision of aids in the home to assist in the toilet, bath and transfer from chairs and getting in and out of bed. The occupational therapists from social services were very helpful at each stage as the equipment itself had to be constantly changed to meet the changing circumstances. The only criticism I have is that every time I had to call them, it was a different person who came to assess the situation. It would have been so much easier if we could have had the same person. Whilst she was still walking however, I observed her hesitation when moving from say a light-coloured carpet to a darker area. I realised that she was not sure what that dark area was; was it a void? Similar hesitation started when getting out of the car at the kerb. That dark area between the car and the pavement must have seemed like some bottomless pit. The only solution was to either park well out from the pavement, not a good idea, park and get her out on the offside and hence into traffic, definitely not a good idea, or put two wheels just on the pavement and attract the dark looks from pedestrians. It really was a no-win situation.

On the same topic of movement, I discovered the safest way for Helen to sit down in a chair was to approach it sideways on, put her hand on the arm rest and sit confident in the knowledge that the chair is in fact there. Think about that next time you go to sit down. Without even thinking, you lower yourself without looking because you know it is there. Someone with dementia needs a little more reassurance. Attend to other things in the home to make it as safe as possible. Get rid of rugs, loose mats and sloppy slippers – they are all accidents just waiting to happen.

It was also during the mid-stages that Helen required increased assistance with eating and drinking. We progressed through two-handled cups to spouts, plate guards, cutting food up for eating with just a fork to my giving everything to her. Because the progress was progressive, and over a period of time, I just adapted as we went along. It was only after a reflective moment that I realised just how much had changed. However we did have a surprise. She started to fill her mouth with food but not chew and swallow. Yet another specialist was introduced and suggested that, although I may be giving Helen her favourite food, her brain was no longer being stimulated enough to want to chew it – in other words, my cooking was bland! Well, I can take criticism when it comes to cooking, as my culinary skill before I became a carer amounted to putting bread in the toaster and opening a can. The solution I was told is to spice things up. I suddenly became an expert (well sort of) in curries and spicy pasta – and it worked. Another problem overcome. I have to admit that I rather enjoyed the change because for many years we had visited our local Indian restaurant and saw no reason to stop just because of Helen's Alzheimer's. We continued to go even when she was in her wheelchair, and needed a plate guard and to be fork fed. All I did was let them know in advance when we wanted to go, agree a quieter time with the restaurant who would hold a table conveniently located for the wheelchair, and Helen would sit quite happily with her back to the room and thoroughly enjoy her meal and, what was more important, enjoy the social stimulation of going out to dinner. Do not hide at home, live as full a life as possible by just careful planning and ensure that the person you are looking after remains within their own comfort zone.

Helen was only 60 when she was first offered by Social Services a place at a day centre. She was invited first to just visit during the day to have a look. Her face was a picture. When she saw the room she turned to me and said 'I don't want to sit with all those old people' but followed it up with an afterthought 'or do they want me to make the teas?' Unfortunately making the teas was not possible, but it still feels like it was a missed opportunity because it was another two years before she agreed to go.

Gradually conversation becomes harder. You learn to deal with repetitive questions but normal discussions also start to fade away. Sentences may commence but do not get finished, but you must try to answer as if they were. I always included her in any conversation I was having, particularly if it involved her, because you never knew just how much she was understanding even if she was incapable of articulating a response or making a contribution. This was important whilst visiting doctors and other medical people where, as the carer, it is up to you to report any changes or new difficulties, but I always made a point of making it a joint report.

Another challenge was the development of double incontinence, but even for this there was help available in terms of bulk supplies of pads delivered to the door. Storage however was another problem as they delivered three months supplies at a time and as the condition changes, the size of the pads increases!

You will realise by now that one is doing many things one never expected ever to do for someone else, from washing, dressing, personal hygiene to buying bras, underwear and ladies' clothes. But I always remembered that although I was doing these things for Helen, it was the last thing she really wanted me to do for her. It is not unreasonable therefore for her to be upset at some of these interventions, so I changed the roles. I started to ask her to help me to do these things – not my helping her. This for a while even produced a few laughs at my so-called incompetence.

Up to this point I have talked about the role of caring. Now it is time to talk about the person doing the caring. Along the pathway you have learned so many new skills and I can assure you that you will never stop learning, but it is time you thought about yourself.

There is a constant strain upon you. For example you must learn to control your emotions; your face is the window to the world for the person you are caring for. You must remain calm, do not show anger or frustration, so when you feel like banging your head against the wall go ahead but just do it in another room. It is inevitable that you will feel lonely, isolated. You will not be able to socialise with friends, they may not call round as much as they used to. This is understandable because they themselves can be upset by the changes they see to their friends – it is not intentional but, as I have said, it is understandable. You will also start to feel inadequate, that you could be doing things better or more effectively, and you may also feel frightened from time to time – frightened about the future, you know where the end of the pathway is, and frightened about your own health. What would happen if you became ill? Remember this, a healthy carer is a good carer, whereas an ill carer means two vulnerable people.

Every carer is entitled to a Carer's Assessment. You will by now be used to a social worker visiting and updating the case notes, but many carers do not have their own. Please ask for a Carer's Assessment if this has not already been offered. Further, do not fill in the form yourself. As a carer I know that I find it difficult to be objective about my own needs. You are under strains that you may not be aware of and therefore with a social worker carefully asking you questions, your real needs start to emerge. One of the things that will probably emerge is the need for respite care. That may be from a few hours to allow you to go to the shops, to go out in the evening to meet friends or the cinema, or to residential care for the person you are caring for to allow you a short holiday – a break from caring. I must say that I resisted respite care for some time. I took a very macho position: 'Oh, I don't need a holiday, I can cope.' Do not do as I did; take it and you will soon realise the benefit. At first I felt terrible when I left Helen in a care home; I felt that somehow I had failed in my duty, that I was being irresponsible. I visited her every day, I could not face up to the idea of going away, but also started to realise how relaxing it was to be able to sit together and not have the responsibility to be doing things for her – just to enjoy her company. Someone else for that week or two weeks would wash, dress, feed and take care of her needs. You could return to that special relationship that a couple have, of friendship, of mutual caring for each other and, at the risk of sounding wildly romantic, your original love for each other without the stresses and strains of dealing with Alzheimer's and caring. It will only take an hour or two, when you return home after the respite break, to be back in your caring routine but hopefully refreshed and your batteries recharged for the fresh challenges that lie ahead.

The later stages: at home and in a home

This is the position on the pathway when you see that there is a junction ahead. One route to a nursing or care home and one route that continues care at home. I am sure every carer would like to look after the person needing care in their own home, but you must consider many different issues. For example, are there medical conditions that require speedy intervention or regular attention? As a carer, is your own health really up to the later stage challenges? In Helen's case, it was the commencement of small seizures that determined the choice of our final route. The seizures left her unable to stand holding on to the various pieces of equipment, which meant that I could no longer wash and dress her by myself.

Some of the things you need to think about if you would like to keep caring at home include your own health, the security of your home, the ability to evacuate in an emergency, particularly important if you live in a block of flats and would need to use emergency stairs. Other issues are things such as noise. Helen for some years has made loud noises when being moved, washed and changed. If you face the same situation, ask yourself how close are you to neighbours? If once again you live in a block of flats, the answer is very close and, although your neighbours may be very understanding, that understanding may be limited if you are disturbing them on a regular basis at irregular hours. The same considerations may well apply if you live in a semidetached or terraced house. Another point to think about is that as you approach the later stages of the pathway, rather tired and weary, you could well find that there will be many things you can no longer do. This could lead to a steady flow of care assistants visiting a few times a day, leaving you always watching the time so that you are ready for their visits (and hoping they will be on time), with the result that home may no longer feel quite like your home.

If you consider residential care, you will never overcome your sense of guilt – should you really be putting someone you have looked after so long into a home? In my case, I had no choice; the medical conditions did it for me. If you have a choice, do plan very carefully. The move from your home into residential care must be the last move the person with dementia makes. Do ask the right questions and ensure that the care home you are considering is capable of looking after someone to the end of the pathway, not just capable of looking after someone as they present at the moment of admission. They and you know full well that the circumstances will change and the care home has a duty to deliver care all the way – otherwise don't go there. Also remember my earlier comments about social stimulation – wall-to-wall daytime TV is not the most suitable form of stimulation. Another advantage is proximity to where you live so that you can pop round as frequently as possible, say around a meal time or afternoon tea, in order that you can continue helping and doing things together.

I hope these notes will be helpful to others following along the same path. I have outlined a few hints to help in the home that certainly made life easier. In a perfect world I would like GPs to monitor the health of the carer just as much as the cared-for person. I would also like GPs to recognise the early stages of dementia and to take carers into their confidence as early as possible. I would like to see continuity of all visiting people including district nurses, social workers and occupational therapists. I certainly welcome many of the recommendations in the National Dementia Strategy which does require extra funding for the earlier stages but long term will produce a far more cost-effective and efficient level of care all along the pathway. I have not mentioned the lack of research, the limited access to dementia specialist drugs or the problems of paying for care. Each is a major issue but I will leave that debate for others, after all, I still have someone to care for.

29

Diagnosing Clapham Junction syndrome

Sir Terry Pratchett

People who have dementia in this country are not heard. I'm fortunate; I can be heard. Regrettably, it's amazing how people listen if you stand up in public and give away $1million for research into the disease, as I have done. Why did I do it? I regarded finding I had a form of Alzheimer's as an insult and decided to do my best to marshal any kind of forces I could against this wretched disease.

I have posterior cortical atrophy or PCA. They say, rather ingenuously, that if you have Alzheimer's it's the best form of Alzheimer's to have. This is a moot point, but what it does do, while gradually robbing you of memory, visual acuity and other things you didn't know you had until you miss them, is leave you more or less as fluent and coherent as you always have been.

I spoke to a fellow sufferer recently (or as I prefer to say, 'a person who is thoroughly annoyed with the fact they have dementia') who talked in the tones of a university lecturer and in every respect was quite capable of taking part in an animated conversation. Nevertheless, he could not see the teacup in front of him. His eyes knew that the cup was there; his brain was not passing along the information. This disease slips you away a little bit at a time and lets you watch it happen.

When I look back now, I suspect there may be some truth in the speculation that dementia (of which Alzheimer's is the most common form) may be present in the body for quite some time before it can be diagnosed. For me, things came to

This chapter is an edited version of Terry Pratchett's article 'I'm slipping away a bit at a time … and all I can do is watch it happen', which appeared in *The Daily Mail* on 7 October 2008. Terry Pratchett is an acclaimed author and the creator of the bestselling *Discworld* series.

a head in the late summer of 2007. My typing had been getting progressively worse and my spelling had become erratic. I grew to recognize what I came to call Clapham Junction days when the demands of the office grew too much to deal with.

I was initially diagnosed not with Alzheimer's but with an ischemic change, a simple loss of brain cells due to normal ageing. That satisfied me until the next Clapham Junction day. I went back to my GP and said I knew there was something more going on. Fortunately, she knew well enough not to bother with the frankly pathetic MMSE test (the 30-point questionnaire used to determine brain function) and sent me to Addenbrooke's Hospital in Cambridge, where, after examination of my MRI scan and an afternoon of complex tests, I was diagnosed with PCA, an uncommon variant of dementia, which had escaped the eagle eye of the original diagnostician.

When in *Paradise Lost* Milton's Satan stood in the pit of hell and raged at heaven, he was merely a trifle miffed compared to how I felt that day. I felt totally alone, with the world receding from me in every direction and you could have used my anger to weld steel. Only my family and the fact I had fans in the medical profession, who gave me useful advice, got me through that moment. I feel very sorry for, and angry on behalf of, the people who don't have the easy ride I had.

It is astonishing how long it takes some people to get diagnosed (I know because they write to me). I cannot help but wonder if this is because doctors are sometimes reluctant to give the patient the stigma of dementia since there is no cure.

I was extremely fortunate in my GP. I think she was amazed to find that of the two specialists in my area, one had no experience of PCA and therefore did not feel he could help me and the other would only take on patients over 65 – at 59 I was clearly too young to have Alzheimer's.

I remember on that day of rage thinking that if I'd been diagnosed with cancer of any kind, at least there would have opened in front of me a trodden path. There would have been specialists, examinations, there would be, in short, some machinery in place. I was not in the mood for a response that said, more or less, 'go away and come back in six years'.

My wife said: 'Thank goodness it isn't a brain tumour', but all I could think then was: 'I know three people who have got better after a brain tumour. I haven't heard of anyone who's got better from Alzheimer's.'

Undeniable signs

It was my typing and spelling that convinced me the diagnosis was right. They had gone haywire. Other problems I put down to my looming 60th birthday. I thought no one else had noticed the fumbling with seat belts and the several attempts to get clothing on properly, but my wife and PA were worrying. We still have the occasional Clapham Junction days, now understood and dealt with.

I have written 47 novels in the past 25 years, but now I have to check the spelling of even quite simple words – they just blank on me at random. I would not dare to write this without the once despised checker, and you would have your work cut out to read it, believe me. On the other hand – and this is very typical of PCA – when the kind lady who periodically checks me out asked me to name as many animals as I can, I started with the rock hyrax, the nearest living relative to the elephant, and thylacine – the probably extinct Tasmanian marsupial wolf. That's the gift or the curse of our little variant. We have problems handling the physical world but can come pretty close to talking our way out of it so you don't notice. We might have our shirts done up wrong, but might be able to convince you it's a new style.

I felt that all I had was a voice, and I should make it heard. It never occurred to me not to use it. I went on the net and told, well, everyone. I wish I could say it was an act of bravery. It wasn't and I find that suggestion very nearly obscene. How brave is it to say you have a disease that does not hint of a dissolute youth, riotous living or even terrible eating habits? Anyone can contract dementia; and every day and with a growing momentum, anybody does.

Disease of knowledge

It occurred to me that at one point it was like I had two diseases – one was Alzheimer's and the other was knowing I had Alzheimer's. There were times when I thought I'd have been much happier not knowing, just accepting that I'd lost brain cells and one day they'd probably grow back or whatever. It is better to know, though, and better for it to be known, because it has got people talking, which I rather think was what I had in mind. The $1 million I pledged to the Alzheimer's Research Trust was just to make them talk louder for a while.

It is a strange life when you 'come out'. People get embarrassed, lower their voices, get lost for words. Fifty per cent of Britons think there is a stigma surrounding dementia but only 25% think there is still a stigma associated with cancer. It seems that when you have cancer you are a brave battler against the disease, but when you have Alzheimer's you are an old fart. That's how people see you. It makes you feel quite alone. It seems to me there's hardly one family in this country that is not touched by the disease somehow. But people don't talk about it because it is so frightening. I swear that people think that if they say the word they're summoning the demon. It used to be the same with cancer.

Journalists, on the other hand – I appreciate that other people living with the disease don't get so much of this – find it hard to talk to me about anything else, and it dominates every interview: Yes, I said I had PCA ten months ago, yes, I still have it, yes, I wish I didn't, no, there is no cure.

I can't really object to all this, but it is strange that a disease that attracts so much attention, awe, fear and superstition is so underfunded in treatment and research. We don't know what causes it, and as far as we know the only way to be sure of not developing it is to die young. Regular exercise and eating sensibly are a good idea, but they don't come with any guarantees. There is no cure. Researchers are talking about the possibility of a whole palette of treatments or regimes to help those people with dementia to live active and satisfying lives, with the disease kept in reasonably permanent check in very much the same way as treatments now exist for HIV. Not so much a cure therefore as – we hope – a permanent reprieve. We hope it will come quickly, and be affordable.

When my father was in his terminal year, I discussed death with him. I recall very clearly his relief that the cancer that was taking him was at least allowing him 'all his marbles'. Dementia in its varied forms is not like cancer. Dad saw the cancer in his pancreas as an invader. But Alzheimer's is me unwinding, losing trust in myself, a butt of my own jokes and on bad days capable of playing hunt the slipper by myself and losing.

You can't battle it, you can't be a plucky 'survivor'. It just steals you from yourself. And I'm 60; that's supposed to be the new 40. The baby boomers are getting older, and will stay older for longer. And they will run right into the dementia firing range. How will a society cope? Especially a society that can't so readily rely on those stable family relationships that traditionally provided the backbone of care?

What is needed is will and determination. The first step is to talk openly about dementia because it's a fact, well enshrined in folklore, that if we are to kill the demon then first we have to say its name. Once we have recognized the demon, without secrecy or shame, we can find its weaknesses. Regrettably one of the best swords for killing demons like this is made of gold – lots of gold. These days we call it funding. I believe the D-day battle on Alzheimer's will be engaged shortly and a lot of things I've heard from experts, not always formally, strengthen that belief. It's a physical disease, not some mystic curse; therefore it will fall to a physical cure. There's time to kill the demon before it grows.

30

My sweet sister and I

Catherine Jenkins

Firstly, let me introduce myself. My name is Catherine Jenkins. I'm 30 years old and currently approaching my second year as a student on the Advanced Diploma in Adult Nursing. Just before the start of my first year of studies, in September 2007, my sister became very ill. I want to share my story with you in hope that it may, no matter how little, make a difference. I hope that with time the stigma attached to people with a mental health illness may be broken down, and the impact not only on the individual, but also on their family, may be understood better.

Jo is my one and only sister. I have no other siblings; it has always been just her and me. She is 18 months older than me, and we have always been very close. We've had our fair share of cat fights like sisters do, but when either one was down or needed a shoulder to cry on, we have always been there for one another. Our mother and father divorced when we were very young, and my mother remarried to a man called Gavin. Gavin was an alcoholic, so, though we also have many happy memories, most of our childhood was spent never quite knowing from one day to the next what the day would bring. He was an intimidating man, and we never knew where we stood. Our mother protected us the best way she could, but as we were all under the same roof there is only so much she could protect us from. At night when the loud music would start, we knew he would be drinking and the night would not end well. We would often sit cuddled together and listen to the abuse he would hurl at my mum. I think because of this my sister and I turned to each other for comfort, and over the years our bond grew from strength to strength.

Fortunately, when I turned 12 my mother left Gavin, and eventually married again to a wonderful man without whom

165

we would be lost. They are deeply in love to this day. OK, a little background out the way, and only a little, to perhaps help paint a picture of how close my sister and I are, and to let you know that from as far back as we can remember, our lives have never been plain sailing.

My sister has always been described as 'happy', 'fun' and 'bubbly' amongst other things, but beneath that there were times when of course she did not feel any of those things. After having her twin girls in 1999 she suffered from postnatal depression. She had never been re-assessed from that diagnosis and had been on antidepressants ever since. I could try to do my sister justice, but I never could in such a short space or time. The best I can say is she is my sister, always has been, always will be. I love her dearly, always will. She is funny (VERY!), entertaining, full of love, sometimes selfish and bossy, and I would not change a thing about her. I would do anything for my sister, as she would me, and her happiness means everything to me.

So I will go back to the summer of 2007. I had returned from nine months away in South America with my daughter. We had missed each other terribly when I was away, and my sister had called me before crying on the phone, desperately asking when I would return. Looking back, I knew things were not going well for her, and had a gut feeling that something was very wrong. It was a large part of my decision to return to England. So when I returned in May, I tried to make up for lost time with her, my toddler nephew aged just one, and two nieces aged nine. However, it was clear after a short time home that things were not right with my sister. I couldn't put my finger on it at first, but she just appeared distant. She was talking a lot, but never listening, and though this was not unusual for Jo, she seemed genuinely unable to concentrate or take in anything I would say to her. I was also surprised at how she seemed to always be busy suddenly. I would ask her if I could come over but she would make excuses about someone else being there and it was often 'later Catherine, call me later'. Then when I did try the calls would divert to voicemail.

Things escalated. By the time the summer month of July arrived my sister had become unrecognisable. She had gone from a size 16 to a size 8, she was spending a lot of time with a friend from her area, and together they were becoming very 'spiritual', reading up on books about healing, and 'connecting with spirits'. Though that may be nothing odd for some, I knew my sister, and the way she was reading into everything was very unlike her. She started to tell me everything had meaning, from the colours I chose to wear that day, to the 'pure virgin olive oil' I had left out on the kitchen worktop! My mum and I were becoming very worried, as she had also confided in me that she had stopped taking her antidepressants, but in her words had 'never felt better' for it.

At the end of July our mum and stepfather took their granddaughters away for a week's holiday. During this time I tried to stay as close to Jo as I could, but it was becoming increasingly difficult as she always had company. One day I called and again she said 'I'm busy Catherine, I'm with my friend, call me later.' I put the phone down and decided I would drive round there, I was her sister, and in my mind there was no reason why we could not see each other even if she had company. When I arrived at her door, it took a short time before she answered. When she did I was shocked. Her eyes looked glazed over, her house was not just messy, it was a total state of chaos. There was food lying on the floor, mess everywhere, and there in the middle of it all was her baby boy. I cannot tell you what that did to me, the feeling it gave me inside. The only way I can explain it is when you are really nervous, you know when you feel like your belly has dropped and your bowels are loosening??!!!! It was like that; I knew from that moment there was something seriously wrong and something bad on the horizon. I spent some time with my sister that day. She was delusional and talking about connecting with spirits and messages she had received. She was talking about cars being colour coded and that she was getting signals from every direction. I tried to reason with her, but when someone believes something so strongly it is near impossible to tell them differently, so in the end I resigned myself to that and just listened. I gently asked if I could give my nephew a 'quick clean up', and did the same with the downstairs to do something, anything. I asked Jo, near begged her, to come back with me that day to stay at mine, but she refused. I asked if I could look after her little boy, my nephew, for the night, but she refused, and in the end I left her there, feeling hopeless inside.

That evening I called my mum who was due home the following day. I told her the seriousness of the situation, but it wasn't until she and my stepfather saw Jo with their own eyes that they realised. In the space of a week Jo had 'gone' to another place. She was with us in body but not in mind, and our worlds were about to collapse in a way we could never have imagined.

The following day my mum arrived home, with my daughter and nieces. I had told mum what to expect but nothing could have prepared her. After dropping the girls with my sister my mum drove immediately back to mine. We could see the worry etched on each others' faces. We knew we had to get her to see a doctor, but Jo was refusing, convinced she never felt better. So we decided that we would try to gently persuade

Jo and the children to stay with mum that night or with me, so that if she would not see the doctor the following day we could get the doctor round to see her. We decided not to put the issue of the doctor upon her till the following day. Jo agreed to stay at mine, but did not want mum anywhere near her as she said she was just interfering and did not understand the new happiness that she had found. I reassured her it would just be us and the children, so later that day my sister arrived with all the children. When she came to my door it was cold. It was 6 p.m. and not a warm evening for a summer month. The girls walked in and her baby boy was in her arms. He was dressed in a nappy and nothing else.

It took me nearly 30 minutes to get Jo through my front door that evening. She was talking about the signals coming through the radio, the colour coding of the cars, how everyone knew who she was and the cars were stopping for her. She was obsessing about the colours I was wearing, what they represented, and kept asking her girls to change clothes with her. She said it was amazing, she had been re-born.

That night the children finally fell asleep around 10 p.m. I stayed up with my sister until I thought she was in bed and near sleeping. At this point it was midnight, and I went to bed myself, worried, scared, and drained. At 1 a.m. I woke with a jump. Jo was at the end of my bed, shaking my feet, telling me I must wake up as she had something to tell me. I said it was late and that we needed to sleep. But she insisted and I could feel her panic so I got up. We went in the kitchen, and I put the kettle on to try and bring some normality into the situation. Jo had a look in her eye that scared me. I put my arms around her; I just wanted to squeeze her so tight, and take all those thoughts in her head away from her. But I couldn't. My sister was totally delusional, chanting, 'casting spells', and believing she was 'the angel Gabriel'. She spoke of a man waiting outside the house, that tonight there would be blood if we did not stop it, and he was out to get us. It was like all the 'positive' delusional thoughts she had prior to that night had suddenly turned dark, and at that time of the night it was very frightening. I asked her to stop but she couldn't. I just didn't know what to do because my mum and stepdad had said under no circumstances to leave her. Jo wouldn't let me use the phone to call them either. It was an awful situation but in the end I was so scared I grabbed my little girl out of bed in the middle of the night in just her nightdress, and left her. Jo shouted at me begging me not to go and that 'they' would get her, but I didn't know what else I could do, I was desperate.

I drove to my mum's and let myself in the house. It was nearly 3 a.m. at this point. My mum was so sick with worry she was still up. I told her what had happened and mum stayed home with my daughter while my stepdad and I went straight back to the house to be with my sister and the children. That night we didn't sleep, none of us, not a wink. In the morning, as soon as it opened, I drove to the doctor's and told him the situation. My mum then brought my sister to the surgery. After five minutes of the doctor reassuring Jo she could speak openly and trust him she spoke freely of all these thoughts and feelings she had been getting and truly believing. Mum took Jo back to mine, where we all sat with her, until finally mental health professionals arrived to assess her. She was immediately admitted to St Agatha's.

Seeing my sister in St Agatha's

My sister was admitted to St Agatha's on 5 September 2007, the day before my mum's birthday. Even now, a year on, I find it very difficult to describe how I felt, seeing my sister there. It was like the final realization. St Agatha's was a hospital for the 'mentally ill', a place for other people's family, not for mine and least of all for my sister. That was MY sister, the other half of me. My sister that watches Little Britain, that can impersonate all the characters to a fine art, my sister that doesn't even know how much strength she gives me, and that without her I am lost, and my sister that's shared my life, who I've cried with, laughed with, loved with and lost with. Even now as I am writing this, a lump is stuck in my throat and my eyes are full of tears. It is raw still today.

The memory is fixed in my mind. When I think back to my sister in St Agatha's, I see her stood there. Brown boots, size 8 jeans, all her womanly curves gone. Her face worn, her eyes lost, her fingers constantly fidgeting, the look on her face of mistrust as I came near her. She rejected me from that moment onwards, till the day she came out. In her eyes I had left her that night, and now she had ended up here, in a scene from *One Flew over the Cuckoo's Nest*, and she couldn't get out.

It turned out that Jo had been taking cocaine. It had started soon after I left for South America the previous year. The guilt I carried for that, it was heavy, and I felt I had totally let my sister down. She had told me she needed me, begged me not to go, but I had gone, and now I saw that my sister was lost, and in my mind it was forever and would be forever because of me. How I did not see the signs. Once we knew that we realised the signs were *so* obvious, textbook almost. But not for one minute did it cross my mind. We had tried things growing up, but only as part of growing up, to experience something new. We didn't 'use' drugs.

But she had stopped taking her antidepressants soon after, and for six weeks prior to being admitted to St Agatha's, Jo had also started using 'speed' ... which would explain her rapid weight loss. I was devastated and felt completely 100% responsible for letting her down, for not being there when she had so desperately needed me. I felt as though she had turned to drugs when she did not know what else she could turn to, through desperation, to escape.

The visits were heartbreaking. My sister didn't want me near her, but I could not go without seeing her. I don't know how any of us got through that time. I would barely sleep. I was looking after my nieces in the early days as well as my daughter. Once university started in October I would take my daughter to school, go to university or placement at the hospital, and afterwards drive to see my sister who would tell me to leave her alone. I just wanted to pull her back, find her, but I couldn't so even if she pushed me away, and accused me of things that had never happened, I would rather that and be near her than nothing at all.

After, I would try to walk out of St Agatha's before breaking down. I would normally make it as far as the car, but on a couple of occasions it would start as soon as I turned my back to walk away and leave my sister in that place again. I would try to cry it out, collect my daughter, put on my happy mummy face and talk about our day (child's version, with added smiles!!), and settle her down for the night, before starting another sleepless night. My life went on like that for the 12 weeks she was in there.

You know when something like that happens, nothing can prepare you for it, nothing can take your pain away, and replace the massive loss and grief you feel. But people can do things to ease it, even if just slightly. When my sister was admitted I noticed different reactions amongst friends and distant family. You see my sister didn't have cancer, she wasn't involved in a road accident and suffering from brain damage. My sister had a serious mental health problem. This is something many people don't understand; maybe don't want to – after all how many people are suffering from mental health problems?? More than we know as it happens. It can be a little too close to home for many.

It is then I also became fully aware of the stigma attached to it, and the discomfort people feel acknowledging it. It was at this time my sister's true friends, and indeed mine, showed themselves, and to those precious few I will be eternally grateful. But I felt so isolated. My mother's grief was so great I could not burden her with mine. My sister was not there to share it with, but she was in fact the one I was grieving for. I had no partner, and I felt that no one really understood me. When I arrived home it was to an empty house, with just my mind and memories haunting me. I would have done anything to share it with someone who really understood. But I knew it was a subject people didn't feel comfortable with, even if the 'subject' happened to be my one and only beautiful sister.

Feeling of isolation

When I used to leave my sister in the hospital, sometimes I was so weak my legs would wobble, my tears would flow before I hit the door, and I would just crave a touch, a smile, someone giving me some feedback, some hope, and if not some hope, a little understanding. But it didn't happen. Of all the times I visited my sister at the hospital, with the exception of one male mental health nurse, no one touched my arm, asked if I was OK, looked into my eyes to acknowledge me, or just even smile. It was like I was almost invisible except for the wonderful lady on reception, or when I had to prove my identity before walking onto the ward. I know my sister was the one ill, was always and must always be at the forefront of their minds, but, not even as a student nurse, but simply as a human being, I could not understand how I was so invisible to others, regardless of how busy they were. I have worked as student nurse on several placements now, rushed off my feet, but have always been aware of families as well as the patient, and what a difference a little support, touch or even a smile can make, not only to patient but to the family as well. That is not something learnt from my experience with my sister, it is something I know, and it's innate in me as a caring human being. I asked if there were any support groups, somewhere I could go to share my feelings. I was pointed in the direction of the leaflets on bipolar disorder, schizophrenia and so on. It was not what I had asked.

I felt increasingly depressed. I felt I had lost a sister, but she was not dead, more in a state of limbo, and I did not know if she would ever, could ever, come back to us. It was not like other troubled times in my life. I felt completely helpless, hopeless. There was nothing I could do, just wait, hope and pray. My doctor wanted to put me on antidepressants but I refused. I felt that with everything going on I could feel nothing but depressed and no medication would change my life situation right now, or how I felt about it. I am very glad now that I made that decision. But I believe that simple little things could have made such a great difference to me at that time. As well as hoping to try to help break some of the stigma attached to people suffering from mental health problems. It is that which is the driving force for me writing this, and giving you my story. My mother felt the same, but of course every story is different through different eyes, and I can only speak for myself.

My sister was diagnosed as suffering from bipolar and drug-induced psychosis. She had to be sectioned after a week in St Agatha's as she was so desperate to leave. After 12 weeks in there, mum and I decided to take her out. Mum had the power to do so if Jo remained in her care. This decision was made not because we had seen an improvement, quite the opposite. We felt she was becoming institutionalised. She was on a ward with many people self-harming. Jo had started to do the same to herself, something she had never done in her lifetime. She felt she just wanted to die, and the last time I saw my sister in there I looked back at her down the long corridor. She was stood talking to herself, swaying back and forth, moving her hands, staying close to her room. A room without colour, a room with a boarded-up window which another patient had smashed. A room where her possessions would go missing constantly, a room with no privacy, a room where any patient or member of staff could walk in and out as they so wished, and a room that looked and felt more like a prison than a home. That night I cried. I cried from the moment my back was turned, and was still crying when I reached home. I called mum, we both agreed – it was time for Jo to come home.

It was a long, slow journey, but after two weeks of my sister being home with my mum the change started, slowly, very slowly. Jo was home in time for Christmas, and with the passing of Christmas and the coming of the New Year, she slowly started to come back to us. It was more than we could have ever hoped or dreamed of, but was a very slow journey and took some time before she could go home. My mum became her carer during this time, and had no support or contact at home from Mental Health Services for some time after discharge from hospital. She just cared for her daughter the only way she knew how, solely driven and directed from love.

Now, just over a year to this day that my sister was admitted, she is back at her home with her beautiful three children. She has come so far. My sister has no idea how proud I am of her, no matter how much I tell her. She still struggles at times, and remains on medication and under the mental health team (who are now very supportive). But she is my sister, my sister as I know her. She may never be entirely the same, as none of us are for having been through this, but she is back. She has and will always have me and my mum there for her, but she is doing so very well by herself and I give her total credit for how far she has come. I do sometimes think though of all the people left in St Agatha's, those without family, or those whose family feel they just cannot cope with it any more.

Because Jo's journey is not over yet, she will battle with this through her life, but medication is only a part of the support system. So many people are just labelled as 'crazy' and 'mad', lost and forgotten in our society, but I think with time, by educating people on mental health issues, and sharing experience, barriers can be broken and better understanding and empathy can grow.

Though I feel I have only touched on my experience, I hope it may bring some points to light, and even if it just makes someone think twice about the care they give in the future, or if this helps someone going through something similar feel less alone, then it will have been worth it for me.

31

My beautiful boy got ill

Maggie Lloyd

The beginning

He was 18 and I thought just being a teenager. He was moody and had headaches and spent a lot of time in his room (which was very untidy). Then one day I got a phone call from a friend who said he thought I should try and get help for Stefan as he saw signs of very strange behaviour. I was distraught and all my other well-meaning friends said don't worry, he is just a teenager and let him be, he will be OK.

Then Stefan started talking to me about his brain being affected and how he had gone to the library and looked up information. He talked about the hypothalamus and was obviously well informed. But then he started refusing to walk through the front door because he said the people in the flats opposite would shoot him, and that he had seen a girl drown when we had been camping in Tenterden, and many more strange memories and ideas.

This is when I started to get really profoundly scared. I turned to my GP to ask for help. He said to me that when the big psychiatric hospitals were open, Stefan would probably be placed there, and medicated until stable, then released. But as it is, he could only put me in touch with Psychiatric Outpatients. After going through our situation with the relevant staff at the Outpatients Centre, we were told that we should go for a few sessions of Family Therapy to work through our problems.

On the day of our first Family Therapy session as the time drew near to leave for the hospital, Stefan became extremely agitated. He voiced his fears in increasingly frantic tones. He was convinced that all of us were going to be executed on arrival. He was screaming that his younger brother had to stay at home so that he would be spared the death that awaited us all. Jonathan, my youngest, was so upset by the bizarre pantomime that he locked himself in his bedroom and refused to come out.

We missed that session.

Our second Family Therapy session went a lot better. By that I mean to say we all got to the hospital, and even into the interview room. We spoke as best we could with a pleasant CPN (community psychiatric nurse), accompanied by the evil glares and muttering we've since come to recognise as the manifestations of Stefan's psychosis.

At one point the CPN had to leave the room and go and do whatever it is that these people do on leaving interview rooms, at which point Stefan leapt to his feet and went into the corridor. I asked why, and he told us all that if we stayed together in the room without a member of staff it would give them the opportunity to gas us.

As time went on Stefan's behaviour was becoming still more bizarre, and we pleaded with the psychiatric staff to tell us how to deal with him day to day. I remember asking outright whether Stefan had schizophrenia. But their responses were always evasive. We asked if we should humour his delusions, or deny them completely …. They wouldn't give us any help or guidance on how we should cope. I felt that I had no support, that my family was completely alone with this familiar-faced monster in our home. An unnamed horror is worse than one you can put a name to, but the mental health workers didn't seem to understand that very basic psychology.

The long nightmare

After a year Stefan was hospitalised, and put on a depot injection (flupenthixol). The side effects were horrendous but he coped and moved to a supported home and then his own flat. I worked part-time in those days and would visit Stefan every day after work. We would walk, have a cup of coffee or sit on the beach. He spent a lot of time on his computer drawing and making his electronic music. It hurt to see him struggling to be normal in spite of severe tremors. He spent loads of his cash on tiny metal models of gaming figures and painted them in beautiful detail. He told me that when concentrating on them he could control the tremors, but when he went to bed and tried to relax it was as if he had cramps all over his body and he couldn't sleep (and doctors blame the patients for not taking the drugs. I think that all doctors should have to take the medications to see what they are asking their patients to go through.)

Then the nightmare started again. Stefan started to get ill because some stupid nurse had said he could refuse his depot, so he did.

I then had to watch him day after day get worse and worse. He wouldn't go to the shops, so I brought him food. He didn't clean the flat, so it was impossible to find a clean cup. They were all in the sink going mouldy. I bought him a washing machine but he refused to wash his clothes because 'the fibres would be altered'. He wouldn't put money into his post office account because he 'wouldn't get the same notes back'. It hurt, all of it hurt, my beautiful clever, talented son wasn't coping, was not normal. I turned to the outpatient mental health team and all they would say was 'He can come and see us'. He wouldn't even go out of his flat! Or they said 'We went to see him and he wouldn't let us in.' That let them off the hook. I felt really isolated.

I was completely confused by the hospital. When Stefan was balanced on his drugs and well they said he must be getting high on the drugs because he was willing to take them. I was told that Stefan would have to have the drugs for the rest of his life but he couldn't have the ones he felt happy with as he might get addicted to them. He had to have them for the rest of his life, so what did it matter if he was addicted to them, if he was happy taking them? I remember one time when Stefan was happy with the balance of the meds, he actually asked me not to let them mess with his medication as he felt OK half an hour after his depot. He must have thought I had some ability to affect the medical gods.

The psychiatrist didn't believe he was as ill as his records made out, and they believed that he was addicted to the medication they were giving him. So, Stefan's medication was 'deferred' to 'see if he is really ill'. He ran away from the hospital again not long after that experiment.

Stefan disappeared for weeks, sometimes months, at a time. Nothing can compare to that constant fear and dread. I became trained like Pavlov's dogs; every time I heard a phone ring, wherever I was, whoever's phone was ringing, my stomach would lurch and I would have to make a conscious effort not to panic. A phone call could be the police phoning to say Stefan had absconded from hospital again, or he had been found in Bedford or Wales, or even Stefan himself phoning in a panic from God knows where. Somewhere I couldn't help him.

I could not get him out of my mind. When it rained I worried whether he had shelter; when it was cold I prayed he had somewhere warm to be. I knew I wasn't being logical as Stefan could be anywhere and just because it was raining here it didn't mean it was raining there.

He was missing for an entire winter and although I functioned, went to work, shopped, cooked etc., I was constantly aware that Stefan was vulnerable and in danger.

The police were very good. I had to phone the police so often during that time that they gave me a direct number so that I didn't have to explain the situation every time I called. I remember one time when Stefan was missing the police phoned to say that the hospital had contacted them. They said that Stefan was no longer in the hospital so they had taken him off section, so he was no longer a missing person. The police asked me if I agreed with this. As no one had seen Stefan for about two weeks, as far as I was concerned he was still missing. I still get angry when I think of this sort of behaviour from the hospital.

Heartache

I was on antidepression tablets for years. I had to carry a water bottle with me as I was thirsty all the time. I always had a pint of water by the bed as I would wake up because my mouth was so dry. And a pint did not last the night. I would wake up and weep until I couldn't cry any more. I often had the radio on all night so if I woke I would have something to listen to, something to distract me from my own thoughts.

I mourn what might have been. While others of Stefan's age have married, split up, had children, got jobs, travelled, bought houses, gone to university, Stefan has been in stasis. He hasn't moved forward. I would visit him in hospital and the only subject he had to talk about was his childhood. Sometimes we would just sit in silence as he would say 'I do nothing, so I have nothing to say'.

Occasionally I see the true Stefan come back. One time he was really animated and exited. He had been taken on an outing with a small group from the ward to Drusilla's Zoo. He obviously really enjoyed it. He loved the animals and the whole event. This brought home to me more than anything else how frighteningly deadening for him it was to be in a locked ward, never going anywhere. He's spent six years locked on a ward, and that's just this time.

And so it goes on

As Stefan eventually started to get better he told me a story of when he was on the streets. It goes like this:

When I was starving, I went into a shop and bought a tin of condensed milk, as I thought it was nutritious and would fill me up, and I had enough money to buy it. But when I got out of the shop I realised I didn't have anything to open the tin with.

He went on to say that he managed to find a stone and smash a hole in the tin. I wanted to cry when he said this.

This is why I have been fighting for years to get help. I have two big files of correspondence with the various authorities. So much of the time it seemed no one listened, and I was dismissed as an over-anxious mother making a fuss. As if Stefan was a small boy with a rash.

But this was a man, my son, who ran from hospital because he was afraid. I have sat beside him in hospitals when he could not speak because the drugs he had been given were so strong. I have seen him stumble because he found it hard to control his limbs and walk. I have seen his limbs contort in reaction to the drugs he was on. I have told every doctor he has seen that he reacts badly to the drugs. I have pointed out that he had been starving and maybe his oedema was caused by malnutrition. I have got angry because Stefan was sleeping in the shower attached to his room and the psychiatrist said he was well enough to be taken off section and released. I have pleaded for help and advice and been dismissed. I have left home at nine in the morning and got back at eleven at night travelling on the trains so that I could spend two hours with him. I visit him knowing he would love to see someone else (he asks me to ask others), but at least I am a visitor. I have learnt that other people voice sympathy but are busy with their own concerns.

I sometimes wonder, when waiting with Stefan to go into a meeting, how the doctors would feel if they had to wait for an interview that would decide their fate, month after month, year after year. They don't let patients or family get angry, and you are either put down as ill or over-emotional. Considering the build-up of pressure before one's monthly trial, I feel that these reactions are normal.

I'm tired seeing my son suffer under medical professionals. I'm tired of their narrow vision. I'm tired of trying to point out to them that maybe he is severely physically ill as well and that if he was physically better he would respond better to his medication. I suppose I am just tired.

32

Archimedes and Rabbit: Me and my brother

Jonathan Lloyd

The stigmatised self is often conferred the identity of the *not quite human and dangerous*. It is very common for those with known mental health problems to be labelled, excluded, dominated and bullied by others, and we welcome stories from this area.

In the guidelines for the contributors to this book I noticed this description. The words '*not quite human and dangerous*' kinda leapt out at me. It made me think of Sci-Fi. I like Sci-Fi. My brother likes Sci-Fi. Our dad liked Sci-Fi. And even our mum, who prefers Jane Austen, is widely read in Sci-Fi, simply because it was littering the shelves of the house. But Sci-Fi in the pages of a book or flashing past on a screen is a very different thing from it happening in your living room at four o'clock in the morning on a school night.

When I was a kid I looked up to my older brother as a little brother should do, at least a little brother in a family to whom the word 'sport' was something that happened to other people. Stefan could draw better than me, he was better at computer games on our BBC Micro, he knew a hell of a lot more than me about everything, as far as I could tell. In fact, I don't remember anything that I asked my brother about that he didn't immediately lecture me on at length. And being the younger brother I had to listen, regardless of whether I'd just wanted a 'no' or a 'yes', otherwise Stef would proceed to tell me about how unimaginably ungrateful and stupid I was.

His cuddly toy was called Archimedes, mine was called Rabbit; need I say more? Then at some point I can't really put my finger on, my older brother started to become less a figure to look up to and idolise and more a person to avoid. Partially for fear of the complicated conversations that cropped up, and partially for a certain late-teen funk that hung in the air about his person.

'Digestive biscuits are a meal unto themselves.'
'What?'
'There are carbohydrates in the cereals; there are proteins in the fats; there is a source of fibre and there are minerals.'
'Um … really?'

He'd take the packet of biscuits upstairs with him, and close his bedroom door behind him. From what I recall, Stefan worked a lot in his bedroom apparently powered entirely by biscuits, and usually wearing one of the sleeping-bags-with-legs that our mum made for us and our friends to combat the bitter cold of our houses.

He worked on his computer producing technical animations for a pneumatics company; probably as interesting as it sounds. And he would stay in his room for days, as far as I could see. Perhaps he left occasionally, but I must have been at school and missed it. He sat in his bedroom, with the curtains closed to stop reflections on his monitor.

His friends, each one living high up on a pedestal of cool in my mind, would pop round, sidle up the stairs and into his room, closing the door after themselves. Even with my ear pressed to the chipped gloss paint I still couldn't make out exactly what they were talking about. I just heard their laughter, smelt the slightly underarm scent of weed creeping out from under the door, and felt pangs of jealousy that I wasn't allowed inside.

Sometimes his friends would leave loudly. Maybe there was a disagreement in his bedroom. Then his door was slammed, and Paul or Ollie or one of the Nicks would thump down the stairs and out the front door.

I may have wondered why one of Stefan's friends was leaving so loudly and angrily, but if I did, I didn't do it for long. Thinking about it now, maybe some truly weird accusations or implications were flying around up there in Stef's bedroom. Things that you could pick to pieces until you were hoarse but my brother wouldn't listen.

Stefan once told me that one of his oldest friends, someone who lived a hundred metres from our front door back then, and lives about two hundred metres from our front door now, had spiked him with LSD. This friend and his girlfriend had done this so that they could trick Stefan into having sex with a dwarf, a dwarf with red hair. They took photos and used them to implicate him as a paedophile.

'Why?' I said. 'Why on Earth would they do that?'

'Because they want me gone. Dealt with. Out of the picture. They did it to my father and now they want to do it to me.'

'He was my dad too, Stef.'

He looked through me with the big black eyes I was learning to hate. My stomach would knot up when I saw them. They really didn't seem like they were his eyes any more. It is a cliché, but they were openings into something else.

When he looks like that, you cannot communicate with my brother. He is another thing; an anti-Stefan. Painful and terrifying things will come out of his mouth. And no matter how much you talk to him you can't convince him that he's wrong. He's always been a bit arrogant. You can sit, talking to him until it's tomorrow and the sun is coming up outside, trying to work with what you understand, what you know is true about the world. But at 15 years of age I was unsure enough about the world and my place in it to make persuading myself an insurmountable problem at times. Let alone my big brother who was the brainiest person I knew.

'You know about DNA, right?'

'Well, yeah, it's two spirals of information that code life and stuff.'

'Exactly, strings, strings of intelligent information. Polymers that control, interact, store knowledge. That's what they're like.'

'I'm sure it doesn't work like ....'

'They can consume someone. Copy them, until the polymer is winding up and down and around and imitating the original person's entire body, mimicking their character and interactions perfectly; a two-dimensional being in three-dimensional form.'

All the while he would be pacing backwards and forwards, backwards and forwards across the living room. It felt like World War Two interrogation methods sometimes, the too-bright central light overhead, the door into the kitchen open, lights out, and the big black windows beyond, Stefan walking back and forth constantly.

It was like being beaten down with truths viewed through lumpy old glass. My brother's paranoia about living in a world of bodysnatching life forms and omnipotent occult groups that toyed with 'standard' humans for sport was turning my life into Room 101. All you can do against that is cling to the sense you were born with.

The worst thing to contend with was the fear. Sometimes his black eyes were very, very scared. So many times he thought that they were coming for him that night. It was a horrible thing seeing my big brother quaking with fear as the appointed hour for his execution came closer.

He was still my big brother though. He still looked out for me in his own way. He would get so protective of me. Telling me I had to stay, hide, keep away. It was almost like being the Chosen One in a Spielberg movie. The whole family couldn't go anywhere together, otherwise *They* could get us all, and all would be lost. At least I had to stay behind, at least me …

Why would anyone be interested in us? Why would clandestine organisations possibly be interested in a family of four living in a terraced house in a seaside town 100 years past its heyday?

The tiniest things grew to be of all-consuming significance: Dad had had two seizures when he was a kid, frozen moments rather than epileptic spasms. Apparently these developed into migraines and nose bleeds in later life. These were clear signs to my brother that something underhand had been done to our dad which had eventually led to his heart attack and death when we were kids. These same insidious tortures were now being inflicted upon Stefan. External forces playing with my brother's mind, his memories and his thought processes.

I have no memory of dad getting migraines. And the only time I saw him have a nose bleed was when I was about six and he was tickling me. I was wriggling and thrashing around and I accidently shoved my entire finger up his nose to the knuckle. It was very warm up there.

When I asked him, again, why anyone would want to do that to him; Stefan, son of Maggie and Dave from Hastings, replied 'Because they can. And because they think it's fun.' What can you say to that? There is no reasoning with a Hollywood villain.

At 18 I moved to Wales, to study animation at university, and to start afresh away from home and all the people who knew me and my family and my friends: just me and the world. Selfish though it may sound, this 18-year-old boy didn't want his bedraggled older brother to visit him at university. He didn't need any one of his new peers to see his skeleton, out of its closet and pacing back and forth in the hallway.

My brother appeared at my place in Wales a few times while I was there at studying. One time he came and I don't remember him being particularly 'mad'. This time he wasn't talking about the Bad Things. But I knew he could, and I knew he had, and I was carrying all I knew of my strange brother around with me. So, when my brother didn't fit in as I felt a person should, I found it acutely embarrassing. He was part of me, my brother, and I was part of him. I was terrified of becoming him, or appearing similar to him in any way. When would this happen to me? Could it happen to me? Was it happening already?

We went to a party. I really didn't want Stefan to go, or to be seen by anyone there. He'd just miss jokes or not realise people were taking the piss. He'd be weird.

Stef made himself a nest and fell asleep resting on a table early in the evening. I hated that he hadn't just gone home. He was like a cat and would find the place he wanted to sleep in and sleep there, regardless. It was a party in a fellow student's house and my brother was asleep in the kitchen, so naturally he was used as a toast rack, a masking tape testing facility, a broken crisp repository and put to all manner of other undignified uses. My stomach churned.

Anyone else who saw an opportunity to have a laugh at their big brother's expense at a university party would probably have found the largest marker pen known to mankind and drawn an oversized Prussian moustache on said sibling's face. I just felt acute embarrassment and guilt and anger. My brother is a freak, and they all must have known it and were taking the piss out of him and, by association, me.

It's amazing how easily you can slip into knowing everyone around you has it in for you.

I just wanted him to disappear.

My brother always managed to maintain contact with me even when not 'absconding' from 'care facilities' where he was 'residing'. Telephones are a wonderful thing. If Stef knew my number he would call up to seven or eight times a day. These were not happy chatty words of advice from older to younger sibling; they were coded texts weighted with alternative meaning; pregnant with subtext and dire plots.

It became a rather cruel sport at times, seeing whether I could ever goad my brother into answering a direct question about any of the things he'd been hinting at bullishly for years. I could picture exactly the look in his eyes as each implication was offered up for me to take on board. But any attempt would end the same with an irate tirade and the sound of a slammed receiver. He would call back without fail, maybe in five minutes, maybe an hour, if I was lucky tomorrow, but he'd definitely call back.

It's difficult to throw oneself into studying the history of Italian Neo-Realist Cinema when that sort of thing is going on. Let alone extracurricular language lessons. There was so much guilt at not being back home helping mum out, supporting her while she watched her oldest child twitching, cracked and shattered. I felt that I should be allowed to do whatever the hell I wanted after speaking to my brother, the universe owed me that. So I did what any self-respecting 'tortured' young person would do: I smoked weed, got drunk, and took pills, HURRAH!

Stef can't just appear at my door anymore for two reasons: first, he has spent the last six years locked up in places he hasn't managed to escape from, and second, I live abroad. We stay in touch by phone, and now that the place he is in allows it, over the internet too.

I only actually meet up with my brother on very rare occasions these days when I am back in the UK. I still feel guilty about not being in the country, not helping enough. But I also feel that I had to get that far away to be able to live for myself, selfish though it sounds. Now, maybe I'd be able to deal with life long-term back in the UK. I've grown up a lot and Stefan's in a lot better way than he has been for a long time.

In spite of all the time that has passed and the things that have been learnt and the resignation acquired, I can still find it difficult sometimes when in my brother's company. I shouldn't, but I still do. I know that you shouldn't judge a person by their appearance. But there's morality, then there's reality.

I hate the odd looks he gets walking around; at least these days it's more for him that I hate them than for me. I hate that people look at him and think 'crazy person'.

His long, uncombed and unwashed hair and his hectically eclectic assortment of clothing aren't important in the grand scheme of things. But the thing is, I know why; I know that washing or cutting or combing his hair could leave parts of himself scattered around for *Anyone* to find, to use against him in some way or to control him.

I also know the sense of social awkwardness that causes him to buy something impetuously, without thinking, and then the sense of moral righteousness that causes him to use the item in spite of everything. This is why I've seen him wearing a hat made for a teenage girl or a jacket four sizes too small. It's the same reason he always carries a bag with him, a bag full to bursting with things. I have no idea what things exactly because he has not once packed or unpacked it in front of me. But I know he thinks if he lets it out of his sight then *Someone* will change the bag or its contents in some way.

The reason is that he still isn't well. He can function better than he could. He can leave the ward these days and go in to town, buy a coffee and browse for comics. And the doctors are starting to talk about sheltered housing and moving him on. But he's still ill. He has headphones in his ears all day, always playing music. He's never said so, but I'm sure it's to drown out the voices.

My brother's lucidity is, in my opinion, 24 hours away from collapse at any one time. All he has to do is miss a few of the pills, pills that he hates taking, and everything that's been built over the last six years of my brother's incarceration will come crashing down. And it'll all start all over again.

Having lived in Barcelona for six years I am now moving to Berlin. I know I should be here to help and support. But I also know that as time moves on, and my mum and my brother get older, it'll be me who has to look after both of them, me on my own. And I have known this for years, almost since he got ill. I have seen how much help other people can and do give. They've all got their own lives and families to cope with. So for now, I am having time for me, just me, till then.

ABUSE AND SURVIVAL

Abuse: The not-so-tender trap

33

Marjorie Holmes

The Corridor People

We are the corridor people,
walking between lines
of despair and hope
illusion and delusion
treading the tightrope.
Hearing voices
out of our past –
crossing the boundaries
causing confusion.

We are the corridor people,
who fly beyond the outer
edge of sanity.
We may touchdown
if we can find reality.
We – the devalued –
move uneasily through space.
Recognise us
who fail to see your face.

We, who stay single,
threaten your ordered universe
with our disordered message,
alternate
between Desire and Apathy.
Do not co-mingle –
Your most exquisite pain
waits poignantly
upon the threshold of our memory.

Unsettled possessors of hearts
that cannot keep up
with your hurrying feet,
we nurse incredible thoughts
resemble refugees
upon your alien street.
Better by far to let us be.
We are the disconnected
beggars of identity.

I am, at present, playing the part of a concerned if nosy neighbour in *Mother Figure*, which is one strand in a cluster of five plays collectively called *Confusions* (written by Alan Ayckbourne) and, no, I am not advertising, simply chalking up this milestone on a rather bumpy road.

I do not easily fit into any of the categories in this book and yet bits of me could be found in all of them. Not that I've ever been in a mental hospital, except when visiting my sons on separate occasions. However this does not mean that I haven't identified with many of the patients when I worked as medical secretary in the psychiatric department of the local one when living in Essex.

When I first attempted to break my bonds as a housebound mother and not only divorce my husband but actually go out to work, I seemed to be walking the tightrope between sanity and craziness. I carried messages from my boss's department (which was concerned with the elderly) to all the other branches and in order to do this I joined the patients walking, as it were, down the long corridor.

My boss was an Indian whose only interest in me, personally, was to try to get me to read sections of the Koran, preferably while photocopying it. As one religion seemed to me to be as unreasonable as the next it was all I could do to finish his workload, let alone read it. My poem *The Corridor People* simply describes my reactions to the patients that I had to hurry past. By contrast, they were doing anything but 'hurry'; one young girl I will never forget was crawling along on her belly, holding her handbag as though it were a raft in a very stormy sea.

My boss did not come across as a life saver, although to be fair he did specialise in what he did, but rather like artists and poets, couldn't cope with the members of staff that he actually bumped into while doing it. I suspected my job had a sell-by date even though it was common knowledge that he had a reputation for being difficult with staff. Be that as it may, because I walked around with the invisible label *I am a victim* etched into my forehead, anyone who raised their voice I automatically saw as a bully! The 'corridor' may have opened out to the sky, in my case, but somewhere there were huge automatic doors that would swing back and lock me inside, and the invisible line that divided me from *The Corridor People* would cancel itself out.

At this point I'd better say that my husband had been volatile and totally unimpressed by any of my forays into writing, believing very much that anything like that would be knocked out of me the moment I realised my true destiny which was to be a mother. Rather like the eldest and most jealous child, the first person I had to pay attention to by way of 'mothering' was him! I could do that by making sure that his house was in tiptop order when he came home from work and that his dinner be served ready on the table. The fact that he was capable of throwing things around when they weren't in place and hitting his wife when she wasn't paying attention was beside the point. For years I really did feel that if I were more organised, moved faster and was firmer with the children – if I was in fact 'normal', he in turn would behave normally to me. I played this game of trying to please and yet trying not to lose my sense of 'self' for too long. Rather like holding onto an extinct Loyalty Card at the supermarket.

I chose not to see, of course, that he was an alcoholic. I wrote a poem called *Destructive Love*, because part of me knew that this 'reward' was never going to happen. That was the trouble, I was splitting into two – the writer in me was telling the woman in me to let go, be realistic. Of course the ironic thing is that most people think poets are dreamers – not that there are times when poems can be the only grip one can have on reality!

It will be a joy (albeit a slightly vengeful one!) for me to play the nosy, if concerned neighbour in Ayckbourne's *Mother Figure*. I too have been besieged by 'concerned' neighbours. Like his fictitious Mother I, too, couldn't see much point in dressing, as there had ceased to be anywhere to go, ceased to be any goals to reach beyond putting the children to bed (always assuming they would go to bed), taking them to school (always assuming they would go to school), feeding them, clothing them and starting all over again the next day! Communication between other people didn't happen. How could it when I was pointed out as a witch, a madwoman or a whore? Only a determined and sustained effort to have a divorce and go out to work was going to reintegrate me.

At least by being a medical secretary (no matter how temporarily) I was in a better position to help myself. I learned, for example, that all drugs have side effects and that the 'know-it-all' attitude of doctors simply disguised their varying abilities at balancing the positive with the negative. This only confirmed how right I was the day I threw my Ativan tablets (for my depression) into the litter bin outside the *Girl Friday Agency*. The *Girl Friday Agency* were first to put me on their books as a temporary secretary, this being a springboard from which I could try my luck at being permanent.

As you can see I was experiencing a lot of rejection, which I responded to by writing a poem called *The Eternal Applicant* and eventually performing it when they were having a party at the job centre! (But that's another story, by then I was in Sussex.) It was time to face my assorted demons especially as they were still insisting that I must be of little value! Fortunately, by now I was in a much healthier relationship which allowed me to not get too stressed over the amount of output my boss seemed to want done and to, instead, go hunting through his files for the address of a counsellor. This led to a year's counselling which, despite my 'happy landing' with a man I was beginning to love, I desperately needed.

At this point I have to say that this was not my first experience of counselling but it was the first time it came over as a therapy. My first counselling experience had taken place with my husband and children at what was then called The Child Guidance Clinic and, as can be inferred by its name, focused mainly on the difficulties of our children. I am not saying that this was wrong. Children who are not turning up for school, not getting a lot of sleep and when not bullying are allowing themselves to be bullied do need attention. I am just saying how it appeared to me.

As far as I was concerned, The Child Guidance Clinic had just joined the ever-lengthening queue of insensitive and obtuse people who failed to see that I was using make-up to camouflage my bruises and that my nerves were shot to pieces while I was sitting there listening to them. I sat with them but cut off from them, as though separated by a panel of glass. Their very efficiency was a threat. In their neat world of Agendas, Diaries and Clipboards everything fell neatly into place; whereas in mine it could only be chaotic.

There was grim satisfaction in knowing that my husband – who had a job and who never stopped letting me know that – was as powerless as I was. Their decision, to ease the boys out of our hands via boarding school and, more particularly, take our younger son into 'voluntary care' seemed to be already made; our part in it to adjust and accept – counselling, as it were, with a purpose – an altogether Hidden Agenda.

By the time I made moves of my own, such as divorcing my husband, throwing out medication (which fortunately I did not take for too long), being tossed around from temporary post to permanent post and back again while still bravely trying to go out to work, meeting up with a male friend I'd met at the poetry society – it was all too late to recover that sad, lost motherhood. From now on everything I achieved, everything I wrote, every friend I made (especially my new man friend) could only be a bonus. The counselling that happened because I wanted it to happen proved therapeutic. It was suddenly as though a light had switched on and someone had confirmed what my unconscious had been telling me all along; that I was allowed to live! I discovered that by aligning myself with that so-called 'dreamer' inside of me, I was in a much safer, happier place. Being *me* wasn't about being selfish, it wasn't about being unaware of other people's needs and it certainly wasn't about being evil!

I have been through mourning since then: the death of my parents and the death of my friend – but what I discovered at that pivotal point did not desert me. In Sussex I went into more counselling via Art Therapy but this was counselling that always moved forward. The bumpy road never gets easier, recovery is never concluded – but this much is certain, I am neither the 'mother' nor the 'neighbour' in a closed-up world where decisions are not my own. I am merely taking part in a play among friends and enjoying myself.

Time to Get SAD

The whole world is crying because it's November;
only yesterday the starlings were feasting –
but now they've disappeared.
Yet the feast remains, bright red berries,
un-squashed, unpicked.
The demarcation line between path and road
is blurring. My windows complain.
Vinegar will do the trick – mingling with rain.

Make this 'wash my windows' day
let the weather do the wash –
Still the feast remains, bright red berries
unpicked, un-squashed, with the raindrops
falling, making stars in puddles.
Why not be depressed? Why look for wellies,
mushroom umbrellas, make a SPLASH?!

Why not be sad for green tomatoes,
clouds emptying overhead?
'Go On! Go on! Go on!' I tell myself,
'Get it over with', for this is the *sad* time,
the bad time,
the time of the living dead.
But when did I fit into labels?

And here comes Joy instead.

Entering and breaking

34

Keith King

My earliest memory is from the age of nine years. Both of my parents were alcoholics and it was clear that I was the reason for their drinking as I had ruined their lives. I paid the price for this every day until their deaths.

My parents would spend each and every lunchtime at a members club, returning home at about three. They would usually be asleep on the couch by the time I got back from school. However, the moment my mother realised that I was home she would wake and ensure that the next three hours until she got ready to go out for the evening would be an absolute misery.

This included verbal abuse, whereby she would detail every aspect of her life that had been blighted by my birth. When verbal abuse did not appear to be having any effect she would become physical, pulling my hair, stubbing cigarettes onto my head, punching and kicking me into submission. This behaviour would continue after midnight when she returned from the club.

Living in such a large home with multiple bedrooms offered a chance to hide out with the hope that she would become exhausted before finding me. However, she would keep hunting, exploring every room, slamming doors as she became angrier. Eventually I would be found, and directed to get out of bed. A refusal was met with continual slaps, punches and aggression. On many occasions I was stabbed with a knife, but this was deflected to some degree by the number of blankets on the bed. However, I still have scars on my arms that prove that it did happen.

Subsequent to the verbal, mental and physical abuse meted out by my mother, I was also sexually abused from the age of nine until I was just over fifteen. Having gifted my mother enough alcohol to render her unconscious, my abuser would, in all knowledge that he wouldn't be disturbed, come up to my bedroom and subject me to various painful and degrading sexual acts. He habitually penetrated me to the point that many times I passed out because the pain was so extreme. Having suffered one too many severe muscle wrenching penetrations, using my initiative I started smearing my anus with Stork margarine as far as I could, usually assisted with a Smarties tube so that I could penetrate / lubricate myself as deep as I anticipated my perpetrator's penis would reach. I have frequently suggested that, as horrendous as the abuse was, it could at least be predicted and the pain level tolerance adjusted accordingly. Given the random attacks of verbal, mental and physical abuse at the hands of my mother, I have never been able to relate to others in the Eastbourne Survivors group who have experienced solely just sexual abuse, which of course has traumatised them in many different emotional and physical ways. This is because, in my experience, I welcomed the sodomy, buggery and forced violent oral sex as respite from the torturous and mental assassinations that I was getting from mother.

From an early age I have had a need to purge my body of the copious amounts of semen that I recollect that I was forced to swallow. Many times it has been suggested that I was bulimic; however, the purging of the body was never about controlling the intake of food or about problems I had with body image, but a subliminal gagging reflex. This was triggered initially when I stuck my fingers down my throat, but after a while I was able to start the convulsions and ultimate vomiting just by thoughts, sights, but more often by smells, especially buttery, oily or margarine-type products.

This purging was a direct contradiction of what I actually wanted my body shape to be. I needed my body to be as large and as repulsive as it could be, as in my mind this would certainly be a 'turn-off' for my current, as well as any future, potential abuser. Other turn-offs would include wetting the bed and ensuring that I was covered in excrement before the attacker came into my room. However, this only served to excite him further and the forceful way in which I was buggered only triggered me to soil myself more as I was unable to control my bowels during any of the penetrations.

As we were living in a home with no electricity, gas or water supply because they had been disconnected at the time, I was unable to make any attempt to get myself clean for school. On many occasions I would have to walk to school in a state of great anxiety, fear, and with tears rolling down my face because I knew exactly the level of abuse I would receive when I entered the playground, because I would still be covered in shit and piss from the night before and the smell was so offensive. On many occasions I would be sat at a desk at the rear of the class with a sold air freshener placed on it by the teacher. I didn't have any friends during primary or secondary school, becoming more and more isolated as well as building up a huge reserve of anger, aggression and hatred. I believe also that this is where I nurtured the beginning of what would later be identified as a severe personality disorder.

At the age of ten I was being physically, mentally and verbally abused by my parents; violently sexually abused by an unknown perpetrator; and then bullied, beaten and humiliated by what seemed the whole of the schools that I attended at the time. By the age of 15 the wall that was to defend me for the next 30 years had its foundations, and got bigger and stronger every year. Now at the age of 43 I must confess that not one person has breached that wall. There are many casualties that lie around the perimeter but still I have the resolve to guard what little mental ability and resolve that I have left.

Having been frequently arrested on charges of fraud and deception, I was eventually imprisoned and given a probation officer. It was only because of the intervention of the probation officer that I was referred to the mental health service. It had been observed that my crime patterns and behaviour were strange. Many of the crimes were seen as a cry for help and not for material gain, in fact most of the 'swag' was given away.

I have had three CPNs, each bringing something different to my recovery. Initially very apprehensive and cynical about the services offered, I now find that the opportunity to discuss my feelings, experiences and fears does assist my ability to survive in a world full of individuals that I do not trust. I certainly need to explore my reactions to others. I feel that my paranoia is at levels that I am unable to contain. I reflect my fears and anxieties onto total strangers and of course these are of a negative nature. I will frequently treat these people with absolute contempt, ensuring that they are aware that I am unapproachable and in no way passive. Many times after my reactions I will discuss them with the CPN who on every occasion will make me aware of other methods that would have been more appropriate.

I have been taking antidepressant medication for many years. I am not necessarily aware that they are helping but I am now too scared to stop taking them in case I get any worse. I dread to think how much lower I could sink if I were not medicated. I do experience side effects including headaches, dizziness and twitching of the eye. I find this bearable and accept it as an 'occupational hazard'. I am loath to discuss this with the GP as I have found a tolerance of the 23 tablets that have been prescribed for other ailments and am inclined to want to 'let sleeping dogs lie'. It has become so easy now to complete the repeat prescription list and have the medication turn up once a month.

Due to my flagging mental health and inability to look after myself I have acquired a list of illnesses, diseases and things that generally just hurt. Currently I have:

- *Diabetes type II*, which is not controlled in any conscious way by me because I just do not have the capabilities or motivation to want to look after myself
- *Polyneuropathy*, which causes tremendous pain in my legs and feet, and is the cause of my constant state of imbalance, subsequent falls, and walking into inanimate objects
- *Post-traumatic stress disorder*
- *Hypertension* (160/102 was the latest reading)

I am constantly being reminded by those who care for me, and by those who treat me, that I am now at constant risk of heart attack, aneurisms, stroke, amputations and of course death. I have to say hand on heart that not one of the grim prospects listed spurs me into any kind of preventative action. Oh how I long for the death option; I walk this Earth knowing that there is the option of death, be it natural, by my hand or by neglecting myself to the point that my organs start to fail me.

Due to severe nerve damage caused by diabetes I have unfortunately acquired erectile dysfunction for which Viagra has been prescribed. This works to some degree, however, because of sexual abuse as a child, I have only ever been able to complete any type of sexual act with the aid of amyl nitrate (poppers). I have been unable for many years to wipe the events from my mind, and any sexual activity is interrupted by the thoughts of what happened to me as a child and therefore sabotages any kind of satisfactory climax. I have found that the effects of poppers allow me for a brief amount of time to be in such a cataclysmic state that I have a brief window of opportunity to forget the trauma that affects me every waking minute. Only having discussed the matter with the GP and researched the matter online have I been made aware of the dangers of combining the two substances and that using poppers and Viagra simultaneously can lead to dangerously low blood pressure, stroke, heart attack, or death. Even with this knowledge I am unable to mentally take on board these dangers, if anything I am reassured that death can be just round the corner.

I am continually having to question my sexuality and whether being frequently raped as a child has changed what I could / would have been. I have always assumed that I am gay, based entirely on the fact that I had experienced gay sex at such a young age, combined with the fact that I have such low self-esteem and feel unable to approach women because of the traumatic and abusive relationship with my mother. Also, the ease in which sex with gay males is accessible, public toilets, websites etc., means that little or no effort is required in finding a sexual partner. But psychologically I believe this is doing me further damage as I feel as if I am being abused over and over again. I have never felt that any of the sexual experiences I have had with men have been fulfilling in any way. Many times, suffering the indignity of a one-night stand has heightened my need to kill myself to put an end to the disgust and self-loathing that engulfs my being. I am continually aware that any relationship that I am involved in, be it one night, short term or long term, has always been one-sided, with me having to go out of my way to please the partner at the time, and unable to allow myself to experience any pleasure at all. This attitude combined with substance abuse has now reached dangerous levels where my body is being abused to levels that cause pain and trauma that continues weeks after the episode – sexual practices that leave little to the imagination and invite risks involving unprotected sex and HIV. Again I do not have the mental resources to prevent this from happening, nor to recognise that I am being further abused and neglecting myself.

My long-term ambitions are very limited and negative and are all based on my eventual suicide. I often mock myself for buying diaries for the New Year when all I seem to use them for is the ongoing CPN appointments, dates for therapy group sessions, hospital and GP appointments. It is very unlikely that a social date will be added to what eventually will be known as the 'Doomsday Book'.

Unable to sustain even a platonic relationship with others is my greatest regret. I long to be able to chat to others about trivial matters, the weather, the cinema, but my personality is such that I am paranoid, suspicious and ultimately *uber* protective of myself. I do not possess the ability now to determine a potential threat, a meaningful relationship or a passing acquaintance in conversation. Everybody is now treated with equal contempt, all a potential abuser. Smiling at me is met with distrust, a whisper as you pass me is treated as a personal slur, and a laugh in my earshot could result in a verbal tirade because you are surely laughing at me. At six feet three inches I appear to be menacing, intimidating and untouchable. I am in fact a ten-year-old boy, hurting, bruised, abused and confused as to who is his friend and who is going to attack him, mock him and bully him. He longs to be loved, he is crying out to be liked but has now got to the stage where he can trust nobody.

I have never perceived that I will have a natural death. I constantly long for an unexpected violent death or a rather subdued overdose on diabetic medication that would render me unconscious and then ultimately comatose; a prolonged coma, whereby my friends and colleagues would have a chance to visit me in the ICU, but then I would feel obliged to take the hand of the Grim Reaper and walk to my final destination.

If, having read this, it has upset you, depressed you, caused you some anxiety or distressed you in any way, please spare a thought for me. I have had to live through it and I continue to live through it. Sometimes my attitude stinks, sometimes I am depressive, frequently I am manic, occasionally I am rude and my humour is black. So many people are intolerant of me and have ditched me, my Facebook friends are barely into double figures and dropping. In a world where I don't feel equipped to cope, inhabited by people I don't trust, I want to say to those people who love me, 'thanks for looking after me, whilst I struggle to look after myself'.

35

Psychiatry's Unholy Trinity: Fraud, Fear and Force

Leonard Roy Frank

In 1959 a revolution took place in Cuba, the Cold War was in full throttle, the Eisenhower era was drawing to a close, and I moved to San Francisco where I would soon find myself in a hellish world of imprisonment and torture.

Born and raised in Brooklyn 27 years earlier, I had graduated from the University of Pennsylvania's Wharton School. After a two-year hitch in the Army, I managed and sold real estate in New York City and southern Florida for several years. Despite a poor record, I continued working in real estate in San Francisco.

A few months into my new job, things began to change for me, more internally, at least at first, than externally. Like so many of my generation, I was highly conventional in thought and lifestyle, and my goal in life was material success – I was a 50s' yuppie. But I began to discover a new world within myself, and the mundane world seemed, comparatively speaking, drab and unfulfilling. I lost interest in my job and, not surprisingly, soon lost the job itself. Thereafter, I spent long hours reading and reflecting on nonfiction books that I found in second-hand bookstores and at the public library.

The book that influenced me most at that time was *An Autobiography: The Story of My Experiments with Truth* by Mohandas K. Gandhi. I adopted for myself his principles of nonviolent resistance, his interest in religion, and his practice of vegetarianism. In that book and other writings of his, Gandhi

This chapter first appeared as an article in the November 2002 issue (pp. 23–27) of *Ideas on Liberty*, edited by Sheldon Richman (Email address: srichman@fee.org). IOL is published by The Foundation for Economic Education, a libertarian publication located in Irvington-on-Hudson, NY 10533, USA.

referred to the works that had helped shape his life. I was soon reading the *Bhagavad Gita,* the *New Testament,* Henry David Thoreau's essay on 'Civil Disobedience', Leo Tolstoy's *The Kingdom of God Is within You,* and the essays of Ralph Waldo Emerson. In keeping with the subtitle of Gandhi's autobiography, I started my own experimenting and this led to a complete revaluation of my previously held values. Towards this end I broadened my reading to include, among many others, the *Old Testament,* Lao-tzu (*Way of Life*), William James (*Varieties of Religious Experience*), Henri Bergson (*Two Sources of Religion and Morality*), Joseph Campbell (*Hero with a Thousand Faces*), and the writings of Abraham Lincoln, Carl Jung, Arnold Toynbee, and Abraham Heschel.

The learning acquired during this exciting, wonder-filled time advanced my self-awareness and my understanding of the world. During this transitional period, however, my parents, who lived in Manhattan and visited me several times in San Francisco, became concerned with the changes they perceived in me. That I was living on my meager savings and not 'gainfully employed' upset them. Perhaps more important, my new-found spiritually centred beliefs and vegetarian practices challenged them in ways they couldn't handle. We were at loggerheads: if one side was right, the other had to be wrong, and neither side was willing to compromise.

The situation seemed to call for a parting of the ways, at least for a time. But my parents weren't willing to back off.

They attributed the rift between us to my having a mental disorder. The changes I regarded as positive they regarded as symptomatic of 'mental illness'. They urged me to consult a psychiatrist. I had done some reading in psychology but, while finding a number of valuable ideas, had rejected its overall approach as being too narrow – psychotherapy was not for me. Over a period of more than two years, the struggle between my parents and me intensified. Eventually, because I wouldn't see a psychiatrist, my parents decided to force the psychiatrists on me. The way that was and still is being done in our society is by commitment, a euphemism for psychiatric incarceration. I was locked up at Mt Zion Hospital in San Francisco on October 17, 1962.

During the same week that the world's attention was focused on the Cuban Missile Crisis and the possibility of nuclear war, two physicians in a San Francisco hospital were focused on me and the possibility of my being mentally ill. They decided I was and gave me a 'tentative diagnosis' of 'schizophrenic reaction'. The case history section of the 'Certificate of Medical Examiners' they signed read in full as follows: 'Reportedly has been showing progressive personality changes over past 2 or 3 years.

Grew withdrawn and asocial, couldn't or wouldn't work. Grew a beard, ate only vegetarian food and lived life of a beatnik – to a certain extent.'

On October 20 I was sent to Napa State Hospital, northeast of San Francisco, and from there, on December 15, to Twin Pines Hospital in Belmont, a suburb south of San Francisco, where I remained through the first week of June 1963. Early on, I was diagnosed as a 'paranoid schizophrenic', a label reserved not only for serial killers but for almost anyone else in a mental institution who refuses to knuckle under to psychiatric authority. Scattered throughout my medical records, 143 pages of which I obtained in 1974, were the 'symptoms' and observations which, according to psychiatric ideology, supported the diagnosis. These included 'condescending superior smile'; 'vegetarian food idiosyncrasies'; 'apathetic, flat affect'; 'has a big black bushy beard and needs a haircut, he is very sloppy in appearance because of his beard'; 'refuses to shave or to accept inoculations or medication'; 'patient declined to comment on whether or not he thought he was a mentally ill person'; 'no insight'; 'impaired judgment'; 'stilted, brief replies, often declines to answer, or comment'; 'autistic'; 'suspicious'; 'delusions of superiority'; 'paranoid delusions'; 'bizarre behavior'; 'seclusive'; 'withdrawn, evasive and uncooperative and delusional'; 'negativism'; 'passively resistive'; 'piercing eyes'; and 'religious preoccupations'.

Soon after being imprisoned, psychiatrists tried to gain my consent to shock treatment – at first electroconvulsive treatment (ECT) but after being transferred to Twin Pines, 'combined insulin coma-convulsive treatment'. When I was 'extremely resistive' to undergoing the latter procedure, the hospital filed for a court order authorising force in administering the procedure. In the closing paragraph of the seven-paragraph letter to the court, the treating psychiatrist wrote, 'In my professional opinion, this man is suffering from a Schizophrenic Reaction, Paranoid Type, Chronic, Severe, but it is felt he should have the benefit of an adequate course of treatment to see if this illness can be helped. In view of the extremes to which the patient carries his beliefs it is felt that the need of hospitalization and treatment under court order is a necessity as he is dangerous to himself and others under these circumstances.'

On January 10, 1963, after a hearing at which I was present, the Superior Court of California in San Mateo County 'ordered [me] committed to Twin Pines Hospital'. The next day, the series began; there were in all 50 insulin coma treatments (ICT) and 35 electroconvulsive treatments.

Combined insulin coma-convulsive treatment was routinely administered to 'schizophrenics' in the US from the late 1930s through the mid-1960s. ECT was sometimes applied while the subject was in the coma phase of the ICT; sometimes the procedures were administered on separate days. Individual insulin sessions lasted from four to five hours. Large doses of injected insulin reduced the blood's sugar content triggering a physiological crisis manifested in the subject by blood pressure, breathing, heart, pulse, and temperature irregularities; flushing and pallor; incontinence and vomiting; moans and screams (referred to in the professional literature as 'noisy excitement'); hunger pains ('hunger excitement); sobbing, salivation, and sweating; restlessness; shaking and spasms, and sometimes convulsions.

The crisis intensified as the subject, after several hours, went into a coma. Brain-cell destruction occurred when the blood was unable to provide the sugar essential to the brain's survival; the sugar-starved brain then began feeding on itself for nourishment. The hour-long coma phase of the procedure ended with the administration of carbohydrates (glucose and sugar) by mouth, injection or stomach tube. If the subject could not be restored to consciousness by this method, they went into what were called 'prolonged comas', which resulted in even more severe brain damage and sometimes death. According to the United States Public Health Service Shock Therapy Survey (October 1941), 122 state hospitals reported an insulin coma treatment mortality rate of 4.9 per cent – 121 deaths among 2,457 cases (Ebaugh, 1943, p. 294).

After gaining my freedom, I tried to find out how psychiatrists justified their use of ICT. One of the clearest statements I uncovered came from Manfred Sakel, the Austrian psychiatrist who introduced the insulin method in 1933 and, after arriving in the United States a few years later, became its most active promoter. In a popular book on the state of psychiatry published in 1942, Dr Sakel was quoted as follows: 'With chronic schizophrenics, as with confirmed criminals, we can't hope for reform. Here the faulty pattern of functioning is irrevocably entrenched. Hence we must use more drastic measures to silence the dysfunctioning [brain] cells and so liberate the activity of the normal cells. This time we must *kill* the too vocal dysfunctioning cells. But can we do this without killing normal cells also? Can we *select* the cells we wish to destroy? I think we can' (Ray, 1942, p. 250).

I didn't see it that way. For me, combined insulin coma-convulsive treatment was an attempt to break my will, to force me back to an earlier phase of my spiritual and intellectual development. It was also the most devastating, painful and humiliating experience of my life. Afterwards, I felt that every part of me was less than what it had been. Except for memory traces, some titles of the many books I had read, for example, my memory for the three preceding years was gone. The wipe-out in my mind was like a path cut across a heavily chalked blackboard with an eraser. I did not know that John F. Kennedy was president although he had been elected two and a half years earlier. There were also big chunks of memory loss for experiences and events spanning my entire life; my high school and college education was effectively destroyed. I came to believe that shock treatment was a brainwashing method. Some years later, I found corroboration for this opinion in a professional journal describing ECT's effect on patients by two psychiatrist-proponents of the procedure: 'Their minds are like clean slates upon which we can write' (Kennedy & Anchel, 1948, p. 318).

Aside from being a flat-out atrocity, the use of combined insulin coma-convulsive treatment necessarily involved the violation of certain human rights; some are proclaimed in the Bill of Rights, all are cherished in a free society:

1. *Freedom from 'cruel and unusual punishments' (Eighth Amendment).* If insulin coma treatment is not a torture, nothing is. Readers of the professional literature, however, receive barely a hint of this reality. The barbaric aspects of the procedure, if mentioned at all, are glossed over in understatement and euphemism; for example, one psychiatrist cautioned against allowing new insulin patients to see other patients further along in their treatment, thus saving them 'the trauma of sudden introduction to the sight of patients in different stages of coma – a sight which is not very pleasant to an unaccustomed eye' (Gralnick, 1944, p. 187).

I recall the horror of coming out of the last coma: severe hunger pains, perspiration, overwhelming fear and disorientation, alternating phases of unconsciousness and consciousness, strangers hovering over my strapped-down body (none of whom I recognised although I had been thrown in with them months before), being punctured with needles, heavily sugared orange juice ravenously drunk, and later being held up by one or two attendants in a shower where the filth was washed away. Brain damage caused by the treatments destroyed my memory of what the previous sessions had been like.

However, I remember what happened a week or two after completing my series when, having returned for lunch from 'occupational therapy', I was sitting in the dayroom which was separated from the insulin-treatment area by a thick metal door. Suddenly I heard an indescribable, other-worldly scream. The metal door had been left slightly ajar and one of the new patients, a young musician, was undergoing insulin coma down the corridor on the other side of that door, and he was venting his pain. Almost immediately an attendent shut the door tight, but the scream, now muffled, lingered on for another few seconds. I don't recall any of my own screams; I will never forget his.

2. *Freedom of thought (implicit in the First Amendment)*. The words of Oliver Wendell Holmes Sr. ring as true today as when he first wrote them in 1860: 'The very aim and end of our institutions is just this: that we may think what we like and say what we think' (Holmes, 1860/1931, ch. 5). The brain-damaging force of insulin coma is second only to the lobotomy operation; it impedes the ability to think, to create, and to generate ideas. Every ICT survivor experiences impaired thinking and knows what it means to lose memories, words (you have the idea but can't call to mind the word to fit it) and trains of thought not just once in a while, but repeatedly hour after hour, day after day. I have keenly felt these losses.

3. *Freedom of religion (First Amendment)*. As noted above, the phrase 'religious preoccupations' was among the symptoms recorded in my psychiatric records. One of these preoccupations concerned my beard, which the staff at both Napa State and Twin Pines Hospitals had been urging me, without success, to remove. In the midst of the series – after I had undergone 14 insulin comas and 17 electroshocks – the treating psychiatrist wrote my father, 'In the last week Leonard was seen by the local rabbi, Rabbi Rosen, who spent a considerable period of time with him discussing the removal of his beard. I felt it was desirable to have the rabbi go over it with him, as Leonard seems to attach a great deal of religious significance to the beard. The rabbi was unable to change Leonard's thinking in this matter.' At this point, the San Francisco psychiatrist who had been advising my father was brought in to interview me. After noting in the 'Report of Consultant' that I was 'essentially as paranoid as ever', he recommended that 'during one of the comas his beard should be removed as a therapeutic device to provoke anxiety and make some change in his body image. Consultation should be obtained from the TP attorney as to the civil rights issues – but I doubt that these are crucial. The therapeutic effort is worth it – inasmuch that he can always grow another.' On March 11, the 'Doctor's Orders' read: 'Pts beard to be shaved off & to be given hair cut – Observe very carefully today & tonite for any unpredictable behavior re suicidal or elopement [escape] REJ.' The same psychiatrist wrote my father ten days later, 'Leonard's beard was removed this last week which caused him no great amount of distress ....' The shock therapy in combination with the beard-

shaving therapy 'worked': I was soon shaving on my own. I have no direct memory of the struggle over my beard or of even having had a beard during this period.

4. *Right to be let alone.* In a 1928 Supreme Court decision (*Olmstead v United States*), Associate Justice Louis D. Brandeis wrote, 'The makers of our Constitution ... conferred, as against the Government, the right to be let alone ... the most comprehensive of rights and the right most valued by civilized men.' Without having been proved guilty of violating anyone else's rights, I had been deprived of my freedom and made to undergo corporal punishment disguised as medical treatment. In the truest sense of the term, I was minding my own business, exercising my right to be let alone. As a young man, I thought that in the United States this right was protected; I was wrong. That was 40 years ago, but it's still happening as literally millions of innocent people every year are being locked up, for short and long periods of time, in psychiatric facilities where their rights are trampled on and they are subjected to psychiatric treatment against their will or without their fully informed consent.

Aside from the serious and permanent memory loss, other effects of those nearly eight months of confinement and forced treatment include a general slowing of the thought processes and a loss of drive and stamina. But by psychiatric standards, I am still 'essentially as paranoid as ever'. I still have my 'vegetarian food idiosyncracies'. I have regrown my 'big black [now graying] bushy beard'. And, what is more, I have maintained all my 'religious preoccupations'.

Aftermath
(written in 1990, modified in 2010)

With 'therapeutic' fury
search-and-destroy doctors
using instruments of infamy
execute electrical lobotomies
in little Auschwitzes called mental hospitals.

Electroshock specialists brainwash
their apologists whitewash
as silenced screams echo
from pain-treatment rooms
down corridors of terror.

Selves diminished
we return
to a world of shrunken dreams
piecing together memory fragments
for the long journey ahead.

From the roadside
dead-faced onlookers
awash in deliberate ignorance
sanction the unspeakable –
silence is complicity is betrayal.

be-ing Twitch

Carol Rambo

be-ing Twitch

I used to hear a small childlike voice in my mind, several times a day, sometimes several times an hour, saying, 'I want to die'. In response, I would run suicide scenarios in my head. They seemed to calm me down and make that stupid, incessant voice go away.

Twitch

While I will attempt to *perform* her in this text, I may only be able to write *about* her at this stage in my life – the story is ongoing and unfinished. I do not have neat conclusions framed by pat theories, which uniquely inform and build on existing academic bodies of knowledge on the effects of childhood sexual abuse. The reader may want me to label the phenomena; I am unsure I can provide one (or want to). I wonder if the existing labels are more enabling (one can know things like this have happened to other people, and not feel alone) or constraining (labels come with baggage, including the idea that one is insane; not whole and usual, but, as Goffman writes in his book *Stigma* (1963), tainted and discounted) when considering the impact of childhood trauma on the experience of the self.

Liminal, ineffable – I like these words but I cannot use them to convey the experience I wish to describe in these pages. They demarcate the contours (or lack thereof) of my problem, but they show nothing; they cop out and fall flat. Because I am unsure of just what 'it' is, I must (I have no choice in the matter, no other methodological tools in the toolkit will do), rely on performance autoethnography (Denzin, 2003) to communicate my experience:

> Performance autoethnographers struggle to put culture in motion .... It values intimacy and involvement as forms of understanding. ... This stance allows the self to be vulnerable to its own experiences as well as to the experiences of the other. (2003, p. 16)

A performance text re-presents lived experience as an immediate and embodied performance in the hopes of evoking in the reader a moment when another's experience comes alive in the reader's self (Denzin, 2003). Thus:

> Dramatic performances occur within the public and democratic spaces of *auto-ethnographic theater*, a safe, sacred aesthetic place, a space where texts, performers, performances, and audiences come together to participate in shared, reflexive performances. (2003, p. 37)

It is my intention to use the pages of this book, *Our Encounters with Madness*, to stage such a performance. For now, I only know to name the performance 'be-ing Twitch'.

Twitch

Curling up, inside and out. A small sensation in the right shoulder. 'It' is here; 'she' is here, peering out at the world through my eyes. My shoulder violently shrugs upwards toward my ear, involuntarily, a coiled, winding, energy that has been sprung.

I write, trying to be and trying to describe. I kind of can't, I sort of can. The more I write like this, typing, reflexive regarding my experience, the more she goes away. But she is here. She is a like a cat – if I am still, she might come out. She tells me things I don't want to know, like now, how sad I am.

Twitch

I am rereading what I wrote about her, days later. My body involuntarily curls inward, protective. At times, parts of me, if I allow it, can flail about oddly, in the air, particularly at distressing passages. Always though, I can clamp down and get a grip on it. Hardly ever is 'it' out of control.

Twitch

I will use a layered account (Rambo Ronai, 1995) in these pages as a writing technique which will enable me to draw on multiple resources for the performance of 'be-ing Twitch'. I will use vignettes from my experiences in childhood, therapy, the experience of writing this text, and observations on the culture of therapy, to sketch for the reader (Rambo, 2007) an impression of Twitch. 'By presenting multiple points of view on a subject, even if they are seemingly contradictory, a picture of the subject can emerge through the layers of interpretive impressions left by the vignettes' (2007, p. 533). The word 'Twitch' will demarcate shifts in perspective and voices in the text.

Twitch

Twitch is a bad name, a joke name, I don't think she likes it but I am afraid of her so I treat her lightly, make a joke of her, like she is no big deal, because to fully own her is to be stark raving mad. But if I have decided to write about her, I must have decided to own her, right? The intellectual part of me has decided that this is not something of which I should be ashamed. If it is a part of me, then it is a part of me. Furthermore, no one should be ashamed, not me, not anyone. Why reject it? Why debate it? Why defend it? But then again, why share it? And risk you thinking I'm nuts, or making it up, or blowing my career sky high?

Twitch

I first met her when I started therapy. I had several articles published regarding my experiences of childhood sexual abuse with my father, a serial child molester, and my mentally disabled mother (we called it retarded back then) (see Rambo Ronai, 1995, 1997 for examples). I read the research, interviewed other survivors – I was an expert! And just when everything was falling into place – marriage, house, kid, and tenure – I started to fall apart. I was faking it at work well enough, but at home

I would sit and stare at nothing for hours. I did not want to move or do anything; I just lived inside my head. At other times I would run for hours. It got to the point where people were asking me if I was anorexic. When I finally went to a therapist, after a few sessions I was sure I had everything under control and that everything was going to be just fine. I had it planned: In therapy, I would explore the meanings I had attributed to the abuse at the hands of my parents, come to understand how those meanings were still steering my life (even though the abuse was over with long ago), and keep the things that were still working for me while getting rid of the ones that were not. It was a straightforward path, predictable and very tidy. I was in good hands and felt relatively safe with my therapist. I was relieved to finally have a plan of attack.

Twitch

It is a beautiful sunny day – peaceful. I am in a medium-sized sailboat, gliding in to shore, getting ready to tie the boat up at the dock. As the boat glides in, suddenly, without warning, the hull gives away, shattering into boards and fragments. I fall through the fragments into the cold blue depths below, flailing, unable to breathe, drowning. I am neither awake nor asleep, but something else, as this unfolds, graphically, in my mind and experience.

Twitch

I am awake, choking, my throat shut, my shoulders pinned to the bed. Nothing is causing this, no one is doing it to me, it is just happening. I roll to the left, twist to the right, tossing, turning, struggling. I manage to shake it off and breathe normally again. I cannot get back to sleep. 'What the fuck was that?'

Twitch

I am now living in a constant state of terror, trying to disguise this fact to the outside world. My affect is so disorganised, I am forced to slow down and think through the most basic of tasks. I startle easy and I tremble a lot. I did not know I was this crazy. It's getting worse.

Twitch

I am going to try it again. I am so confused. I keep ending up back on the freeway. For the third time, I get on the exit ramp, approach the intersection to join regular traffic, get into the turn lane and – damn it! I am back on the freeway again. I'm weeping behind the wheel. I wish I could call someone to come get me but I can't. I don't have a phone; don't know who to call, or who could find me if I did. If I pull over, I may be in no better a position than I am in now, I could just end up trapped with traffic flowing all around me, maybe I would get hit. I'm shaking badly as I shift lanes again, quickly, so that I can get back onto the exit ramp. And I do it again! God I'm so fucking stupid, maybe I shouldn't be alive. It takes me more tries than I can count to finally get my car into the correct lane and move on to my destination. I'm glad no one is watching.

Twitch

The small, childlike, voice, the one that says 'I want to die', the one that I went to therapy to get rid of, is with me almost always now.

Twitch

I awake, frequently, choking, my throat shut, my shoulders pinned to the bed. Nothing is causing this, no one is doing it to me, it is just happening. I still don't know what the fuck it is, but I can't tell anyone, not the therapist, no one. This is stark raving mad and I am going to have to figure out how to deal with this on top of everything else.

Twitch

My therapist is upset with me. 'Why didn't you call me? That's why I gave you the number.'

'I didn't know that had anything to do with childhood sexual abuse,' I say, genuinely shocked. 'I didn't want to bother you or seem needy. I thought I was to call only during a real emergency.' What I don't say is that I am afraid more is wrong with me than I first thought, and I am hiding it.

'Everyone goes through it differently, does different things, has different experiences,' he says. 'While there is a path for healing from sexual abuse that is as straightforward as healing a broken bone, there are a lot of different things that can happen on the way. Unfortunately, the younger you were when it happened and the longer it went on, the weirder things can get.'

Twitch

I lay on the ground relaxed, palms open, facing up. I am following my therapist's advice and opening to 'it'. After a bit of internal dialogue where I tell myself this is stupid, I try to quiet my mind. After all, telling myself this is stupid is not being open. There is a now familiar sensation in my shoulder, which grows and takes over my arm. My arm goes up, involuntarily. I am no longer prone. The arm feels as if it is being pulled straight up. I weep. I don't know why this gesture keeps happening over and over again. It never goes anywhere; it doesn't mean anything. I cry like an idiot with my arm stuck in the air.

Twitch

Repeat this scene frequently, with slight variations. Know there are things I am not willing to tell you about yet, because they still scare the shit out of me (or maybe I am ashamed).

Twitch

I am running at the track. I feel burning sensations gently brushing the tops of my thighs. I stop to look at my thighs and nothing is happening, no rash, no discoloration, nothing. I feel little round burning spots landing, as if it was a light afternoon shower of small flames. I vigorously brush the tops of my thighs, decide to ignore it, and go on running.

Twitch

Repeat this scene as well, with slight variations.

Twitch

My therapist has read some of my work and remarked how clearly, and in graphic detail, I seem to remember events and write about them. I am quietly proud of this. I know other people have repressed memories (I have read about them). None of that for me, I remember everything, every bit of it. My memory is rock solid.

Twitch

My throat is tightening now as I type the above. I have more ease with Twitch, I don't fight her anymore because she has never really hurt me or done anything stupid to blow something for me. But I do need to breathe and swallow.

Twitch

My father beat me, performed oral sex on me, and put his fingers in me, but that is it. That is what I have always told myself. Then one day while processing a therapy session afterwards, I asked myself, directly, 'Did you ever perform oral sex on your father?' I had never asked myself that question directly before. I just assumed I had not because I didn't remember it.

It was like wandering around in a big house, going into halls and rooms you don't go into much, but you know are there. It was as if I turned a corner, took a bend in my mind, and there it was. It had always been there, I just had never looked at it, but the scene unfolded in my mind with revolting clarity.

Twitch

I am probably three or four years old. We are living in an abandoned house on the side of a mountain in Pennsylvania. My father is on the bed and I am between his legs, masturbating him. He and my mother, who is sitting in a chair to the left of him, are laughing. The whole atmosphere is 'playful'. My father and mother often chased through the house laughing, naked, and would end up having sex; they did nothing to hide this from me. At times, I did not think much of it, and just went on playing. At other times, knowing I could get dragged into it, I would quietly go elsewhere. When they brought me into it, sometimes it seemed loving, and at other times I didn't want to do it and complained, cried, or even fought with him. This particular time, I am sort of OK with what is happening, but also uneasy and suspicious.

They are instructing me regarding how to handle my father's penis. I don't want to handle it at all but stroking it did not seem to be a big deal. Then my father says, 'Put it in your mouth.'

I say, 'I don't want to.'

He says, 'It's fun.' Then he says to my mother, 'Tell her how she can do it Suzy.'

She laughs and says, 'There's two ways you can do it. You can lick it like an ice-cream cone.'

'Show her,' he says, interrupting her. My mother makes a gesture as if she is licking on an ice-cream cone.

'Or you can suck it like a lollypop,' she says, gesturing as if she were putting a whole lollypop into her mouth.

'Which would you like to do?' my father asks.

I decide that the ice-cream cone is a much better idea. I know what comes out of the tip of that thing.

Twitch

My memory fails me after this point. My throat constricts as I type this and my shoulder is jumping.

Twitch

After talking to my therapist about this memory of performing oral sex on my father, I decide to bring it up with my mother the next time I talk with her on the phone. When I do so, she denies everything. In her whiney, childish, mentally retarded voice, she says, 'He never did that to you, I told him to never, ever, do that to you.' I am so dumbfounded by her denial that it is only later that I am struck by the irony. Should any mother *have* to tell any father that he should *not* have his daughter fellate him? What she said next threw me worse.

'He did burn you with the cigarette lighter in the car. I told him not to do that to you either.'

Twitch

Again, it was as if I had turned a corner and took another bend in my mind, and there it was. It had always been there, I just never looked straight at it before. And both my forearms and upper thighs felt tiny little burning sensations gently brushing them, as if there was a light afternoon shower of small flames.

Twitch

I am seated between them in the car. We have just pulled into a park where there are children playing on a carousel. We are homeless and living out of the car, we are probably going to try to stay the night. I want to go play on the carousel so bad. Not only have I never seen a carousel before, I don't get to play with other kids much. I ask if I can go and I am told 'no' by my father because it is too much trouble. In retrospect, I can see why he did not want to attract attention to us by having me outside, playing.

I ask again and I am told 'no' again. I turn to my mother and plead to be let out of the car. I start to climb over her.

My father slams me back down in the seat, enraged, and says, 'I said no' and presses the cigarette lighter in on the console. My mother begs him, 'Don't do that.'

He tells her, 'Shut up.'

He takes the cigarette lighter out and holds it briefly to the top of my thigh. I cry out in pain. He tells me, 'Don't cry or I'll give you something to cry about.'

My mother repeatedly begs him to stop what he is doing. He tells her to shut up or he will make it worse. He applies the lighter to the tops of my thighs, and then the tops of my forearms. I am paralyzed; my eyes are wide open, straining against my eye sockets. I do this partially to stay alert, and partially to prevent myself from crying. If I don't blink, I won't drop tears from my eyes. If I keep them open wide enough, it creates a split second where the tears can dry a little and perhaps not fall at all. I don't dare move, I don't dare flinch. I understand what he wants from me. He wants me to take the pain, and pretend I don't feel it.

Twitch

Twitch has asked me to tell you something. How do I know this? I had an idea about something to write and then thought better of it. My arm, and particularly my hand, waved around involuntarily. My body curled inward. When I asked myself the question, 'Does Twitch want me to write about this?' I started to cry involuntarily.

Twitch

Let me restate. I am crying involuntarily. I am not screaming but I could. But it is not me. Best to just tell you, to get this to stop.

Twitch

He ran experiments and tests on little Carol, all the time. I remember it as a kind of fact, some of it a little more clearly than that. He would do things and demand that I not express emotions, or he would ask me how they felt and would want detailed feedback. Sometimes I would lie to him, just to mess with him. It was a small expression of power, that he did not totally own me. Sometimes he would suspect I was lying, get angry, and hit me. This is obviously a new quagmire that has opened up for me writing this manuscript and I won't get it resolved here, today. Working through these issues is like that, it takes time, and I don't always have time. Got a deadline to meet getting this article to the editors.

Twitch

When I have the courage to open up to her, Twitch leaves me gifts. After hearing my mother say that my father burned me with the car lighter, and remembering it, never again did I have the burning sensations on the tops of my thighs, jogging. The gift is not only the memory, but also remembering how it felt, and integrating that into my understanding of who I am, and into my lived experience of being in the world. I hope that doesn't sound like bull-shitty-psycho-babble. Knowing it happened gives me the capacity to have compassion for myself. Once I have genuine compassion for myself and what it was like being their kid, I have a deeper understanding of people in general, who they often are, the way they might live insulated from their painful lives in isolated bubbles, and how sometimes slowing down and trying to understand is a better option than judging or attacking if one is attacked.

Twitch

The narrative is that I am supposed to be better after therapy. And I am mind-blowingly, rock-solid stable, so much so it is almost boring. I am a tenured Associate Professor of Sociology, an editor of a journal, a wife, a mother, and other very normal things to other very normal people. I have a cat that sometimes sleeps in my lap when I write on my computer. I have paid off my student loans, my home, my modest car, and my credit cards. I am sensible, often shopping at thrift-stores for my clothing, always looking for a good deal. I have little need of electronic gadgets and no need for conspicuous consumption. I shop and cook organic food for my family and go out to dinner once or twice a week to a nice restaurant. We do not eat 'fast food'. I garden some. I have found that it is good for my mental health to avoid eating too much sugar, and to get exercise – all very ordinary.

Yet late at night, when the hour stretches and creeps into the morning, she emerges, still. I worry you are going to read this and think I am still crazy. At times I do too.

When I release deeply into it, she takes over. My perception can become horribly disorganised, but not always. Sometimes I coexist with her, and wonder at it, as it takes over my body and shows me things in the strangest ways. But that will be for another time, and another manuscript.

Twitch

Twitch makes no sense according to the everyday stories I carry around with me about how people are, it is only when I go to the psychology literature that some of this starts to look 'normal'. One of the reasons I believe I am having such a difficult time working with this aspect of myself is because of the culture I find myself located in. Some might read this text and decide Twitch is a 'body memory', or an 'abreaction'. Others may interpret her as a cast-off fragment of a personality that I have not incorporated into myself. A therapist once described me as having PTSD with 'dissociative features'. Some of the difficulty in dealing with it is the fear and the shame. The resources for interpreting an experience like mine are relegated to the discourse of psychology and mental illness. It is ghettoised, stigmatised, set off from the rest of the world because it is considered to be outside the norm and problematic. Things that are considered problematic interfere with the smooth flow of social interaction, therefore, as a culture, we quarantine them to be dealt with on the sidelines. Psychology as a discipline is that sideline, that quarantine, that ghetto.

I would like to use the occasion of this performance to suggest that perhaps my so-called 'mental illness' is in fact simply 'everyday life'. By pathologising it, it is almost exclusively examined through medical frames. But what if Twitch were to be perceived as ordinary? And what if Twitch, or something like her, exists for a large number of people?

I would like to ask the reader to consider the possibility that modern life itself is traumatic. Never mind the statistics we have on the prevalence of childhood sexual abuse, child abuse, child neglect, domestic violence, etc. Never mind the violent neighbourhoods many are currently forced to live in. Never mind the PTSD that soldiers come home from war with. We certainly know that ordinary modern life is 'stressful' and that stress places a burden on the body (you can google *cortisol* and *stress* and find a number of articles quickly on the topic; though I am not a physiologist nor a psychologist, I do like David Baldwin's Trauma Information Pages). If stress and trauma are thought to exist on a continuum, and if it is the case that having a part of yourself fragment off, unavailable to yourself, is a coping mechanism, then why can't it be the case that this fragmenting, in one form or another, is in fact very common?

I am open to the idea that I am just working through my own shame and lack of acceptance of Twitch by making this observation. Maybe I want it to be more common because I want to normalise my own pathology. If there are a good number of people numb to their stress/trauma, constantly avoiding how they feel (denying, alcohol, drugs, diversion into other addictions and splintering off in the manner I describe by performing 'being Twitch'), then I believe we would have an explanation for many of the issues that we label 'social problems'. How could people in touch with how trauma feels hurt and exploit others? How could they hurt and exploit animals? How could they pollute and damage the planet? How could they hurt themselves? Perhaps the culture itself is suffering from PTSD with 'dissociative features'. What would it mean if, as a collective, we made it our project to get to the bottom of that?

I am one woman exploring the continuing impact of trauma on her daily experience. Because the vocabulary of mental illness frames my experience as pathological, I must struggle, co-existing with my experiences with Twitch and having a workable definition of self. I am an Associate Professor of Sociology. Perhaps I have blown my chance at promotion to Full Professor by choosing to write this; time will tell. But being an Associate Professor, with tenure, gives me identity resources and a platform to explore this issue in public with less fear of consequences than most. I probably won't lose my job, but then again, I did not tell my departmental chair exactly what this paper would be about. Most people do not have the privileges I enjoy. If they are lucky, they skulk on the sidelines, in private, with their therapists, and hope that they can reach a place where they are happy, functioning, and that few find out that they ever needed 'help'. If they are not so lucky, they do not get the space to deal with the effects of stress and trauma, at all.

If we were to slow down our lives and listen, if we were to open ourselves to it and watch, what would it be that we are trying to tell ourselves but can't? That life is going too fast? That we are making demands on ourselves that are unreasonable, unnecessary, and unsustainable? That we are in pain and using short-term fixes to numb it that end up hurting us in the long term?

I have spent the pages of this manuscript be-ing Twitch. She insists she is a being, though I have my doubts about just what she is. I am both grateful for the therapy I had and find myself questioning the therapeutic culture and society at large. Being afraid to get help, on both the individual and collective level, is not helpful. Yet this is how things currently stand. be-ing Twitch should not be scary because be-ings were born from fear and of necessity.

37

My Life:
My encounters with insanity

Fran Biley

Diary entry, sometime in about 1965

I'm about 7 years old; I accompany my father to visit a colleague of his who has been admitted to the local lunatic asylum. We walk through long empty corridors and enter an almost empty, neutral-coloured bedroom. My father and his colleague talk for a while, the man seems quite normal, I don't know why he is in hospital. Afterwards, my father and I go for a walk in the woods and I play in a stream. The sun is shining.

I began my career in mental health nursing in 1976, to be precise, at lunchtime on August 14. I walked, somewhat bemused and not quite sure what I was letting myself in for, into a forgotten, musty ward situated at the back of one of the finest and most expensive private psychiatric hospitals in the country. I was 18 years old, and self-conscious of wearing the new white, bright white, legitimizing white, coat of office. Instantly I became one of three members of staff who cared for a motley group of about 30 aimlessly wandering accidents, aimlessly wandering accidents of psychiatry. Mere shadows of former people. Gross institutionalisation, post-war pre-frontal leucotomies, deep insulin therapy, ECT for practically everyone, 20 years of thioridazine and addiction to the then wonder drug, phenobarbitone, had removed most of their will to live, and, it appeared, almost all of their interest in life. John's main job, he was the nurse in charge, was to administer medication in the form of endless rounds of sedatory syrup,

Acknowledgement is given to SAGE Publications Ltd for kind permission to reprint this chapter.

crushed-tablet deception and non-compliance distrust. He also distributed cigarettes and chocolate, and sometimes, the contents of food parcels sent by geographically or emotionally distant relatives. Patients would queue anxiously; seemingly eager to burn their fingers on short cigarette butts and to use chocolate to further rot their already rotten teeth. Bert was the third member of staff. He was the ward domestic, a kind-hearted chain-smoking Irishman who did his best to feed and water the patients three times a day. He did that every day, for years, perhaps even for decades. Food was the only other thing that seemed to get the patients excited. He also made attempts to keep the grimy, tobacco-stained yellow ward clean, a futile activity. But he did his best to keep the dust, the forever present silverfish and cockroaches, the finally exhausted cigarette butts, the spat-out tablets and the other detritus of shadowy lives, to a minimum.

I entered formal nurse training a few months later; and was taught all about psychiatry, the signs and symptoms of psychiatric disorders and practical procedures such as giving injections. 'Paraldehyde has to be given in a glass syringe; it will melt the plastic ones', the not-far-off-retiring clinical tutor told us, about that now-long-gone but at the time, vile-smelling stuff. We practised bandaging techniques. Three years of practical ward experience was supplemented with quite an extensive lecture programme. Top psychiatrists taught us all about psychiatry and mental 'diseases'. We, that is, I and my fellow nursing students, all had the one textbook that was available to mental health nurses at that time, which I have on my bookshelf to this day.

Then it started to go wrong

Diary entry, sometime in 1978

There was a commotion in one of the bedrooms. It sounded as though two people were fighting so I dived in between them to try to stop anyone from getting hurt. The big guy was on top, beating the smaller one, probably a teenager. I seem to remember that I managed to stop the fight. The big guy was the nurse in charge. The smaller one was the patient. These things happened. He was a nasty piece of work, that charge nurse.

We used a lot of ECT in the 'nest'. We used diazepam, chlorpromazine, and thioridazine; chemical restraint. We used additional drugs in order to minimise the side effects; but on the way to and from work you could always catch one or two of the solitary inmates taking one of those gait-altered, not quite there, walks around the hospital grounds. The side effects had been minimally minimised. In addition to chemical restraints and locked doors, we 'managed' the patients using a system of token economy; and if the patients behaved badly and didn't earn their tokens they got a nasty-tasting protein drink instead of a meal.

And you had to watch your back. Turn your back on one of the 'inmates' and you got thumped. We carried attack alarms and in the worst of the cuckoo's nests we had at least one member of staff to every patient. 'Controlling' these patients was a dangerous activity. Perhaps they resented not being able to get their proper meals. To this day, if I am anywhere in public, such as a restaurant, I will always try to sit with my back to a wall so I won't get thumped from behind.

I didn't understand why many of the people were in hospital. As a result of their hospitalisation they had become grossly institutionalised; passive and disinterested shells of former beings and could never ever live independent or even semi-independent lives again. One patient had stolen a push bike and had been committed 50 years earlier. Another had become pregnant and as a result, had been declared insane. Another talked too much and had been told so many times to shut up that she had been mute for the last 40 years. Others, over decades, had developed bizarre and sometimes frightening coping rituals; too complex to describe here, perhaps designed to preserve some kind of personal identity and integrity. Most of us had forgotten (perhaps we never really knew), why these patients had been admitted in the first place.

Some patients came and went of course. Often they came and went, and came and went again. And again. And again. Unable to cope with their life with depression, schizophrenia, homosexuality, or addiction. Or perhaps they were unable to cope with society's response to their depression, schizophrenia, homosexuality, or addiction? So we did the required first aid and critical care, perhaps a course of ECT, modified narcosis or, of course, the psychiatrist's selection from the usual menu of mind-altering drugs; they reached a stage of being fit enough to be able to do without asylum, and they went, back into their former lives. There was a perpetuating cycle of dependency and of course for the professionals, employment.

Things were starting to go wrong. I was starting to think about what I was doing. Although I frequently, perhaps predominantly, witnessed exemplary compassionate behaviour from my fellow nurses, I was always uneasy with what I perceived to be the attempts at what I was starting to perceive was mindless (biology-based) psychiatry (Keen, 2003) and control of deviance. In my mind, the control of what others seem to perceive as political and social deviants was not only in operation in the former Soviet Bloc, it existed just under the surface in our own back yard. And I was part of that system, and felt uneasy. I locked doors and administered mind-numbing medication. I don't want to sound negative, and I know that the situation was a complex interplay between a range of social forces; but that was the situation as I saw it and as I experienced it in the late 70s and early 80s. I didn't understand why I was getting lectures on the psychiatric abnormality of homosexuality, I didn't understand why some cultural and ethnic groups were more likely to be diagnosed with particular mental health problems than white people; I couldn't understand why diagnosis was related to socio-economic status and class (it seemed as though if you were rich and mad then you were eccentric, if you were poor and mad then you were just that, mad).

Diary entry, sometime in 2003

insulin therapy
barbiturates
chlorpromazine and thioridazine
the benzodiazepines; diazepam and lorazepam
fluphenazine decanoate and Depixol
Prozac
paroxetine and clozapine
Psychiatric success stories?
trifluoperazine – that's a good one – it enables one woman I know
to get out the corner of her bedroom that she occasionally finds
herself stuck in for days on end, too scared to move. It also reduces
the number of insects she feels she has crawling all over her.
Trouble is it makes her fat, destroys her libido and other things.
Never mind, the Seroxat she also takes can control those things.

I had to get out. In the UK, we have had some sort of specialised direct-entry mental health nurse training for almost 100 years, it is not an adult nursing add-on, as it was, and often still is, in many countries (Welch, 1995). I went and did adult nursing training. It seemed to be a sensible option, as just before I went I was working with people who were experiencing issues related to substance use and they often had associated physical problems either as a result of their substance use or, or more frequently, and at least in the shortterm, as a result of the treatment of their problems. Adult nurse training was interesting, I seemed to be able to get to talk to more people who seemed to have genuine, although short-term and still medically induced, problems. Dealing with pre-operative anxiety, death anxiety and the reassurance of worried or grieving relatives were all in the job description. I completed my adult nurse training and went back to psychiatry, but only for a few months. After undertaking further university-based education – I wanted to find out what nursing really should be rather than what it was – I went back to a general hospital, and only did a bit of occasional consultation work with psychiatric nurses. That was in 1987. Since that time I have never been back, so my continued presence in mental health nursing could be called a bit of a fraud; on the other hand, perhaps it isn't. It is somewhat ironic that I now feel much more at home with my mental health nursing colleagues both where I work and in the rest of the UK (at least the more radical, anti-establishment colleagues) and for the last ten years in Germany, for longer than that in the USA. We seem to hold the same core values.

Diary entry, sometime in 1980

Her name was Betty, a dear old lady who I remember was in her 60s. She had severe brain damage, I can't remember why, and 'behavioural' (with an emphasis there) problems. She was admitted to the unit, and systematically and rapidly institutionalised, rapidly stripped of her own identity so that we could begin her 'therapy' (another emphasis), which was to be token economy behaviour modification. She gave in and complied, except on one account. She always insisted on carrying around her handbag, something she had probably done for most of her years. The staff didn't like that – and she started to get that nasty protein drink instead of her meals. She still kept her handbag. I didn't like the staff not liking her having her handbag, I didn't like the punitive nature of the punishment (they called the regime rewarding, I called it punishment). I got moved to a different clinical area, I clearly wasn't suited for that sort of work, they more than implied.

In the mental health nursing of today there are a number of key issues that are driving the profession forward. Those key issues could officially include, but may not be limited to: developments in nursing education, with the move into higher education, the improvement in the educational standards of mental health nurses and the development of specialist mental health nursing courses and roles (including the role of cognitive, cognitive-behavioural, psychodynamic etc., etc. therapist) and an increasing emphasis on undertaking research into mental health nursing activity and related issues; rapid, brief interventions as a response to, for example, deliberate self-harm; early and/or psychosocial interventions for serious mental illness. In addition, there is collaborative, inter-professional care and changes in the health and social care interface and the gradual erosion of the role of the mental health nurse and the blurring or disappearance of traditional professional boundaries. Finally, there are developments in the care of older people with mental health problems, an emerging struggle between the different schools of psychiatric and/or mental health nursing (yes, there is a difference that is more than semantic), and the mindless-brainless, biological-social paradigms, perhaps the death of humanist-based 'interventions' (with emphasis); and finally the development of 24-hour community services and assertive outreach programs to provide adequate care in the community.

That would be my official list, but my unofficial list would be quite different.

Diary entry, sometime in November 1994

I'm sitting in a window seat in a diner on Times Square, New York, having just finished the plate of spaghetti that was my dinner. As anybody who's been to America knows, the portions are huge and I'd left a substantial amount on my plate. All of a sudden, a young Black woman rushes in, like a tornado, and sits opposite me. She could be pretty, but she's filthy and covered in sores, she's shivering and wet from the autumn rain and hardly dressed in dirt-grey rags. She snatches the left spaghetti, and eats it, like some kind of very, very hungry wild animal. I could see the fear and madness in her eyes. 'Is she troubling you?' asks the waiter. 'No,' I reply, 'let her finish.'

There is evidence that, as a result of Governmental policy in the UK, care is becoming 'increasingly coercive [and] compulsory' (Hannigan & Cutcliffe, 2002). There seems to be a shift away from community mental healthcare towards custodial acute inpatient care, and the meteoric rise of the forensic services might be symptomatic of that. With claims to greater professionalism and the adoption of new ways of working, combined with attempts at a range of quasi-psychotherapeutic activity (including cognitive-behavioural therapy, brief intervention therapy and so on), the true role of the mental health 'nurse' seems to be rapidly disappearing, morphing into something akin to a generic mental health worker. Keen (2003) looked to an allied professionals' definition of the mental health–psychiatric nurses' role and found them saying that:

> The nurses' role has become one of assessing symptoms and risk and maintaining safety and administering medicines. The provision of therapeutic and recreational activities is thought of as somebody else's job ...

Added to this is the humanistic–biological debate with the new biological absolutism (Keen, 2003) and strict systems of diagnosis that emerged as a response to the near collapse of psychiatry created by the psychodynamic movement.

I went off to university to find out about nursing, because although I was a nurse, I was worried that I didn't know what nursing was. I didn't seem to do much of it. And I had the opportunity to repeat a phrase here that I repeated to myself on many occasions, that is, 'Nursing is not what nurses do', or at least 'Nursing is not what they think they do'. At university I studied real nursing; for three years, full time. I learnt about the philosophical basis of nursing, and the potential of nursing therapy. I began to really realise what was wrong with psychiatric nursing – and its biggest problem – that it was not psychiatric nursing at all. It was being a gaoler, and pharmacist, a pseudo-psychiatrist or pseudo-psychologist or pseudo-analyst. It was a pseudo-everything and nothing at all.

There were solutions to this problem. For me, nursing could be defined and was deeply rooted in firstly Betty Neuman's Health Care Systems Model, later Roy's Adaptation Model, before I finally settled on Martha Rogers' Science of Unitary Human Beings. The latter has dominated my work for the last 20 years (although that includes excursions into the wonderfully stimulating worlds of Watson's Caring Theory, Newman's Health as Expanding Consciousness and Parse's Human Becoming). I began to discover real nursing, and real nursing therapy.

Diary entry, sometime in the mid-1990s

Brian, a staff nurse on a medical ward, had just spent the last half an hour with an elderly Jewish lady. Her husband had just died, suddenly but not together in silence; true presence by anybody's definition. When it came to the time for them to part, Brian reached into his pocket and found a poem, one from a number that he carries around with him for just that reason. The lady left the ward, carrying the memories of her husband of over 50 years; healed just a little bit perhaps by Brian's presence. And the poem.

In order to avoid the future risk of ...

A potent synthesis of neurological knowledge, genetic mapping and technologies, orthomolecular biology and psychopharmacology will pervade deeply into an increasingly tense, stupidly violent yet over-managed and risk-aversed culture. (Keen, 2003)

... it is vital that we begin to discover what real nursing is all about. This seems to be at odds with the earlier predictions, and perhaps a midpoint on what the literature seems to call the Barker–Gournay axis might be reached. In this preceding text, I've tried to hint at what the Gournay end of the psychiatric–mental health worker continuum might be. In a gross over-simplification and perhaps a misrepresentation of such a predicted situation, I've tried to show a world dominated by psycho-pharmacology, with nursing activity subservient to psychiatry, medicine and ultimately the pharmacological industry. This has been called the reductive-pharmacological camp (Clarke, 2002). The Barker end of the continuum is represented by nursing activity defined by the Tidal Model, an emergent nursing theory that will, no doubt, create as much reactionary hostility as the nursing theories that have gone before it. However, I want to assert that the future of mental health *nursing* lies in the acceptance and adoption of grand nursing theory and in particular, the Tidal Model and similar emergent activity. Without it, psychiatric *nursing*, mental health *nursing* or psychiatric–mental health *nursing* will disappear.

The Tidal Model emerged from a five-year study, carried out by Barker and others, of what people '... need psychiatric nurses for' (Barker, 2002). It is a

... *radical* reconceptualization of mental health problems, by framing these, unequivocally, as *human*, rather than psychological, social, or physical problems.

Really, there should be space in this journal to do full justice to the work, perhaps it might be a future consideration, as I can only provide a brief overview here. Simply, early findings of the study (Barker et al, 1999) constructed the idea that the central issue was based on a complex set of 'knowing you, knowing me' relationships, where nurses moved between and presented either their 'Ordinary Me' (OM – truthfulness and honesty in the revelation of aspects of their lives and the relationship with the patient), their 'Pseudo-ordinary or Engineered Me' (POEM – limited and superficial dialogue and life event disclosure) or their 'Professional Me' (PM – characterised by the maintenance of distance and detachment). The Tidal Model built on this, and the foundation of Peplau's interpersonal model, identifying a number of concepts, including the care continuum, consisting of critical, transitional and developmental components. In a manner than clearly parallels Parse's Theory of Human Becoming, and Richard Cowling's profound and innovative work on Unitary Appreciative Inquiry, the Tidal Model concentrates on 'contacting the person' rather than 'engaging with the illness'(Barker, 2001) with the aim of understanding the person and their world. In the Tidal Model, personhood is represented by three dimensions; 'world' (where the focus is on the person's need to be understood and validated by others), 'self' (where the emphasis is on exploring and responding to the person's need for safety and security) and 'others' (where the need for support and services that might be required in order to lead an 'ordinary life' are explored). The nurse aims to establish a therapeutic alliance in order to explore these areas of concern through the use of narrative and with the eventual aim of determining and contributing to interventions that might meet a person's aims. The Tidal Model 'assumes that nurses need to get close to the people in their care, so that they might explore (together) the experience of health and illness' (Barker, 2001). This seems to have been recognised by certain members of the psychiatric–mental health nursing community, and there is considerable evidence to suggest that the Tidal Model is gaining in popularity throughout the world.

In my final paragraph I would like to offer a minor moderating point, perhaps more to deflect any potential criticism than for any other reason. Burnard (2002) identifies that …

> …'the walking alongside' of Barker can, most usefully, be supplemented by the 'technology' of Gournay.

… a position that is echoed by Barker (2002) himself, although he would maintain that the Tidal Model is fully capable of encompassing Gournay's 'technological' position. Engaging in the Barker–Gournayism debate is little more than academic posturing and vying for position, visibility and status. In constructing this paper for you, I am as guilty of this as the rest. However, I, like Barker (2001), am unhappy to accept that nursing has to adopt '… a subordinate role within a medically dominated mental health service' and I urge you all to take the same view, not just for the well-being of the profession and to secure its continued existence, but in order to fully, or at least partially, realise the vast therapeutic potential of real nursing practice that authentically engages with the person rather than hides behind the shadowy veil of drug-induced anonymity.

An epilogue: Shifting sands

38

Fran Biley and Hannah Walker

Recently, and with ever-increasing momentum, mental healthcare seems to have been becoming more humanised. And by that we mean that the person, the 'human' behind the disorder, the 'disease', the psychiatric diagnosis, is starting to be acknowledged. We are not sure when this movement started. Perhaps it was with the work of Carl Rogers in the 1950s, perhaps William Sargant, R.D. Laing, and of course Thomas Szasz. Perhaps it was Enoch Powell's drive towards the importance of promoting community rather than asylum-based care.

Although the original idea of the 'asylum' may have been admirable and it may have served a purpose for many people, in retrospect it also seemed to fail in so many ways. Care was institutional, ineffective, disempowering and very frequently dehumanising. Fashionable treatments such as deep insulin therapy, ECT, pre-frontal leucotomies and a whole host of chemical interventions, from paraldehyde to amphetamines, the phenothiazines and benzodiazapines, more or less came and went as they were often found wanting, but of course may have been useful for some people.

In the 1970s, as the large Victorian asylums were closed, or 'decanted' as the contemporary terminology would have it (which was a good indicator of the status of asylum 'inmates' at the time), patients became ex-patients (and ideally perhaps people) as they moved back into the communities from whence they came. The institutionalised no longer had an institution. Community care was inadequate and patchy. Ten or twenty years on, professional community care has become more sophisticated, service user and survivor groups have found much more of a voice, and the role of 'experts by experience' is becoming more prominent. Peer or user-led initiatives now often drive local and national policy, including Governmental activity. They drive treatment, care and support innovations, and so on.

Central to this pattern of change and development must be the rise in significance of the Recovery movement in the UK and perhaps parallel initiatives such as the IAPT (Improving Access to Psychological Therapies), the latter giving greater opportunity to receive a range of psychological treatments. Recovery, in its simplest sense and as we interpret it, may be different from *clinical* recovery but should help to restore hope and meaning in a person after they have experienced a catastrophic mental health event. It should empower the person to enable them to take part in collaborative activity aimed at optimising personal potential, whatever that might entail.

The enormity of this paradigm shift is manifest in, for example, the development of peer support workers, who work alongside professionals and in a similar capacity to them, and are qualified to do so because of their experience, rather than any professional qualification. It is also manifest as people being able to dictate the contents and direction of care programme approach meetings, how personal-budget direct payments may be spent, service user representation on commissioning boards, NHS Trust and Foundation Trust boards, research ethics committees, educational advisory groups, psycho-educational groups, participation in student mental health professional education and the strong emergence of user-led research groups.

All this sounds very formal. And it is. And it is also reinforced by a whole range of important but more informal service user-led activity that has the same recovery aims. In addition, organisations exist such as Rethink, who give voice to those who have experienced severe mental health problems; Mind, who offer similar national services; Together, who work to recovery principles; the Mental Health Alliance, who work mainly on positively changing national policies; and Time to Change, whose primary aim is to tackle stigma and discrimination in almost the same way as some of the aims of Mad Pride. There are of course local service user forums and informal support groups as well.

Often, the above groups will engage in activities that may certainly be therapeutic, but they are not aligned to the traditional medical model response to the need for 'treatment'. These activities – and we hesitate to use the word treatment, although in reality they may be as effective as more orthodox medical/psychiatric treatments – can include using photography workshops to explore and express our worlds, and creative writing groups that can be used for the same purpose. There may be two-

and three-dimensional art groups, sports and leisure activity programmes, gardening, green gym and cookery groups, or peer-led hearing voices groups where people can simply, and very effectively, discuss their voices in a safe and supportive environment.

Out of all this, that is, the trend towards humanising mental healthcare and the greater involvement of experts by experience in all aspects of mental healthcare, came the idea for this text.

We were aware that experts by experience were often called into meeting rooms and classrooms to speak to mental healthcare professionals and students about their experience of the mental healthcare system. There is also a body of work, prose, poetry, stories, narratives and autobiographies written by these experts, by service users, by those that have experienced mental health challenges, that describes, often in very vivid and powerful ways, the 'human', the 'lived experience', the 'lifeworld' of the mental health service user. This work, presenting the 'true' and authentic voice of those who have experienced mental health events rather than disembodied academic textbook interpretations by professionals, often appeared in disparate places, in blogs, on scattered and transient websites, in small circulation magazines and newsletters and so on. Some work was yet to be written. Clearly, the task to hand was to collect some of this work together so that it could be presented as a lifeworld-led, real-world aide and supplement to textbook learning and expert by experience monologue and lecture.

The troops were mobilised. A proposal was written, a publisher sought (and found). Contacts were contacted, and contributions were promised and most were delivered, sometimes with a little cajoling. But it was not that simple. We were dealing with emotions and experiences that were often still painful and current. Some who we approached felt unable to reveal those aspects of themselves that were still too raw. One didn't like our title, considering it to be too emotive and sensationalising. But on the whole, people enthusiastically engaged with the project. They were often more than willing to share their words.

Personally, we were driven primarily by two imperatives. Firstly, we wanted to be able to fully present, and therefore honour, the words of the individuals who contributed to this book. This would have to be without resorting to any editorial interference, beyond making very minor syntactical or stylistic corrections. Preserving the original writing as far as we could was felt to be the only way forward if the text were to be fully authentic. Secondly, unlike many of the academic or professional texts currently on the market, many of which have appeared very recently, we were averse to adding any sort of commentary, interpretation, value statement or diagnosis. To have done so, in our minds, would have been to contribute to the further oppression (and suppression) of the authentic service user voice, thus instantly destroying our prime motivation.

Of course, the human experience is infinitely variable. And so are the stories that have emerged and that have been included here. It is safe to say that this process has been serendipitous, at least to some degree. We have attempted to include voices, words, that represent as wide a range of experience and situations as possible. However, this could never be, or even attempt to be, comprehensive. There are gaps. There always will be gaps, however all-encompassing we try to be. Such is the nature of human experience.

Finally, we hope that this book and the work contained within it will contribute perhaps in some small way to a better understanding of the human experience of mental health events, to greater insights by mental healthcare professionals into the real world and the lived experience of those who have experienced, or are challenged by, mental ill health. As editors, it has been a pleasure to work together on this small project, this small potential contribution to the development of the service user-led movement. It has been a pleasure to have had the opportunity to work with such a wide variety of individuals who have been so enthusiastic about the project and about sharing their own, often painful memories in such a meaningful and powerful way.

Contributors

Fran Biley (1958-2012)

Francis C. Biley initially trained as a mental health and an adult nurse and after holding a range of clinical and practice development posts moved into undergraduate and postgraduate research and teaching. He was an Associate Professor in the Centre for Qualitative Research at Bournemouth University, UK and an Adjunct Professor of Nursing at Seton Hall University, New Jersey, USA. In addition he was a Governor of a local Foundation Trust hospital.

Terry Bowyer

I have been using services since 1998. In the last several years I have been in recovery and have enjoyed a longer period of stability. This has enabled me to do some involvement work in mental health. I started in recovery research, did some campaigning, fund raising and activism, and more. I recently became a peer support worker for Rethink and the Dorset Mental Health Forum.

John Evans

I was born in South Wales in 1980. I studied History at the University of Leicester, where I was diagnosed with anorexia nervosa within the first six weeks. I gradually restored weight and by the time I graduated I was back living an active life. After moving to Manchester and then Poole, my weight began to slide again and I was eventually admitted to hospital for three months. After discharge I began a Mental Health Nursing course at Bournemouth University, but quit before completing the first year when my anorexia came back with a vengeance. In December 2009, I decided to fight back one more time. A second, four-month admission has set me on the road to a full recovery. I hope to start a Masters Degree course in Information and History Studies in April 2011.

Leonard Roy Frank

After being released from Twin Pines Hospital in 1963, Leonard Roy Frank spent the next six years in study, reeducating himself. Since the early 1970s he has been active in the psychiatric survivors movement, first as a staff member of *Madness Network News* (1972) and then as the co-founder of the Network Against Psychiatric Assault (1974) – both based in San Francisco and dedicated to ending abuses in the psychiatric system. In 1978 he edited and published *The History of Shock Treatment*. Since 1995, three books of quotations he edited have been published: *Influencing Minds: A Reader in Quotations*, *Random House Webster's Quotationary*, and *Random House Webster's Wit & Humor Quotationary*. He can be contacted at: lfrank@igc.org

Alec Grant

Alec is Reader in Narrative Mental Health in the School of Health Sciences at the University of Brighton. He qualified as a mental health nurse in the mid-1970s and went on to study psychology, social science and psychotherapy. He's proud of being widely published, in the fields of ethnography, autoethnography, clinical supervision, cognitive behavioural psychotherapy, and communication and interpersonal skills. He's also passionate about his current and developing research interests, which coalesce in the area of narrative inquiry. As he heads towards old age, he wants to represent his life as a whole rather than in artificially fragmented parts, by role-modelling anti-stigmatising/othering practices. He tries to do this by being open about his mental health history and difficulties, and how these are positively fused with his academic concerns in a vulnerable embodied scholarship. He can be contacted at: A.Grant@bton.ac.uk

Judith Haire

Judith was born in Kent in 1955. She left school at 15 and worked for an estate agent and then in a London advertising agency before going to college where she passed her A and S levels. After working for a further year she went to Sheffield University to read Political Theory and Institutions, graduating in 1981. She returned to work in advertising and then spent 11 years in the civil service in Sheffield and London. At 37 her career was cut short when she experienced an acute psychotic episode which was to change her life radically. Once recovered she worked in the voluntary sector and continued to study part time at college. Judith's first article appeared in *Mental Health Practice* magazine in 2007. Her first book *Don't Mind Me* was published in 2008 (Chipmunkapublishing). She wrote this book to help others as well as herself and to inform mental health professionals and anyone wanting to gain an insight into mental illness. She lives by the sea with her husband Ken and their cat Smudge. She can be contacted at: www.judithhaire.vpweb.co.uk

Marjorie Holmes

The journey between my two poems *The Corridor People* and *Time to Get SAD* is a story from the inside out. I am naturally an introvert but it seemed to me that all the routes back to the real world of people where there was warmth, inspiration and laughter had been blocked or cut off unwittingly by my estranged husband. *Time to Get SAD* (in upper case because it stands for Seasonal Affective Disorder) is really 'time to be joyful'. My cup that was half empty has mysteriously become half full. I do not easily make friends but the friends I make appreciate me completely and I can take their criticism without coming to the weird conclusion that they have turned into enemies. Making people laugh is all about timing and can therefore disastrously fail but being able to laugh is the torch that I carry.

Catherine Jenkins

It is hard to write a biography in so few words but here is a very brief rundown. Names have been changed to maintain confidentiality. My name is Catherine Jenkins. I was born in 1978 and have one sister 18 months older than me named Jo. We were brought up by our mother, and the three of us together have a very close relationship. We shared our home for most of our childhood with our stepfather who was an alcoholic, and intimidating aggressive man, more so when drunk.

Difficulties through my childhood surfaced during my teenage years, and I chose a path that was frowned upon by my biological father. At the age of 20 I gave birth to my beautiful daughter who I adore, and have done what I can from that day onwards to support her alone as best I can. At the age of 27, I started university and began my training as a general adult nurse. My life has been full of challenges so far, too many of which to begin to explore, but some of the darkest days are described in this narrative beginning at the start of my nurse training. I transferred from General Adult Nursing to Mental Health Nursing largely due to what you will read, a decision I have not regretted for a moment, and am now a qualified mental health nurse. I hope that people reading this will gain something, be it comfort from similar experience, or insight into how a mental health illness has a profound effect on all those concerned. I also hope it may make those working within psychiatry reflect on the way the patient, and family, are viewed and considered. I feel honoured to be able to share this with you all and hope you enjoy reading it.

Keith King

I am 44 years old and single (not by choice). I have always lived in Eastbourne; I have had dreams of moving but have never found the guts to do so. I am educated to A-Level standard. This is my first foray into writing of any kind. My career path to date includes, cinema usher, jewellery shop assistant, barman and an off-licence manager.

Henry Laxton

Suffering from bipolar disorder and alcoholism has for me been like navigating a schooner through the most dangerous oceans without a compass, and with a very poor crew. However, I would not change anything about my life. If it had not been for my last visit to a psychiatric hospital, I would not be where I am today, and would not have met my dear sweet Ely. We met in hospital and, although not the ideal place to start a relationship (with someone who also suffers from mental health issues), it has worked for us. We have been together now for eight years, and married for just over six, and we support each other when either is suffering.

Alcoholism and bipolar disorder never go away, and sometimes I suffer in a big way, but I have learned a lot about these sicknesses of the soul and now have in place a step-by-step plan which helps me get back on track. The worst thing I can do when unwell is to isolate, go to ground and cut myself off from the fellowship of friends, family, and those in the medical profession who would help me. I usually become arrogant, and ego-driven when unwell, and feel I can do this on my own (usually when in the manic part of the illness). I would not ask for help at this stage. After some time, could be days but usually weeks, I go into the depressive stage of the illness. At this time, I do one of two things: I ask for help from the psychiatric team or I isolate.

As more and more time passes, I learn to sharpen my skills of putting my pride in my pocket and asking for help. The help comes in two ways: medication and the fellowship of other people I can trust, and who listen and care for me enough to give me their time. People who give me direction, and tell me what to do, I choose not to return to. People who suggest and share back to me their own experience become my friends, and I return to them, not just when I'm unwell but also when I'm well, and I am also there for them when they need to talk. I just want to thank my family and the wealth of friends I have made on this journey, but especially I want to thank my dear sweet wife who is the driving force in my recovery.

Helen Leigh-Phippard

Helen has a PhD in international relations and was a university lecturer until she developed mental health problems in the late 1990s and was diagnosed with psychotic depression. In late 2004 she joined Brighton and Hove MIND's LiVE (Listening to the Voice of Experience) Project and since that time has been actively engaged in local service user participation. She contributes to the development and delivery of training to local mental health service providers, to the training of nurses at Brighton University, and to the development of research within Sussex Partnership Trust as a member of the Trust's Lived Experience Advisory Forum (LEAF).

Maggie Lloyd

I come from a small family and was initially brought up in various countries in Africa. At ten years of age, I was sent to boarding school in England. I grew up being self-reliant. I went to art school in 1967 and dropped out three years later, joining the civil service. I lived in a commune for a few years, got married and had two children, both boys. When they were 13 and 11, my husband died following a major heart attack. When my older son Stefan was 18 he began to show signs of mental ill health. Stefan's first hospitalisation came one year after, and since that time he's had further admissions to a variety of hospitals. After 18 years of being ill, he now seems to be making progress and is on an open ward. Those 18 years have left me tired.

Jonathan Richard Lloyd

Jonathan was born and brought up in Hastings, East Sussex by two former art students and influenced greatly by everyone around him, including his big brother Stefan.

While Jonathan was just a bun in the oven, Stefan begged the former art students for a little brother called Richard. They spent so much time preparing Stefan for the disappointment of a little sister that he was quite surprised when he got the brother he wanted so much. The art students decided they couldn't give Stefan everything he wanted, and slapped Richard in as a middle name.

Fortunately Stefan and Jonathan (Richard) had their own rooms by the time Stefan's illness began to manifest. This gave Jonathan somewhere in the house where he could close the door and get on with his teenage angst in peace.

At 18, Jonathan went to university in Wales to get an education in more ways than one. Rather awkwardly his brother kept turning up unwelcomely unwell, much to Jonathan's dismay.

After finishing his degree Jonathan went to Spain. There, he and his brother could stay in contact via telephone and the internet, and unannounced visits were highly unlikely.

Homes away from home include Barcelona and Berlin, so far. But he doesn't want to restrict himself to just those locations, and remains open to suggestions. This includes work, as his job making digital copies of prison/shopping centre toilets has become a bit of a grind no matter which cosmopolitan mainland city he does it in.

John Major

John and Helen Major moved to Bournemouth from London in 1988. It was in 1995 that they realised that they had a problem and Helen received a diagnosis of Alzheimer's when she was in her mid-fifties. Although he assumed the role of carer straight away, it was not until 2003 that Helen's condition progressed to the point when John had to take early retirement. Since then, John has devoted himself to not only caring for Helen, but also campaigned with the Alzheimer's Society fully aware that any improvements he was able to achieve would not benefit Helen, but he was determined that those following should have a smoother pathway. At the time of writing Helen is in a nursing home. John was able to look after her at home for almost 13 years and visits her most afternoons.

Sarah Nayler

I was born in 1973 in Sussex, South East England. I had a very happy childhood, living with my parents and older brother. I have always loved meeting people and have a passion for music.

Unfortunately I was unable to finish my schooling as my mental health became very fragile. About a year later (at the age of 16) I was diagnosed with bipolar affective disorder. This has had a huge impact on my life and on my family.

Although my working life has been very up and down, I have gained qualifications and work-based experience in retail and administration. I have undertaken voluntary work for many charities including Age Concern, Relate and Mind.

For the past ten years I have worked in the mental health field. I started out as a group facilitator for a local self-help group. I then progressed to becoming a part-time lecturer for a university.

I now do occasional work as a service user consultant for a mental health trust. My duties include training staff, assessing ward environments and sitting on interview panels.

I am passionate about sharing my experience of living with mental illness and hope to help others understand and reduce stigma and prejudice.

Amanda Nicol

I was born in Glasgow in 1966, moved to Germany where my parents worked with the British forces in 1974 and in 1977 went to boarding school in Hertfordshire. After school I studied the conservation and restoration of oil paintings in Hastings, then moved to London where I worked as an assistant restorer in the Old Master trade for many years. After hospitalisation I did a Foundation course in Art and Design at Kingston Polytechnic. Some years later I began a degree in Art History at Birkbeck College, London but soon realised that the writing I wanted to do was not academic. I didn't finish the course. In 1999, ten years after my hospitalisation, I wrote *House of Bread*, a novel based on my own experiences, and in 2001 I left London. I now live in Hastings with my husband and our dog, where I continue to write, paint and restore paintings.

Nicola Oliver

Nicola first succumbed to mental illness in the form of bipolar disorder in 2007 at the age of 35. Prior to her illness she had a successful career as a process improvement consultant. Her breakdown followed a period of extreme work stress. Following her breakdown she became an artist (www.artbynicola.co.uk) and an author in her quest to make sense of her illness.

Today she works for a number of mental health charities in the hope that she can use her experience to help others. She also works part time for the Centre for Mental Health (www.centreformentalhealth.org.uk).

Richard Leopold Peacocke

Richard was in the Army for 14 years as an Ammunition Technician on bomb disposal duties. He retired to join the Prison Service, where he trained to be a Hospital Officer.

He has gained a BSc Hons in Psychology (OU), a Cert in Health Promotion (OU), a Mental Health Nursing Diploma with Registration (Bournemouth), an MSc in Investigative Psychology (Liverpool), and a PG Dip in Forensic and Biological Anthropology (Bournemouth). Richard is now in the final year of a Doctor of Professional Practice course (Bournemouth).

He is a Consultant Peer Support Specialist with Dorset Mental Health Forum, and a Mental Health Act Hospital Manager Associate with both Dorset Primary Care Trust and Dorset Healthcare NHS Foundation Trust. Richard's particular interests are in helping the move away from the medical model towards a more recovery-oriented approach to care. He can be contacted at: richard.peacocke@btinternet.com

Ali Quant

Ali Quant is an online survivor activist in the fields of self-harm, hearing voices, OCD (otherwise known as 'Marigolditis') and social policy. She is a moderator on a peer-support forum and has previously worked in service provision in the voluntary sector. She has written for nursing journals and articles used within nurse education. She's a keen Trekkie, wine gum and Marmite disciple who plays the piano, guitar and drums and enjoys baking chocolate bonios.

Carol Rambo

Carol Rambo is Associate Professor of Sociology at The University of Memphis in Memphis, Tennessee, and the current editor of *Symbolic Interaction*. She has written on topics such as exotic dancing, childhood sexual abuse, and intellectually disabled parenting. Carol has published in journals such as *Deviant Behavior, Journal of Contemporary Ethnography, Qualitative Inquiry, Mental Retardation,* and *Journal of Aging Studies*. Her current research interests include the intersections of trauma, narrative, the economy, and the environment.

Nigel Short

In April 1994 I was working for a 'case management' team [now Assertive Outreach Team] in Hastings. I experienced my first period of depression. I was given a few months off of work and prescribed antidepressant medication. I spent many days and weeks landscaping the garden in a new family home. I returned to work and felt much better.

In January 2000 I was now working as a nurse cognitive behaviour psychotherapist. I was experiencing my second period of depression. This time an inpatient stay was recommended. In many contemporary inpatient units patients [people] are sometimes discussed as deviants, hopeless, manipulative or burnt out. I had read these descriptions of me. How can this dominant discourse be dismantled? How can we become interesting, worth-getting-to-know people? Possibly through eliciting our narratives? This small contribution may go some ways to letting people into my stories, my narrative.

Andrew Voyce

Andrew says of his experiences: Let there be no return to asylum life. If my written narratives and digital cartoons of the waste and inequities of the old mental hospitals serve any purpose, it is to say 'don't let this happen again'. There is today great benefit to be had from shining a light on mental health, so if you get the chance, say your piece. Website: http://www.slideshare.net/AndrewsAsylumLife

Hannah Walker

Hannah was adopted at 4 months and brought up on the Isle of Wight. She went to grammar school and had a place at Warwick University to read Philosophy and Logic, but joined the RAF instead. After a highly successful career she was invalided out for being bipolar. Hannah got married, got separated and retrained as a therapist – the last two events being very helpful and liberating. She worked for six years on an acute psychiatric ward until she was invalided out of that as well. Now retired, she spends her time fly fishing and looking after three cats. She can be contacted at: piglet292@talktalk.net

Margaret Walker

I grew up and went to school in Chichester in the seventies. When I was about 14 I decided I wanted to study languages at Cambridge, like my father had. I particularly wanted to learn Russian and I liked to imagine being approached by MI5 one day and asked to become a spy! However, by the time I was 16, not only was I far too idle and distracted by my social life to contemplate Cambridge, I also became ill, following a period of high mood, with a severe and long-lasting depression which effectively terminated my education. The reality of my life ended up quite different from what I had imagined.

I seemed to spend the next 25 years trying to catch up on education and a career. I trained to be a nurse, then went to University to do a degree in Cognitive Sciences, then further nurse training, then a Master's degree in research. I was not good at clinical nursing work as I was far too indecisive and neurotic. So, instead of proper work, I enjoyed an office-based role in audit and research until 2003. I have had long periods of being perfectly well, but also long periods of being ill, causing interruptions in my life. I spent all of 1996 in and out of hospital.

In 2004 I left my audit and research job during a period of depression and became self-employed, selling books on the internet. The high and low episode described in my narrative occurred at this time, when I was 44.

I now work in the local Jobcentre, in Hastings, assessing eligibility for help with mortgage payments for people on benefits. I enjoy it very much, and it suits me as the work is complex enough to be stimulating but the stress levels are generally manageable. I may not have become a spy dodging poison darts from umbrellas, as I had planned, but I am very happy that I am well enough, unlike many others, to be in relatively secure paid employment at all.

References

Aldridge, S & Stuart, A (1998) *The Willow Scheme: An innovative project offering befriending support to young carers living with a severely mentally ill relative.* Presentation at National Children's Bureau Conference on 'Mentally Ill Parents and their Children', London.

Ashmore, R, Cutcliffe, J & Collier, E (2002) An examination of the last ten years of mental health nursing. *British Journal of Nursing, 11,* 503–5.

Baldwin, D (nd) David Baldwin's Trauma Information Pages. Retrieved on February 26, 2011 from http://www.trauma-pages.com/

Barker, P (2001) The Tidal Model: Developing an empowering, person-centred approach to recovery within psychiatric and mental health nursing. *Journal of Psychiatric and Mental Health Nursing 8,* 233–40.

Barker, P (2002) Doing what needs to be done: A respectful response to Burnard and Grant. *Journal of Psychiatric and Mental Health Nursing, 9,* 232–6.

Barker, P, Jackson, S & Stevenson, C (1999) The need for psychiatric nursing: Toward a multidimensional theory of caring. *Nursing Inquiry 6,* 103–11.

Burnard, P (2002) Not waving but drowning: A personal response to Barker and Grant. *Journal of Psychiatric and Mental Health Nursing 9,* 229–32.

Campbell, J (2005) Recovery in mental illness: Broadening our understanding of wellness. *PsyCRITIQUES, 50*(46), 3.

Clarke, L (2002) Doubts and certainties in the nursing profession: A commentary. *Journal of Psychiatric and Mental Health Nursing 9,* 225–9.

Deegan, PE (1988) Recovery: The lived experience of rehabilitation. *Psychosocial Rehabilitation Journal. 11*(4), 11–19.

Denzin, NK (2003) *Performance Ethnography: Critical pedagogy and the politics of culture.* Sage: Thousand Oaks, CA.

Ebaugh, FG (1943, March) A review of the drastic shock therapies in the treatment of the psychoses. *Annals of Internal Medicine.*

Falcov, A (1998) *Crossing Bridges: Training resources for working with mentally ill parents and their children. Reader for managers, practitioners and trainers.* Brighton: Pavilion Publishing, commissioned by the Department of Health.

Frank, AW (1995) *The Wounded Storyteller: Body, illness, and ethics.* Chicago/ London: University of Chicago Press.

Goffman, E (1963) *Stigma: Notes on the management of spoiled identity.* Englewood Cliffs, NJ: Prentice Hall.

Gralnick, A (1944) Psychotherapeutic and interpersonal aspects of insulin treatment. *Psychiatric Quarterly, 18,* 187.

Hannigan, B & Cutcliffe, J (2002) Challenging contemporary mental health policy: Time to assuage the coercion? *Journal of Advanced Nursing 37,* 477–84.

Holmes, OW (1931) *The Professor at the Breakfast Table.* New York: EP Dutton. [Original work published 1860]

Jacobson, E (1938) *Progressive Relaxation.* Chicago: University of Chicago Press.

Keen, TM (2003) Post-psychiatry: Paradigm shift or wishful thinking: A speculative review of future possibles for psychiatry. *Journal of Psychiatric and Mental Health Nursing, 10,* 29–37.

Kennedy, CJC & Anchel, D (1948) Regressive elecric-shock in schizophrenics refractory to other shock therapies. *Psychiatric Quarterly, 22,* 318.

Markowitz, LJ & Purdon, C (2008) Predictors and consequences of suppressing obsessional thoughts. *Behavioural and Cognitive Psychotherapy, 36,* 179–92.

Nicol, A (2009) *House of Bread.* Eastbourne: Antony Rowe Publishing.

Pennebaker, JW (2004) *Writing to Heal. A guided journal for recovering from trauma and emotional upheaval.* Oakland, CA: New Harbinger Publications, Inc.

Rambo Ronai, C (1995) Multiple reflections of childhood sexual abuse. *Journal of Contemporary Ethnography, 23,* 395–426.

Rambo Ronai, C (1996) My mother is mentally retarded. In A Bochner & C Ellis (Eds) *Composing Ethnography* (pp. 109–31). Walnut Creek, CA: Altamira Press.

Rambo Ronai, C (1997) On loving and hating my mentally retarded mother. *Mental Retardation, 35,* 417–32.

Rambo, C (2007) Sketching as autoethnographic practice. *Symbolic Interaction, 30,* 531–42.

Ray, MB (1942) *Doctors of the Mind: The story of psychiatry.* Boston: Little, Brown.

Stockwell, F (1984) *The Unpopular Patient.* London: Routledge.

Tillmann-Healy, LM (1996) A secret life in a culture of thinness. Reflections on body, food, and bulimia. In A Bochner & C Ellis (Eds) *Composing Ethnography* (pp. 76–108). Walnut Creek, CA: Altamira Press.

Welch, M (1995) Recent developments in psychiatric nurse education in the countries of Central and Eastern Europe. *International Journal of Nursing Studies, 32,* 366–72.